WITHDRAWN

Excess and Restraint

in the Novels
of Charles Dickens

Excess
and
Restraint

in the Novels of
Charles Dickens

John Kucich

The University of Georgia Press
Athens

Set in 11 on 14 point Century Expanded type
Printed in the United States of America
Design by Martyn Hitchcock

Library of Congress Cataloging in Publication Data

Kucich, John.
    Excess and restraint in the novels of Charles Dickens.

    Includes bibliographical references and index.
    1. Dickens, Charles, 1812–1870—Criticism and in-
terpretation.   I. Title.
PR4588.K8   1981   823'.8   81-1286
ISBN 0-8203-0576-6   AACR2

For the Egg

He tried a new direction, but made nothing of it; walls, dark doorways, flights of stairs and rooms, were too abundant. And, like most people so puzzled, he again and again described a circle, and found himself at the point from which he had begun. "This is like what I have read in narratives of escape from prison," said he, "where the little track of the fugitives in the night always seems to take the shape of the great round world, on which they wander; as if it were a secret law."

—*Our Mutual Friend*

contents

acknowledgments

Appropriately, my chief debts are dialectical. Roy Roussel's example convinced me that literary criticism could be an expansive form of thought, and while his sense of Dickens also lies behind much of this study, that larger inspiration was the more valuable gift. Joseph Fradin guided me through the hard work of revision and clarification, and his class on Dickens—as well as his own work on Dickensian aggression—helped me shape my own insights.

For help with the various stages of this manuscript, thanks to William F. Axton, Edgar Dryden, Garrett Stewart, and Bill Warner.

Less directly, I am indebted to Elliot Krieger, John McGowan, David Myers, and Jim Weis for their often unsuspecting help, and for their standards. I want also to acknowledge the intellectual environment of the State University of New York at Buffalo for the sense of community (and outrage) it engendered.

Portions of this manuscript, in altered form, have appeared in *Dickens Studies Annual, Nineteenth-Century Fiction*, and *PMLA*.

a note on texts

Except where otherwise noted, all references to Dickens'
novels are to the Penguin edition (Baltimore and London:
1965–76). In the absence of any text with cachet, this edition seemed to me to be a good compromise between faithful editing and general availability. For the sake of readers
using other editions, however, all references will be given
to chapter numbers, or to volume and chapter numbers,
and not to page numbers.

introduction

Assuming that an introduction should define for the reader the method and scope of the work before him, but wanting to avoid boring the reader with a colorless map of the boundaries of my subject, I would like to provide such a framework by tracing the course of my thought about Dickens during the time before I began this study. Such a history, I hope, will interest the reader who, besides wanting a general orientation, also wants to know the reasons why I approached Dickens the way I did. In the current state of literary criticism, in which no paradigm is ever clear-cut, let alone pervasive, the reasoning behind any particular study is rarely obvious. I realize, however, that a longer kind of explanation can also become tiresome—or bumptious—and therefore, like Fielding in *Joseph Andrews*, I invite the more restless reader to read no more of these introductory pages than he likes and to plunge right into the first chapter whenever he has had enough.

This study of Dickens began with my sense of a special concentration of energy in Dickens' prose, and with my frustration at not being able to talk about that energy in any but the most vague and uselessly eulogistic of terms. From this point of view, the entire work is a springboard for the penultimate chapter, which concentrates on narrative energy in Dickens' writing style itself. But to say, even now, that it was energy that fascinated me in Dickens sounds merely rhapsodic; what I really mean to say is that Dickens' novels generate a series of explosions, in which the energy of characters or narrators is repeatedly concentrated against rigid limits to thought and action. The profundity and the persistence of the limits intrigued me as much as the irrepressibility of the energy. But these generalizations still do not convey what I have in mind—the book as a whole must do that. Let it suffice to say that I began by trying to articulate a special kind of tension between energy and limits that I found in reading Dickens.

Several things should immediately be clear. Since my discussion focuses primarily on Dickens' texts as literary experiences, this study is inevitably aesthetic rather than sociological, atemporal rather than historical. I do not reject other approaches; in fact, I have benefited more than I can say from the research of cultural historians like Raymond Williams, or, in a narrower sphere, George Ford and Philip Collins. But I have everywhere used the research of their critical studies as a tool toward a better understanding of Dickens' relationship to his readers, and not as a model for my own goals. My work on Dickens tries only to specify a certain quality in the novels. In the process, it indicates how that quality is projected by Dickens as a goal for culture, but it stops short of examining the consequences of Dickens' vision of culture either for Victorian society or as an ideal for our own. This is not to say that such work would not be valuable, or that it would be incompatible with my approach. That my work on Dickens' novels as literary experiences does not leave me room for an evaluation of the full implications of those experiences for culture, which would be a project of some complexity in itself, is, in fact, the chief of my many regrets. I do hope, however, that I have indicated how such an evaluation can proceed.

At the same time, I have avoided either a relativistic and personal approach or a narrowly stylistic one. On the one hand, I have avoided any tendency to root the works in the psychology of their author or in the localized responses of particular readers, although at times I have used psychoanalytic insights—particularly those of Sigmund Freud and Norman O. Brown. On the other hand, I have tried not to revere Dickens' novels as aesthetic totalities, in the style of New Criticism or structuralism—totalities whose ultimate goal is a hypostatized balance of forces, or whose significance lies entirely in an internal logic of coherence. My interest was in Dickens' excessive energy insofar as it seemed a model for one fundamental kind of human energy, and, as a result, I wanted to move freely between the confluence of literary forces in the texts and their impact on, and meaning for, most readers.

Though I have borrowed insights from other disciplines, my approach has remained somewhat uncomfortably within the eclectic field of postmodernist literary criticism, which in the last twenty years or so has begun to define itself as a science in its own right, using a vocabulary that mediates between philosophy, linguistics, history, anthropology, and psychology. It is difficult to define this kind of criticism, since it bears the same problematic relationship to other disciplines that literature itself bears to life, being at once rational and intuitional, rigorous and playful, scientifically precise and humanistically discursive. As Paul de Man notes, however, there is one important assumption in recent criticism that distinguishes it from earlier literary study: the assumption that literature is not a privileged gesture made by rarefied, aestheticized sensibilities. Such criticism considers literature as an act with no more authority than all other acts, even though—like other acts, too—it retains its own unique characteristics, the chief one being that it is explicitly invented.[1] That is to say, the kind of criticism that has been most helpful to me in my study of energy in Dickens—the work of J. Hillis Miller, Frank Kermode, Edward W. Said, Jean Starobinski, Roland Barthes, and others—has been the kind of criticism that puts into question the relationship between fictional experience and real experience. So it was, too, with my sense of energy in Dickens; there is something in Dickens unlike the energies of real life—a purely verbal excessiveness, one which does not produce human meaning—but at the same time, there is something about that excessiveness that seems to have a particular relevance for everyday energies. Dickens' narrative energy thus presents the relationship between the fictional and the real as an important one. In no other novelist, in fact, has the tension between imaginative and mimetic energies been such a perennial subject for debate.

Therefore, as I tried to define the special kind of energy that I found in Dickens' writing, I kept one eye on contemporary theoretical discussions, hoping to find there some critical vocabulary that would suit my sense of that energy. As I have been hinting, however, I do have one important reservation about those recent discussions. Inevitably, I employ many of the propositions of postmodernism—particularly, the general assumption that moral and intellectual assertions are fictional in origin, nonmimetic, and therefore can be shown to dissolve into contradictions or "constructions" under scrutiny—propositions which have led many critics to an absolute kind of skepticism about the referential abilities of language. But I remain interested in literature as an image of human satisfactions apart from epistemological projects; in this sense, I assume that literature is in some way mimetic of human desires.[2] I use the term "mimetic" not to signify a one-to-one correspondence between literary experience and human reality, but to indicate simply a belief in the usefulness of evaluating literary assertions as they refer to desires whose source lies outside of language. Stanley Diamond, an avowedly antistructuralist anthropologist, has argued that primitive societies use myth and ritual to understand and to use rational contradictions, rather than—as Lévi-Strauss believes—to repress them;[3] in other words, their rituals are "expressive" rather than "binding."[4] A similar argument could be made for literature; only by discovering the seams in rationality, the points at which our values represent impossible or fictional solutions, can we begin to make informed choices about them— for, as Diamond says, more elaborately, some myths *are* better than others.[5] One practical result of this theoretical attitude has been my attention to a synthetic attitude held by Dickens, who I believe affirms moral and social values even as he demonstrates their manipulable, or even dangerously double, natures.[6]

Consequently, although I have profited from contemporary theoretical discussions in ways that I cannot begin to acknowledge, I found that I was repeatedly dissatisfied with the vocabulary of presence and absence that seems to dominate them. Within the strict terms of this vocabulary, contemporary theoreticians for the most part discover the nonprivileged status of literature—and the impossibility of establishing any privileged language to express meaning—over and over again; or they thematize this discovery—designating it as an authorial inten-

tion—in the work of novelists. The discovery itself did not of-
fend me; the constant repetition of the discovery did, since the
failure of language to produce "presence" seemed to me to be a
necessary preliminary assumption, but no more. A description
of the theoretical vocabularies of two of the most influential of
these critics pinpoints my dissatisfactions.

Jacques Derrida's fundamental contribution to literary studies is his systematic attack on Western attempts to formulate
transcendence, an attack that is based in the semiological concept that around any assertion—even self-consciously critical
ones—there is a suppressed field of discourse. According to
structural linguistics, when this suppressed field is recovered,
it reveals that the assertion is bound by a play of differences
within language, rather than being free to signify, in an absolute
way, something outside of language. For instance, one cannot
understand the concept "truth" without a concept "falsehood";
therefore, one understands truth not in terms of itself, but in
terms of its opposite, solely as a stress within a language system. In much more convoluted but essentially similar ways,
every term in language can be shown to suppress its necessary
relationship to its opposite—and, by extension, to all of language. For Derrida, this relational aspect of signification is the
condition for the failure of language to make any extralinguistic
concept present to consciousness, including those of philosophy
and the history of ideas. Most important, Derrida claims that
Western culture is always frustrated in its attempts to transcend the insubstantiality of human meaning and to arrive at
an unqualified apprehension of truth—at "presence"—by the
structure of language itself. For Derrida, language is always absence that masquerades as presence; the word never arrives at
the thing itself. In fact, "things themselves" are only signs.[7] A
second critic, Paul de Man, although he looks at Derrida crit-
ically, comes to a similar conclusion; de Man asserts that language has an inherent weakness for desiring presence—de Man
calls this the "blindness" of language—and that to make an authentic statement one must take apart this search for presence

indirectly, almost despite itself. De Man calls this "insight."[8] Both these critics, rejecting presence as a possibility but leaving man to desire it eternally, even against his will, describe what amounts to an aesthetics of failure.[9] Following Lévi-Strauss, Derrida concedes that texts may lapse into empirical statements in good faith—since they must lapse in any case—only insofar as they use empirical tools to further deconstruct the notion of presence.[10] De Man extends this logic to the conclusion that great literature always anticipates the critic and deconstructs itself,[11] a notion developed more systematically in the work of J. Hillis Miller, who thematizes deconstruction in the writers he studies partly in order to make deconstructive criticism amenable to traditional classroom approaches.[12]

However, we should also note—as a paradox that will help us with the complexities of energy in Dickens—that Derrida and de Man tacitly privilege a kind of cool, detached rationality—their own—which is playful but never exuberant, and which very gracefully, even coyly articulates its limits, being content to unravel complexities within those limits. Derrida and de Man themselves thus pretend to a kind of ultimate indifference, an *askesis*, a bland willingness to throw away what man has always held dear—the quest for Truth, or Meaning. Through this flaunted indifference, they deliberately irritate more humanistic critics; the very "superiority" of Derrida and de Man, at least in literary circles, comes from their flagrant, seemingly transcendent willingness to abandon human strongholds that others—presumably less daring—are not willing to risk.

Putting aside the great usefulness of these discussions of presence and absence, I found that none of them seemed to help me with my sense of Dickens' energy, for in Dickens, energy is not tolerant or cool. It does not brook limitations, nor does it seem to serve any metaphysical superiority, stated or unstated. Moreover, I began to suspect that narrative energy in Dickens does not aspire to presence at all, but that it seems to enjoy consuming itself before the reader's eyes, without necessarily leaving the trace of a meaning. If anything, it seems to pursue absence, a deliberate, rational negativity. In Dickens, the signs of this drive beyond significance are the extravagant wordplays, the inflated and mock-pompous diction, and the impossible characterizations, all of which seem somehow separate from meaning in the sense that, being satirical of so many things—and, at the same time, of nothing in particular—they imply no single, serious base.

To use more traditional terms, in Dickens there is a high level of nonsense. By nonsense, however, I do not mean that which is lacking in sense; I mean that which actively empties sense of its content, or that which reveals the normal itself to be absurd. This war on sense is at the very heart of parody and caricature, which transform the commonplace into the ridiculous, and Dickens' parodic style seemed to me deliberately subversive of conventional sense, rather than being merely capricious.[13] Similarly, Dickens' irrational excesses of sentimentality and melodramatic violence defeat the narrow claims of ideology through a kind of emotional nonsense, since extravagances of feeling in Dickens often seek to surpass the values they support and to revel in a world of pure feeling. The assertions are there, of course, in Dickens—the values of hearth and home, the puritanical moralism, the doctrine of the heart. But in Dickens' novels, as I hope to show, there seems to be a greater glee in dismantling the world of sense and the assertive behavior of others than there is in making direct counterassertions.[14]

Ultimately, of course, the recuperated meaning—the "blindness"—in Dickens can be formulated. But the enthusiasm for dilapidations of sense in Dickens seemed to contrast strikingly with the cool detachment from stable meaning propounded by poststructuralism. On a theoretical level, this meant that what I had found lacking in Derrida and de Man was precisely their unwillingness or inability to account for the negative pleasure they themselves take in deconstruction—which is, in one sense, just a more pedestrian version of parody. Why, too, the insistence that such pleasure must be willed; why do theorists seem to find deconstruction and the idea of absence so liberating if, according to their principles, man's fundamental desires all run the other way, toward presence? The notion of "play," as formulated by Derrida or Barthes, seems inadequate to explain this sense of liberation, since it lacks all urgency.[15] Is there something more dynamic to be said for the discovery of absence, that is, for the avowedly irresponsible project of *giving up* desires for significance and meaning, a giving up that corresponds to the more agreeable satisfactions of nonsense in Dickens?

At the same time, interestingly enough, I found the more traditional critics of Dickens laboring with the same problem of negative satisfactions, albeit in a slightly different form. Many of these critics seem to read Dickens in terms of a similar thematics of failure, this one taking the form of moral renunciation, that is, the allegory of defeated expectations. For traditional critics, Dickens' ultimate lesson is his belief in the impossibility and the cruelty of any assertion of radical individuality; Dickens, they say, urges us instead to humble ourselves before our dependence on and our identity with the community of man. Curiously, the pattern may be more moral and less elaborate, but it is essentially the same as the pattern in Derrida and de Man; both humanists and structuralists agree that we should not presume to break the bonds of our humanity, either by asserting a radical individuality or by asserting a radical presence, and that we must learn instead to humble ourselves before these bonds, to recognize the fundamental sameness of all fallen humanity— whether the bond that unites us is the humanists' bond of "responsibility" and "dependence" or Derrida's linguistic "inscription." Despite their differences—the moral warmth of the humanists and the cold scientism of Derrida—the overall pattern of rejected hubris is the same. It is a pattern as old as Western civilization, as old as Adam and Eve, and it is a pattern that all of us find deeply reassuring on some level, no matter which literary camp appeals to us more.

But Dickens was not a very humble man. Neither, I dare say, are Jacques Derrida and Paul de Man, and the same might be said of any number of Dickens critics. This is not an *ad hominem* argument; my point is simply the obvious objection that the meaning of a dogma depends as much on its tone as on its rational content. To take the argument to ridiculous lengths, neither is moral Western civilization a humble civilization. Why, then, this radical division: why does a culture that rewards self-assertion and dynamic energy simultaneously profess a dogma of moral or philosophical renunciation and a thematics of individual failure? The insistent repetition of the pattern in Western culture seems to indicate either that the lesson is one we never adequately learn, or that the nature of resignation is transformed during the course of the allegory and offers satisfactions that are not readily apparent—or that are deliberately masked.

It occurred to me at this point that the opposition between presence and absence, or between radical individuality and resigned communality, is a false opposition. Between the polarity of transcendent assertions of difference and complete absorption into the sameness of the group, the commonly opposed images of human action, there is a third possibility: nontranscendent difference. Between hubris and humility there remains the possibility of isolation from the rest of humanity that does not include the consolation of radically focused individuality. This third state, as an image of man's condition, seems particularly pertinent to the novel, which begins and often ends in the conviction that we are all separated both from each other and from a higher completion in the world beyond us.

In these terms, radical assertion and radical humility have an unexpectedly common goal; both overcome the loneliness or the restricted significance of nontranscendent separateness, either by achieving a hubristic union with absolute "Meaning" or by dissolving us into a humble but "meaningful" union with the group. Both achieve contact with otherness by dissolving the limitations of mere individuality. From this point of view, the relationship between Derridean and humanist is more complex than it might appear, since both achieve the general goal of self-assertion—union with an authenticity prior to the self—in the same general way, by means of a self-denial, a renunciation. Hence, the frequent and disturbing tendency of self-assertion in either group to disguise itself as self-effacement—Pecksniffism; hence, in particular, Derrida and de Man's tacit but unmistakable claims to a metaphysical superiority grounded in their very renunciation of individual differences. The vocabulary of presence and absence itself seemed to me to be a good way to capitalize on a kind of psychological *felix culpa*; that is, by discovering the inevitability of absence and, therefore, our collective unity within a sovereign language—which is ultimately a nostalgic idealization of primal forces—critics are able to realize, through an extravagance of resignation, a kind of bliss and a fracturing of deeply felt isolation. This dissolution into language is one that strongly resembles the bliss that is the object of the assertive struggles for meaning they seem to reject.

It is not my purpose here to unravel the complexities of hubris and humility as theoretical or behavioral strategies; I only wish to point out how the distinction between the two can blur. In general, the literary theorists' opposition between presence and absence, as well as the more traditional opposition of individualism and surrender, began to collapse for me in my thinking about Dickens into a new dialectic whose poles were separateness and nonseparateness. I began to think of Dickens' energy in particular as the expression of a desire to annihilate separateness and everything that defines separateness—the world of sense, of personality, of money, of status, and of all worldly object and purpose. Realizing full well that, as Derrida and de Man teach us, this kind of project is at least potentially aggressive—and also potentially terrifying in its emptiness—I began to suspect also that nonsense and morality were not just casually related in Dickens.

What finally catalyzed these thoughts for me, both in theoretical terms and in my study of Dickens, was my reading of contemporary literary studies of erotic energy, the work of critics superficially as diverse as Roland Barthes, Norman O. Brown, Morse Peckham, and, most especially, Georges Bataille.[16] The "mimetic" aspect of my work, in fact, is grounded in a model of human psychology derived from these writers. The fundamental issue they share is their sense of a crisis in the old-fashioned distinction between creative and destructive energies, and the collapsing of these categories seemed peculiarly relevant to my own problems wth presence and absence, meaning and nonsense. Of course, it would be impossible to make this collection of writers into anything like a school; nor is it possible, in light of all their differences, to summarize in any fair way the common elements of their thought. Yet, in all modesty, I am in many respects only an instrument of the ideas of others, and some sort of outline of these ideas seems necessary. Given this dilemma, then, the most convenient approach for me is to summarize only the ideas of Bataille, who is, in fact, the most influential of these thinkers in my work, and the most convincing theoretician of eroticism, as well as the writer whose works best encompass the relevant positions of the rest. By no means does Bataille stand alone as a theoretician, but a brief summary of the ideas in Bataille that I found useful is the easiest way for me to make it clear how I began to organize a vocabulary that exchanges problems of meaning—of presence and absence—for problems of separateness, which are erotic problems, problems of energy.

First, Bataille maintains that, contrary to the Freudian notion that there is a deep gulf between erotic, life principles and a "death instinct,"[17] man is devoted to death to precisely the same degree that he is devoted to life. In other words, because our primary dissatisfaction in life is our sense of being separate, of being isolated from the world and from each other in a way that renders all experience inauthentic—limited as it is by our personalities, our bodies, our minds, our culture—any attempts to overcome the inertia of these limitations and truly to live tend also toward our desire to experience death, which is the final and the only complete dissolution of everything that limits us in life. According to Bataille, man does not desire death, exactly, but he does desire the state of primal unity, continuity, and formlessness that he imagines must lie on the other side of death, a state of wholeness that must be ontologically prior to the discontinuity and fragmentation of biological life. To be fully human, for Bataille, means to consent to life up to the point of death.[18]

Second, since man is also terrified by death and the abyss of formlessness that it represents—as terrified of death as he is terrified of being constrained by life's limits—man finds ways of staging imitations of death within life. Ideally, these experiences imitate the formlessness, the loss of control, and the freedom from slavish desires to conserve life that death brings, but without actual dissolution. Sex is such an experience, involving both a penetration of physical limits and a dizzying loss of control. Violence is another. But the release need not be so extreme, and correlative experiences are numerous. The same sensation of limitlessness can be produced by lavish spending, or by play, or by generosity—in short, by any experience that implies a willingness to risk life or the means of conserving it. The notion of transgression is especially important here, though, since to transgress a taboo is to cross a limit that carries with it the threat of death as punishment. Hence, every transgression is a risking of life, and every risking of life is also potentially a transgression—the presence of anxiety signaled by transgression is essential to confirm the proximity of death in any particular experience. The notion of sacrifice is also important, since in sacrifice the survivors can identify vicariously with the death of the victim.[19] Obviously, the vicarious experience of death is an important aspect of reading, too, since literature is able to present metaphors for death—for example, in the form of a character's abandonment to experiences that rupture normalcy—without the reader's having to take dangerous risks himself. In my study of Dickens, I have designated these temporal experiences of timeless release from discontinuity by a litany of names, according to shades of context—"expenditure," "excess," "limit experience," and I have opposed to them another list—"restraint," "economy," "conservation." It should be clear by now, also, that I use terms like "excess," not in the sense of a surplus, but in the sense of an opposition, that is, to refer to something that defies the necessary human limits of order, meaning, economy.

Third, because these staged deaths are only representations, they have a component of reserve and are caught up again in the very economy of life they sought to overcome. Self-sacrifice, which attempts to dissolve the ego, can be put in service of prestige; lavish spending, which can free us from the restrictions of our economic class, can become the mark of social status. Neither, then, achieves a complete release. In another form, this is the problem of hubris and humility; one often annihilates self-interest only to gain something back. The structure of the act, whether conscious or not, is the same, since only in death is loss final and complete. Not only do we actively desire a reconciliation of expenditure with temporal experience, such a reconciliation is inevitable unless we actually die, and it brings with it both new reassurances and new frustrations. Hence, the need to evaluate carefully both the completeness of experiences of release and the desirability of the recuperated forms they take. In his eagerness to stress the significance of expenditure, Bataille himself often underplays the inevitability of this recycling of limit experience back into form.[20] On these grounds, and because the concept of expenditure carries with it a fashionable rakishness which I hope to moderate, Bataille sometimes invites the charge of decadence.[21]

There are a number of permutations of these ideas—the opposition between the world of work and the world of play, for example—but the germ of the thought is here. In all of these ideas, the fulcrum is a dialectical relationship between our willingness to experience loss and our need to incorporate loss within the normal world of meaning, survival, and restraining affection—to merge loss with significance or, more dynamically, to found significance on the idea or the experience of our mortality. Thus, when I claim that Dickens' work features nonsense as a violation of significance, I do not mean that Dickens advocates an ethos of irresponsibility and a philosophy of nihilism; I mean only that Dickens tries to violate the world of common sense to stage liberating encounters with the freedom represented by death, and that these encounters take place in a way that legitimates the expenditure within a more conservative framework of values. I do not advocate one need at the expense of the other, nor, I will argue, does Dickens. I discuss the relationship of expenditure and restraint in Dickens' novels as a dialectical human problem, and not as a partisan issue. Of course, the nature of this study demands that excess be weighted as the more significant term, since it is the problem of excess that most dramatically defines the scope of my discussions; I am always aware, however, that impulses toward excess cannot be considered apart from reciprocal desires for order.[22] Ultimately, I see in Dickens a constructive myth, based in a struggle to confront death and nonmeaning, and to put them into a relationship with orthodoxy and tradition that does not compromise the nonrecuperable nature of such excess.

The idea of desired death is an old one, and a simple one—so old and so simple that it surprised me how little it has found its way into the study of Dickens, or into the study of literature in general. The idea seemed to fit especially well with my sense of Dickensian energy, though, since everywhere in Dickens there is a tendency to defy the limits of signification, of representation, of characterization. And in a late novel like *Our Mutual Friend*, the connection between this imaginative exuberance and death is even made explicit, through Jenny Wren's invitation to "Come up and be dead!" (2.5) and through the good characters' necessary, revitalizing "deaths" by drowning. The connection between death and liberation is drawn earlier, of course, though in less clearly positive ways, as in the death of Anthony Chuzzlewit. "It was frightful to see how the principle of life, shut up within his withered frame, fought like a strong devil, mad to be released, and rent its ancient prison-house" (18). Strangely, too, I found myself able to use Bataille's vocabulary in ways that ultimately support more humanistic values

than are currently in vogue in lite
even foreign to Bataille, given over s
lent side of the dialectic: values like cha
and love—all of which are methods of exp
through the exercise of excessive energy.

In this work, I have extended the notion o
separate but overlapping levels. The first two cha
the question of excess in terms of Dickens' relatio
readers, a relationship that is dominated by problem
lence and of communality. In the next three chapters, I
these questions as explicit concerns of the novels themselves,
issues that are thematized through Dickens' efforts to differenti
ate between good and evil drives toward excess and to formulate the possibility of a social order based in excess. And in the
last two chapters, I discuss the ways in which Dickens' texts
feature excessive energy in broader stylistic strategies. The organization is significant: Dickens' unique relationship to his
readers, I will argue, successfully resolves problems of excess
and restraint in ways that are not available to us today; the novels themselves announce why this failure in time must occur;
and Dickens' style provides the most permanent—because the
most insubstantial—means of aesthetically fulfilling our twin
needs for liberation and for conservative meaning.

There remains one formal point. In chapters where my generalizations do not require the extended proofs of the traditional
reading of a novel, I have drawn from all of Dickens; but in the
chapters in which closely read, extended proofs or the total organization of a novel seemed important—that is, in chapters
three, four, and five—I have kept for the sake of greater clarity
to only four novels. Reluctant to marshal the massive details of
the Dickens corpus in my analyses of the internal workings of
the novels—for the reader's sanity as well as for my own—I
have concentrated on *The Old Curiosity Shop, Bleak House, A
Tale of Two Cities*, and *Great Expectations*. These novels were
selected, from one point of view, to establish the widest possible
base; they cover the early, middle, and late periods of Dickens'

ges; one is a pica-
ne historical, and
hough, these four
f Dickens' novels
raint. Each novel
eath and Sydney
Estella, and the
which represent
r to heal the gap
tically, that be-
xpress Dickens'
time, however,
ate loss as the
arton and Nell
viving groups;
ella leads him to a new

self-integration and interpersonal responsibility; and Esther, Jarndyce, and Woodcourt, I will argue, relive in an acceptable way the transgressions of Lady Dedlock and Nemo. This kind of integration is clearly not present in a novel like *Barnaby Rudge,* in which violence fails to contribute to a formulation of new values, but is random, dominant, and dissipating instead. Conversely, a novel like *Little Dorrit* describes a predominantly closed world, and the Christmas stories embody solely Dickens' conservative, social impulses. While any restricted treatment of Dickens' novels must result in imbalances—these occur, most particularly, in the chapter on villains—I have done my best to shore up thinner areas with interpolated examples from other novels.

Chapter 1

Storytelling

I am rebegot
Of absence, darkness, death:
Things which are not.

     —John Donne

One way to approach a writer's work is to look at the way he formulates his own role, as artist, within it. The motif of the actor in *Hamlet*, for example, carries in embryo a good many issues that are taken up in broader contexts by Shakespeare's play—problems of self-detachment, of indirect influence, and of action. In *Paradise Lost*, the tension between the privileged position of the poet and his simultaneous inadequacy to describe underlies much of the concern of the poem with the status of human knowledge. Dickens, more than most novelists, perhaps, rewards a similar kind of study, for Dickens frequently employs artistic characters, even in a number of unlikely guises: the circus performer, the craftsman, and—in Mr. Venus—the anatomist. And while we should be careful not to equate fictional idealizations of the artist with Dickens' success in realizing the ideal, these artist figures can help us define for his novels the sphere of their author's intentions.

Many readers have noticed that Dickens uses the broad notion of the fictional as a metaphor for the arbitrariness and the willed quality of personal identity. Those readers have also noticed that this function of art in Dickens' novels is hardly celebrated. On the one hand, self-conscious fictionalizing can be liberating, as in John Harmon's playing the role of John Rokesmith. But in this case artistry is a subordinate issue; Harmon's experience as an "artist" is not as significant as the change he produces in Bella; his fiction is a means, not an end. On the other hand—and this is more often the case in Dickens—fictionalizing can limit personality to a lie. *Little Dorrit* expresses this claustrophobic fear acutely in Merdle's fiction of wealth, Flora's fiction about the persistence of her past, Little Dorrit's fiction of perpetual childhood, her father's fiction of patriarchy, and Clennam's fiction that he feels no love—to name a few. In other novels Dickens satirizes with more humor this negative but awesome power of fiction to imprison character within an artificial, inauthentic self: through Bounderby's fiction about his childhood independence, for example, or through Sarah Gamp's imaginary Mrs. Harris, or through Joey Bagstock's fictional magnanimity. It is a common enough observation to say that characters in Dickens are defined by their adherence to invented beliefs and imaginary priorities—to fictions.

This kind of fiction in Dickens is also related to problems of subjective interpretation; every attempt at understanding is a fiction—either an approximation or a projection—and, therefore, a restrictive distortion.[1] Mrs. Snagsby's perceptions about her husband are a fiction, as are Mark Tapley's notion that cheerfulness in adversity is the greatest possible virtue, and the Pickwickians' many conjectures about the hieroglyphic they happen to find on a stone. Joe's "reading" in *Great Expectations*, which consists of identifying "J-O's," is a concise image of the solipsisms of reading as interpretation.[2] In this way, Dickens shows us that interpretations of the external world as well as performances of the hidden self result in fraudulent fictions, leaving a vacant spot where genuine identity and knowledge should be. Thus, characters in the third-person narrative of *Bleak House* pore over documents and other clues about events only to develop competing versions of the truth about Lady Dedlock's guilt; and Esther, in the first-person narrative, presents us with a carefully contrived, if naive, self as a strategy for guiltlessness. Similarly, Pip struggles to "read" his own destiny and personality in signs written in the external world, only to be misled by them into a false conception of himself. In Dickens' world, perception and identity are both made up, and they combine to make all human existence a mere fabrication.[3] So it is that David Copperfield tells us he will not be able to decide whether "I shall turn out to be the hero of my own life, or whether that station will be held by anybody else" (1) until his autobiography is actually written, that is, until real life, which is multivalent, is committed to a particular fiction, a particular version of the reality.

We should remember, however, that this description of fiction in Dickens as a reflection of the fabricated quality of human existence is emphatically a modern one, and that it involves distortions of its own. While Dickens does seem obsessed by the inauthenticities of his characters' individual lives, and while the fabrications of imagination and interpretation do become oppressive for those characters, there is another kind of artistic or fictional energy in Dickens that shatters the oppressions of artificiality. The specific role of the storyteller—and the artist generally—in Dickens does not parallel his characters' broadly fictional attempts to create personal identities and perceptive truths. Instead, there is another goal of storytelling in Dickens, a goal that is opposed to all stability, order, and closure, regardless of their artificial or organic status. In fact, there is a way in which Dickens sees storytelling as a defiance of the very arbitrariness and fixity threatened by personal identity and perception. The fundamental impulse underlying this kind of fiction in Dickens is not fabrication; necessarily, it is violence.

Of course, the violent side of Dickens and of his artistic figures—Jasper, Gowan, Jenny Wren—has been noted before. Even John Harmon's fiction involves a kind of manipulative violence if we take into account its effect on Bella, who is Harmon's principal audience. But this violence is often considered only as a kind of frustrated rage or an inarticulate restlessness. If, however, we take our notion of rigid, fraudulent existence to be a central problem in Dickens, and if we look closely at the actual narratives and storytellers in the novels as they affect others— readers and audiences—rather than at characters' purely subjective uses of "fiction," we can uncover a more important goal for the violence of Dickens' artists: a passionate quest for authenticity. Storytelling in Dickens is always an interpersonal act, and the interpersonal relationship it figures for us is often violent, but always as a means to a profound kind of fullness.

Dickens' interest in the violence of art shows up even in an early novel like *The Old Curiosity Shop*. One of the odder intrusions in the plot is the single gentleman's "most extraordinary and remarkable interest in the exhibition of Punch" (37). It is strange, in a novel rotten with physical deformity and tense with the threat of violence to Nell, to find one of the heroes fascinated by a play that thrives on violence. Though the story varies from performance to performance, the puppet Punch regularly kills some or all of the other characters in the play, including the man sent to execute him, and swears himself ready for combat with the Devil himself. Of course, the single gentleman has a deeper purpose; he is trying to trace Nell and her grandfather by finding the puppet-show exhibitors they had been seen traveling with. But our introduction to the single gentleman's obsession with the puppet show, before we learn his underlying motives, leads us to believe that his interest in Punch as a performance, however secondary that interest turns out to be, is quite real. The single gentleman is not content simply to interrogate the exhibitors; instead, he brings the puppet show back to Bevis Marks, has it set up in the street in front of Sampson Brass's house, and watches the performance from the privileged viewpoint of his first-floor window. Because of the latent similarity between Punch's violence and the single gentleman's volatility, we are led to feel that a love of the puppet show is simply one of the single gentleman's "peculiarities." And as if to reinforce the acceptability of the single gentleman's fascination, Dickens makes an appreciation of the Quilpian Punch a criterion of virtue. Dick Swiveller, Sally Brass (at a point when we think that Dick may have won her over to amicability), and Nell's grandfather all share the single gentleman's enjoyment, while only Sampson Brass is opposed.

The grounds for this moral distinction lie, paradoxically, in the violence itself. For the audience to the performance, Punch's violence functions as a liberation from the mundane, morally negative world of mere human endurance. Punch, we are told, is a relief from the staid, repressed world of business and law, the restrictively economic world, the normal world. He is deliberately ranged against the values of work;[4] in Bevis Marks, right outside the stifling office of Sampson Brass himself, "the entertainment would proceed, with all its exciting accompaniments of

fife and drum and shout, to the excessive consternation of all so-
ber votaries of business in that silent thoroughfare." Swiveller,
too, agrees that "looking at a Punch, or indeed looking at anything out of window, was better than working." For Sampson,
the "screamers and roarers" who flock to the performance have
the terrible effect of "distracting one from business," and Sampson underscores the opposition between the excessiveness of violence and the restrictiveness of economic reality with his own
cheapness. "If I could get a break and four blood horses to cut
into the Marks when the crowd is at its thickest, I'd give eighteenpence and never grudge it."

Sampson's whining, sterile presence makes it clear why the
aesthetic violence in Punch is a shot of life. The energy Punch so
refreshingly unleashes from its established channels—the reckless, gratuitous energy of violence—is flagrantly opposed to the
calculated, economical, carefully conserved energy of business.
Punch's performance—and all entertainment, for that matter,
including Dickens' novel—is excessive in the sense that it is unnecessary for biological life; it is an unremunerative interruption
of the struggle for survival, implying a vital willingness to suspend concern for the economic self. Therefore, it is an assertion
of human freedom.

Significantly enough, in *The Old Curiosity Shop* this freedom is displayed through the economic liberality of the poor,
lower-class audience after the show is over, a release from economic limits that the puppet-show exhibitors depend upon; "voluntary contributions were showered in with a liberality which
testified yet more strongly to the general delight" (16). Metaphorically, this economic liberality indicates a willingness for the
conservative self to "die" momentarily, to run an economic risk
in a world (or a novel) that insistently identifies economic circumspection with the inhumanity of survival: through Nell's
grandfather's obsession with money as the preserver of Nell's
life, through Swiveller's assumption of an insufferable job because his rich aunt fails him, and through endless portraits of
the lower classes at work—digging graves, slaving in the facto-

ries, even bearing the daytime burden of the puppet show that, dismantled, is only a means for Codlin to make money. In contrast, Punch, through explicit violence, makes the audience's violation of conservative economic control through art a joyous one. To underscore this positive relationship, Dickens has Kit, while at play with his family, "hit a man on the head with the handkerchief of apples for 'scrowdging' his parent with unnecessary violence." The narrator comments, "all this was looked upon as quite a capital joke, and an essential part of the entertainment" (39). For Dickens, the radically liberating quality of art is foregrounded in the explicit violence of both Kit and the puppet show, which, when it is performed for an audience as entertainment, becomes an alternative energy to that of the working self.

The enthusiasm of Punch's audience implies that the act of violation is directly related to what makes human life authentically human rather than merely mechanical or biological: spontaneity, flexibility, enthusiasm. Violence is not necessarily the product of aggressive self-interest; in this case, it is a reflection of human needs for expansion and release. Through violence, the audience devotes itself to a world in which personal limits have been transcended, a world in which authenticity is no longer falsified by the self. To affirm this violence as a performance, then, is, in some qualified way, to affirm human life. Buried at the heart of *The Old Curiosity Shop*, a novel that seems to celebrate death through Nell, the story of Punch adds a radical new dimension to the abyss of death; violent death is the final, ultimate form of human liberation, when liberation is conceived in terms of a violation and not a preservation or an elaboration, of selfhood. In a paradoxical way, we realize our humanity most fully by opening ourselves to the profundity of death—to that which is usually considered nonhuman.

Of course, the problem of violence in art is a complex one, and it would be idle to assume that Dickens intended Punch only as a veiled indulgence in outright violence for his readers—especially because we see only the reactions of Punch's audience and not the actual violence of the play itself. The most obvious complication to the problem of violence is our fear of death, and of the abyss of formlessness outside personality, which is as strong as, if not stronger than, our desire to violate stifling human limits. In *The Sickness Unto Death*, Kierkegaard specifies these twin fears as the inevitable result of our human situation, which suspends us between finitude and infinitude.[5] But for the moment at least, it is clear that the role of violence, once seen in its metaphysical aspect as a liberation of consciousness, can help us to understand a basic tension within all art—which can shield us from our fear by making violence vicarious—and within Dickens' art in particular, a tension which is usually slighted in favor of the ability of art to order reality for us.

It is important to recognize, for instance, that the problem of excessive violence in Dickens is not merely a personal one.[6] In fact, the theme of violence and transgression is a central one for all novelists. The censure of the novel by countless eighteenth-century commentators points up a nearly universal fear; initially, the novel genre was felt to be inherently subversive in its mimetic attention to violence and to moral transgression in general, which always implies a violation of limits. The argument usually ran this way: because of its close scrutiny of everyday life, the depiction of wrongdoing in the novel would easily give rise to imitation, even if that wrongdoing were rebuked by the novelist's narrator.[7] And although it is easy to scorn such a fear from this distance in time—in view of the relative moderation of those early novels and the foreignness of older conventions of modesty—we may have to admit that those critics were basically right. It is clear, at least, that the contemporary liberal argument that TV violence encourages imitation is not so very different. And although novelists from Defoe through Nabokov have employed the convention (sometimes satiric) of an endorsed moral "lesson" meant to extenuate the presence of sin in their novels, that homiletic frame does little to conceal the overriding appeal of sin's excessiveness. Can we really deny the prominence of transgression in a genre whose early classics include Pamela's threatened virginity, Clarissa's rape, Tom Jones' fornication and putative incest, Moll Flanders' career of vice, and Roderick Random's robust, burlesque violence? Unwittingly, what the critics—old and new—tell us is that transgressive behavior naturally attracts realistic narrative forms, perhaps because we all find transgression deeply interesting as we move from abstract modes of thought to more phenomenal ones. The problem is epitomized by Satan in *Paradise Lost*; evil often becomes attractive once it has been personified or dramatized. The narrator of *Dombey and Son* expresses this difficulty through Sol Gills' anxiety that his stories about shipwrecks—intended to deter Walter Gay from going to sea—only encourage Walter to associate the risk of violent death with vitality and adventure. "It would seem as if there never was a book written, or a story told, expressly with the object of keeping boys on shore, which did not lure and charm them to the ocean, as a matter of course" (4).

It is difficult to approach Dickens' work without considering the place of transgression in it, if only because we know so much about Dickens' own fascination with crime. A casual look at *Bentley's Miscellany*, which resembles *True Detective* or *The National Enquirer* in its array of sensational reports of murders and robberies—lurid factual accounts that run side-by-side with the fictional text of *Oliver Twist*—confirms the prominence, in Dickens and in his audience, of an interest in violence. But it is crucial to overcome our tendency to assume that Dickens' featured violence is an inarticulate prurience and to suspend for a moment strict notions about morality. Dickens does not clandestinely indulge a pathological yearning for violence. On the contrary, in the novels the fascination of violence is overtly made a principle of the artwork. Through Punch, as we have seen, aesthetic violence is exalted (in a tongue-in-cheek way, Punch clearly being vulgar entertainment) as a matter of content, since it is represented violence that appeals to Punch's audience. But elsewhere in Dickens, the function of violence within storytelling is dramatized in a profounder way, as a function inseparable from the relationship of the storyteller to his audience. In Dickens, the very notion of storytelling hinges on a relationship of latent violence; rather than merely witnessing violation, the audience is itself jolted.

Captain Cuttle in *Dombey and Son* provides perhaps the most obvious example of this relationship. When Cuttle undertakes the job of presenting the recovered Walter Gay to Florence, he does it—elaborately, and over something like a thirty-six-hour period—in the form of a carefully contrived, suspenseful fiction, to which Florence becomes the audience. First, he takes to reminding Florence incessantly of Walter's death. Then, he tells her a protracted story about a shipwreck at sea and about the possibility of a single man's surviving that wreck. Finally, Cuttle has Walter appear in the shop at the climax of his story, when Florence's agitation is at its height. There is no rationale proposed for this eccentric storytelling; we can assume that Cuttle, in his odd way, is trying to soften the blow to Florence, especially since he has received a garbled message from Walter about "existing circumstances" and "coming prepared." Yet it is not impertinent to wonder whether the shock is made worse through the suspense that Cuttle creates for Florence— and for the reader as well—by acting out a part and by drawing out the revelation. His often repeated "Poor Wal'r. Aye, aye! Drownded. An't he?" (49) may or may not be calculated to mollify, but its effect on Florence is to reopen old sores without soothing them. These reopened doubts produce pain enough in Florence, who does not know their groundlessness, to make Cuttle's pretense seem positively cruel. While Cuttle is "preparing" Florence by dwelling obsessively on Walter's death, we are told:

Florence was very sorry that she should unwittingly, though naturally, have awakened these associations in the mind of her protector, by taking refuge there; and sitting down before the little table where the Captain had arranged the telescope and song-book, and those other rarities, thought of Walter, and of all that was connected with him in the past, until she could have almost wished to lie down on her

bed and fade away. But in her lonely yearning to the dead whom she
had loved, no thought of home—no possibility of going back—no presentation of it as yet existing, or as sheltering her father—once en-
tered her thoughts. She had seen the murder done. In the last
lingering natural aspect in which she had cherished him through so
much, he had been torn out of her heart, defaced, and slain. The
thought of it was so appalling to her, that she covered her eyes, and
shrunk trembling from the least remembrance of the deed, or of the
cruel hand that did it.

It is significant that the death of Walter should become associated in Florence's mind with her flight from her father, and not
only because it was through her father's hardheartedness that
Walter was sent to sea in the first place. Both Walter's death and
Florence's flight represent radical release and "dying"—one
irredeemably grievous, but the other potentially liberating.
Florence's agitation, heightened by Cuttle, embodies both the
attractive and the terrible aspects of release.

Cuttle's exacerbation of Florence's distress could be considered simple ineptitude if it were not for deliberate hints from
Dickens that, on some level, her distress is desired. To intensify
the potential for violation in their relationship, Cuttle and Florence are repeatedly paired as beauty and the beast: "There
could scarcely be a more decided contrast than between Florence in her delicate youth and beauty, and Captain Cuttle with
his knobby face, his great broad weather-beaten person, and his
gruff voice." Thus, a "wandering princess and a good monster in
a story-book might have sat by the fireside, and talked as Captain Cuttle and poor Florence talked—and not have looked very
much unlike them." Cuttle frequently reinforces this image by
calling Florence "my beauty" and "my pretty" during the period
of his fiction. Then, too, while Florence lives in Cuttle's house,
we see him peering through her door while she sleeps—protec-
tively, to be sure—more than once; we hear his "growling whisper" about Walter; and we see him acting ambiguously nervous
and embarrassed. More strikingly, at the very moment when
the revelation of Walter is at hand, at the moment when Flor-

ence is almost undone with anxiety, Cuttle cuts off the story tantalizingly and focuses our attention on his own monstrousness. "The Captain, without knowing what he did, had cut a slice of bread from the loaf, and put it on his hook (which was his usual toasting-fork), on which he now held it to the fire; looking behind Florence with great emotion in his face, and suffering the bread to blaze and burn like fuel." Florence and the slice of bread, both blazing and both the prisoners of Cuttle, are linked in a way that becomes comical once it has been pointed out, especially because Cuttle and Florence pause over the word "spared."

Cuttle, of course, is far from being malevolent. His status is more properly ambiguous—he is a good monster. It is no accident, however, that Cuttle is a man frustrated in love, in the sense that the hoary old bachelor is constantly threatened by the matrimonial designs of Mrs. MacStinger. That is to say, Captain Cuttle is haunted by the restrictive potential in sexual relationships; as a result, he appears to be fortified in his bachelorhood. Interestingly, at the end of this chapter Cuttle dreams that Mrs. MacStinger has been married off to Sol Gills and that she keeps him "prisoner . . . in a secret chamber on a short allowance of victuals." Moreover, Cuttle meets with Mr. Toots, the frustrated aspirant to Florence, just before he enters on his fictional project, and banishes him forever from Florence's presence—he and Toots are identified in this scene, if only in their mutual bachelorhood and in Cuttle's sudden "tender pity" for Toots, but Cuttle takes on himself the office of dismissing Toots and remains with Florence alone. Cuttle's frustrated singleness, his momentary identification with Toots, his monstrousness, his dismissal of Toots—all point up his eroticized relationship to Florence. Then, too, our attention is so frequently called to Cuttle's careful modesty around Florence during these scenes that we cannot help but be aware of the erotic situation created by her presence in his house. When she first arrives at his door and passes out, Cuttle, after commenting on her recently attained womanhood, "was so respectful of her, and had such a reverence

for her, in this new character, that he would not have held her in
his arms, while she was unconscious, for a thousand pounds"
(48). And later on the narrator explicitly tells us, "As the Captain sat, and smoked, and looked at Florence, God knows what
impossible pictures, in which she was the principal figure, presented themselves to his mind" (49). Captain Cuttle's fiction
takes on a new dimension in this context; it is as if, through Florence—a literally captive audience—Cuttle gains some kind of
momentary, violent release from erotic inhibitions.

The important point, however, is that Captain Cuttle's resolution of the situation is aesthetic and imaginative. Through the
emotionally violent medium of story, Cuttle shares in the release
featured in the erotic reunion of Florence and Walter without
committing an actual transgression, and he manages to participate in that union innocently, vicariously. "The fulness of the
glow he shed around him could only have been engendered in his
contemplation of the two together, and in all the fancies springing out of that association, that came sparkling and beaming into
his head, and danced about it." Although Cuttle stages an act of
violation, he does so in an imaginary and not a real way. Cuttle
thus becomes a meeting ground for several Dickensian themes:
romantic love, violence, and storytelling seen as the conjunction
of these two themes in the socially legitimate relationship of narrator to audience. In fact, Cuttle's legitimately erotic relationship to Florence as storyteller supplies much of the sexual
atmosphere Dickens refuses to associate even with Walter, who
must be returned to Florence as a "brother" and not as a lover.
In Cuttle and Florence, the relationship of narrator to audience
is a "harmless" version of the relationship of the beast to beauty,
so much so that it is finally impossible to say who takes the
greater satisfaction, the violator or the violated, the cunning
narrator or the dizzied audience. We cannot help sharing in the
pleasure of witnessing Florence's agitation, if we suspect that
she will finally be overwhelmed with good news—just as we
might enjoy the distress of a child if we can see both its "harm-
lessness" and the prospect of its immediate relief; or, if we have

not yet guessed the truth, we can easily understand through our own reactions how Florence's pleasure is the greater for her moments of panic and doubt. The arousal and the release of both storyteller and audience is a common one. It would be heavy-handed to call this kind of pleasure sadistic or masochistic, but it cannot be denied that the pleasure depends on a manipulation designed to evoke disorientation, fear, and hope, followed by a shock—that is, an eroticized release from the stable, restricted self and, therefore, a temporary dissolution of that self into intense emotion.

This same symbolic drama is enacted in a briefer form in *A Tale of Two Cities*. In this late novel, it is Mr. Lorry, the old bachelor and banker, who presents to Lucie Manette, the virginal princess, news that her father is still alive and that she is about to see him. This recitation, too, is conducted by Lorry in the form of a fiction, "a story of one of our customers." Here the story is explicitly presented as an attempt to soften the blow, an attempt that fails. Despite Lorry's "protective" fiction, Lucie swoons, and Miss Pross then accuses Lorry, "couldn't you tell her what you had to tell her, without frightening her to death?" (1.4). Lorry may be less implicated in the violence of this story than Cuttle is in his own, but the violence proves to be there nonetheless, in the structure of storytelling itself, which mixes suspense and the implication of an urgent meaning with a sudden, terribly anticipated revelation. Dickens' repetition of this motif in two novels separated from each other by roughly twelve years is an indication of its prominence in his imagination as an image of the role of the storyteller.

No doubt, the horror stories Dickens' nurse told him as a child—stories like the tale of Captain Murderer, which Dickens later set down in print—exerted a powerful influence on him as an image of his craft. Magwitch's story about the "young man" who will eat Pip's heart is an echo of this potential for violence and horror in stories, as are many of the stories that interrupt *The Pickwick Papers*, and the same role is played in more sophisticated ways by other Dickensian storytellers. Tulkinghorn, in *Bleak House*, probes Lady Dedlock's heart by telling her story to Sir Leicester's circle in her presence, disguising it in the form of a fiction. In the same novel, Bucket holds Sir Leicester captive while he dramatizes before his very eyes, playing the role of stage director, the same story. Noddy Boffin's hoax in *Our Mutual Friend* is a subtle version of this motif of violation; his pretended cruelty is the very substance of his fiction. More subtly, Dickens frequently associates his storytellers and artist figures with death through images of waste and decay. The image of the puppet Punch in *The Old Curiosity Shop*, lifeless and disfigured, "perched cross-legged upon a tombstone" (16), most vividly illustrates the parallel. Similarly, Jenny Wren in *Our Mutual Friend* uses her own hair to make dolls, as well as bits of cast-off wood and cloth. John Jasper compares the sordid visions of the "haggard woman" of the opium den (1) to his own, and even Mr. Dick's inability to turn the head of Charles I into art suggests by analogy an element of human waste present in David Copperfield's more successful attempts to turn his dead past into a "Memorial." In addition, many of the articles in *Household Words* about various arts and crafts demonstrate an inordinate interest on Dickens' part in the way waste materials can be turned into art.[8]

In some way, all of Dickens' stories and storytellers feature violence. Nevertheless, there is another dimension to storytelling among Dickens' good characters that counters its potential for shock. It would be only half right to argue that storytelling for Dickens is simply a staging of violation—whether of character or of the reader. For instance, the spectators in *The Old Curiosity Shop* are not Quilp, no matter how much they enjoy the violence in the puppet show. To take up our first three examples: Punch, Cuttle, and Lorry make it clear that a dimension of violence is inevitable in stories, since even a character like Lorry, who tries not to shock, is caught up in narrative violence through the very mechanisms of storytelling. At the same time, however, the Punch show is a harmless, convivial performance, Cuttle is a good monster, and both he and Lorry are the bearers

of good, not evil tidings. Just as important as the aestheticized
violation inherent in these stories is their contrary function for
their audiences as vehicles of restoration. Through story, impulses toward violation are reconciled with the gratification of
more conservative desires.

Cuttle and Lorry, though they exacerbate the pain and suffering, the torture, of their auditors, finally fracture the suspense and release their auditors from distress by presenting
them with a *happy* ending. In this way, restoration is embodied
as violation, violation is redeemed by restoration. Pain, suffering, and intense loss are fused with the conservative values of
the happy reunion. Story, thus, becomes a magical vehicle of
protection and fulfillment, gratifying the listener who gives himself up to it completely, at the same time that it is the condition
for the erotic shock of a liberation. So it is that many of Dickens'
happy endings are themselves presented as stories within the
novel. Oliver Twist's story, for example, is finally told by
Brownlow, and, at Brownlow's insistence, by Monks; old Martin
Chuzzlewit satisfies his family and friends with a recitation of
his strategy for undermining Pecksniff; Sydney Carton imagines
his martyrdom told to Darnay's grandson as a story; Kit tells the
story of Nell's death to his children; and Boffin explains how his
miserliness was a pretense. Through the patriarchal voice of
these storytellers, we feel plot to be a kind of happy, fixed destiny. Ideally, of course, as with Cuttle and Lorry, these two elements—suspense or violation and the happiness, restoration,
survival of the conclusion—are fused. Dickens' entire art might
be capsulized as the delicate balancing of these two opposite and
equal but mutually exclusive satisfactions.

The puppet show in Punch provides a more obscure but perhaps a more convincing example of this fusion. Punch's audience
sustains an experience of violence, but they also survive. And
these two conflicting human needs do not simply coexist in the
puppet show; the one produces and transforms—it is made manifest in—the other. The feeling of "continuity"[9] with otherness
that is the goal of violent release is recreated on this side of

death in the audience's heightened sense of fraternal union. So it is that Nell's grandfather is a changed man in the afterglow of Punch's performance. "He, happily insensible to every care and anxiety, sat listening with a vacant smile and admiring face to all that his new friends said" (16). Only the puppet show can release the old man from his jealous economic fears about the rest of mankind and generate in him a kind of selfless bliss. Similarly, the puppet show provides an occasion for a greater intimacy between Swiveller and Sally Brass; Dick had been "at some pains to awaken in his fellow-clerk a sense of [the puppet show's] beauties and manifold deserts; . . . The glass being dim, Mr. Swiveller, agreeably to a friendly convention which he had established between them, hitched off the brown head-dress from Miss Sally's head, and dusted it carefully therewith" (37). Shortly afterward, too, the Nubbles family, Barbara, and her mother see a play that lifts them out of their workaday lives into a fellow-feeling so strong that the narrator speculates "there were not six happier people in the world" (39); the play reflects, in part, the melodramatic violence of *The Old Curiosity Shop* itself; "the forlorn lady, who made [Barbara] cry—the tyrant, who made her tremble—the man who sang the song with the lady's maid and danced the chorus, who made her laugh—the pony who reared up on his hind legs when he saw the murderer."

Through these performances, violence can be experienced within a form that paradoxically increases the fraternity of the audience. The authenticity of limitlessness that is the object of violence is thereby recreated on this side of death in the fraternal, egoless union of the audience. Death is given a form in life by the audience's collectivity, their mutual relaxation of personal limits. The great instance of this paradox in *The Old Curiosity Shop* is Nell's fictional death itself, which is the crucial instance of the dynamic Punch foreshadows; the curious thing about Nell's death is that she was recovered by Victorian England as a cultural symbol of loss. As the popular response to her death seems to indicate, she is an invitation to a common mourning and a corresponding sense of recovered community. It is the publicness of Nell's death, the blatant invitation to join in the event, that induces embarrassment in those who are more alienated from public society. A broader illustration of Dickens' interest in this kind of resolution is his imagistic treatment of fire. Most of the scenes of violence and destruction in Dickens are accentuated by fire, and yet it is the hearth, the fire brought inside the home, that becomes indispensible to the world of the good characters, who often seek to discover themselves by staring into the flames—Lizzie Hexam, Louisa Gradgrind, even Nell in the factory all gaze meditatively into fires; and Joe's forge in *Great Expectations* has the same vital but reassuring imagistic value.[10] These kinds of resolution indicate a vision of culture that bases meaning and collective union on a reverence for death and for meaninglessness.

It should be noted, too, that the violence of story, which we have seen as both the violence of the storyteller against his audience and as the content of particular performances that an audience—like Punch's—finds attractive, can be much more subtle; it can simply be the violation of temporal self-consciousness that occurs when we give ourselves up to the linear, alternative time of story. For example, David Copperfield's portrait of himself as the audience to eighteenth-century novels hints at this subtle violation; David sinks himself into his reading to escape his actual relationship to the Murdstones, and his enthusiasm testifies to the success of his release. "I have been Tom Jones (a child's Tom Jones, a harmless creature) for a week together. I have sustained my own idea of Roderick Random for a month at a stretch, I verily believe" (4). Young David, by dissolving himself in an identification with his fictional heroes, violates the deadliness of his enslavement at the Murdstones and finds freedom. Yet the alterations—"a child's Tom Jones," "my own idea of Roderick Random"—are significant. This is an escape, but an escape of a particular kind. Through story, David manages to restore to himself a satisfactory image of himself and of his world. This restoration extends to all the features of his immediate surroundings.

Every barn in the neighbourhood, every stone in the church, and every foot of the churchyard, had some association of its own, in my mind, connected with these books, and stood for some locality made famous in them. I have seen Tom Pipes go climbing up the church-steeple; I have watched Strap, with the knapsack on his back, stopping to rest himself upon the wicket-gate; and I *know* that Commodore Trunnion held that club with Mr. Pickle, in the parlour of our little village alehouse.

The world, previously alien, oppressive, and restrictive, is restored to David as an open-ended place through the synthesis of fiction and reality. David's entire autobiography, in which he fuses the griefs of his own life with the fictional conventions of *Tom Jones* and *Roderick Random*, is a realization of this synthesis, a synthesis that subsumes the tension between violent loss and recovered meaning.

As we might expect, these fictional formulations of the storyteller's violent relationship to his audience are paralleled in Dickens' own career as a storyteller in ways that are too striking to go unmentioned. Dickens undoubtedly had a very special relationship with his own audience—though one wonders whether this actual relationship may not simply be the incarnation of every novelist's projected relationship with his reader. Most significantly, both Dickens and his readers participated in an artistic medium in which violent excess could be experienced as harmless at the same time that community offered a kind of shelter that was not burdened with the usual restrictions represented by social life.

Much has been said recently of the violent side of Dickens' relationship to his readers.[11] Certainly, we have Dickens' own words to testify to it. After reading "The Chimes" to a small group of friends, Dickens wrote to his wife, "If you had seen Macready last night, undisguisedly sobbing and crying on the sofa as I read, you would have felt, as I did, what a thing it is to have power."[12] Dickens' insistence on reading Nancy's murder from *Oliver Twist*, even against the advice of his doctors when it became evident he was overstraining himself, further testifies to his love of terrifying audiences. Not only in his pathetic and in his violent propensities, but in his comic impulses, too, Dickens displayed a desire to shock and overpower his audience; Forster reports that in his school days Dickens and his friends used to affect a foreign-sounding lingo to astound passersby, and one of Dickens' favorite pranks as a young man was to knock on a strange door, lie down on the doorstep, and, when the door was opened, jump up frantically and run away.[13] This violence in relation to his audience, his desire to shock and disturb them, was an adjunct of Dickens' generally violent attitude toward his writing itself. Dickens often expressed a rough-and-tumble attitude toward his characters; he "had fallen on him [Oliver Twist] tooth and nail," he once wrote to Forster.[14] And in *Martin Chuzzlewit*, the narrator opens a chapter in this malicious way. "As the surgeon's first care after amputating a limb is to take up the arteries the cruel knife has severed, so it is the duty of this history, which in its remorseless course has cut from the Pecksniffian trunk its right arm, Mercy, to look to the parent stem and see how in all its various ramifications it got on without her" (30).

Furthermore, Dickens always conceived the mimetic aspect of writing as a violent one. Dickens' own image of the violence latent in writing as mimesis is Mr. Venus in *Our Mutual Friend*; as emblems of their shared interest in violence, Mr. Venus is said to have a statue on his desk of two toads fighting a duel with swords, one of them in process of being run through; and Forster tells us that on Dickens' writing desk there was a similar statue.[15] The artistic analogy is apt in this sense; Mr. Venus, as the "articulator of human bones"—and, like Dickens in later life, as the man frustrated in love—routinely expresses the representations of his anatomizing craft in terms of violence. "You've no idea how small you'd come out, if I had the articulating of you" (1.7), he says to a pesty boy. Jenny Wren, who sticks pins in the dolls she has made to resemble people she hates is yet another example of the same aggressive quality in representation. In more general ways, literally all of Dickens' writers and artist figures are potentially violent. Jasper claims that "even a poor monotonous chorister and grinder" of music like himself can be given to restless, desperate urges (2); Henry Gowan's dog "Lion" seems to be the embodiment of his own repressed violence; and Tom Pinch, the mild organist, is capable of flooring Jonas Chuzzlewit with one blow.

But Dickens, in his use of authorial violence, neither affirms violence in general nor bewails it as an inevitable element in man's will. Instead, Dickens turns the violence of writing into spectacle—which is why he is so willing to display its presence through storytelling motifs—in order to make the meaning of loss, and, therefore, the authentic meaning of man, stripped of his artificial identity, present on this side of death. It is essential, in this dynamic, to confine violence, or to displace it in such a way that it is not actually carried out, that is, to make it a performance that has meaning for a receptive, nonviolent audience. Bataille formulates this necessity concisely.

For man to be finally revealed to himself he would have to die, but he would have to do so while living—while watching himself cease to be. In other words, death itself would have to become (self)consciousness at the very moment when it annihilates conscious being. In a sense this is what takes place (or at least is on the point of taking place, or which takes place in a fugitive, ungraspable manner) by means of a subterfuge. In sacrifice, the sacrificer identifies with the animal struck by death. Thus he dies while watching himself die, and even, after a fashion, dies of his own volition, as one with the sacrificial arm. . . . This difficulty foreshadows the necessity of *spectacle*, or generally of *representation*, without the repetition of which we could remain foreign to and ignorant of death, as animals apparently remain.[16]

Of course, art is much more complicated than sacrifice, but it is clear that Dickens' work shares with sacrifice the desire to present violence within a closed form. Through both the content and the performance of the art work, Dickens sought such a synthesis; his violent relation with the world as a storyteller had the paradoxical effect of creating for him a reassuring, understanding, complicit community that shared in this aestheticized violence.

Dickens was extremely careful to make his relationship with his readers a sustained as well as a violent one. He very scrupulously calculated when to stop serial publication in order to give his readers a rest, which characters would have the most popular appeal, and how far he could go to shock his audience without losing them. For instance, he once asked Forster if he thought that his plans for a dissipated Walter Gay would anger readers, and, on Forster's advice that it would, he changed his mind.[17] Contrary to his assertion that he never read reviews, it has been proved that Dickens *did* read them, and George Ford hypothesizes that it was because of the reviews that Dickens changed direction between the disastrously received, sardonic *Martin Chuzzlewit* and the successful *Dombey and Son*, supplying his readers in the later novels with more of the pathos they had liked in his earlier work.[18] Then, too, Dickens did not hesitate to advocate the use of conventions to other writers in the interest of sustaining the bond between author and audience; when advising one of his contributors to *Household Words* to revise a story to make it more palatable to readers, he wrote, "You write to be read, of course."[19] This advocacy of convention was not merely an interest in driving up sales, for Dickens seems to have been genuinely fond of his audience. For instance, he loved to repeat an incident that occurred on one of his reading expeditions, when a woman asked to "touch the hand that has filled my house with many friends."[20] And Dickens never tired of dwelling somewhat sentimentally on the sustained affection his audience felt for him. "The affectionate regard of the people exceeds all bounds and is shown in every way," he once wrote to Forster. "The audiences do everything but embrace me, and take as much pains with the readings as I do."[21] Jack Lindsay proposes that the readings themselves were Dickens' attempt to reassure himself about his community of readers at a time when he felt his creative powers waning, and at a time when he risked scandal through his affair with Ellen Ternan. In other words, at the moment when Dickens broke the limits of society, he sought to reestablish contact with his own society of readers, to feel his actions confirmed in them.[22]

The important point here, though, is that the community that contains and conserves the violence of Dickens' writing is not a social community but a fictional one, a community of his own creation. Only in this way can Dickens moderate the restrictive side of conservation and avoid being too rigidly bound to the requirements of a social group. During the time of his break-up with Kate, Dickens told Forster, "I have written to little purpose, if I cannot write myself right."[23] And Dickens' faith in the magical powers of the word to create an unworldly, insubstantial community is demonstrated by his "personal" message in *Household Words*, in which he lies to his readers, telling them that his domestic troubles have been "amicably composed" and that all rumors about his love life are false.[24] By the sheer power of the pen, Dickens hoped to sustain the readership he had gained through the pen, and his readers' willingness to accept the lie testifies to their reciprocal need to participate in a community well-removed from the normal one. Dickens' figural community, created by and sustained in language, offered him a transformed, unburdened version of what reassurance and permanent love—or, in a sense, meaning—would ideally be like: an unlimited vessel of receptivity, and a field for the sublimated exercise of writerly violence and excess. Dickens' relationship to his readers is the real marriage that the conventional marriages in his novels figure—the closest thing to the containment of excess within an insubstantial form that Dickens could create in real life. In a letter to Forster, Dickens makes this transposition of the notion of marriage from wife to audience explicit.

Quite dismiss from your mind any reference whatever to present circumstances at home. Nothing can put *them* right, until we are all dead and buried and risen. . . . A dismal failure has to be borne, and there's an end. Will you then try to think of this reading project (as I do) apart from all personal likings and dislikings, and solely with a view to its effect on that particular relation (personally affectionate and like no other man's) which subsists between me and the public?[25]

If marriage was too restrictive for Dickens, his relationship with the public was not, if only because, just as the violence in storytelling is "unreal" violence, so, too, his community of readers was an "unreal" community, brought into being as it was by Dickens himself and capable of being sustained by his imagination in some vague, sentimental way as "the public."

Ultimately, Dickens tried to move his sense of his audience directly into the writing itself. Perhaps the ideal image of the fictional space in Dickens that aspires to resolve expenditure and restraint, to contain and make loss present in a conservative but insubstantial medium, is the image we have of Dickens at work provided by his daughter Mamie, who secretly glimpsed him writing.

For some time there was no sound to be heard in the room but the rapid working of the pen, when suddenly he jumped up, went to the looking glass, rushed back to his writing table, and jotted down a few words; back to the glass again, this time talking to his own reflection, or rather to the simulated expression he saw there, and was trying to catch before drawing it in words, then back again to his writing. After a while he got up again, and stood with his back to the glass, talking softly and rapidly for a long time, then looking at his daughter, but certainly never seeing her, then once more back to his table, and to steady writing until luncheon time.[26]

Dickens, here, is totally absorbed into the purely fictional meeting ground of expenditure (writing's self-abandonment) and restraint (the ever-present audience's consciousness that Dickens seems to have internalized). The audience is now that part of himself that watches and tries to catch his movements in the mirror. The extent of Dickens' own absorption into his imaginary world can only be estimated, but what can we make of the purely linguistic habitations of a man who consummated his tabooed love relationship with—of all people—an actress, a player of parts, a girl whose first name he could shorten affectionately to "Nell"?

As we shall see, the natures of violation and restraint, which Dickens adumbrates in his conception of storytelling and develops more fully in every aspect of his work, are such that a complete synthesis is possible, finally, only within imagination. And yet, to say that is not to take away from the remarkably real form—the insurpassable social phenomenon—Dickens was able to create out of this imaginative harmony with his audience. Nor should it distract us from more explicit formulations in the novels about how such resolutions can be actualized. Still, it must be admitted that the violence expressed through the storytelling of Cuttle or Lorry and the violence present in Dickens' own storytelling is not ultimately disturbing. Problems arise when the violent impulses behind storytelling are revealed as the primary impulses underlying other, nonartistic kinds of human activity. Storytelling in itself is therefore not a solution to problems of excess and restriction in Dickens; it offers only an idealized resolution, one that the characters and the narrators in his world struggle to achieve—with varying degrees of success.

Chapter 2

Melodrama and Sentimentality

There have been men indeed splendidly wicked, whose endowments threw such a brightness on their crimes and whom scarce any villainy made perfectly detestable, because they never could be wholly divested of their excellencies; but such have been in all ages the great corrupters of the world, and their resemblances ought no more to be preserved than the art of murdering without pain.

—Samuel Johnson

The panting pursuit of danger is the pursuit of life itself, in which danger awaits us possibly at every step and faces us at every turn; so that the dream of an intenser experience easily becomes rather some vision of a sublime security like that enjoyed on the flowery plains of heaven, where we may conceive ourselves proceeding in ecstasy from one prodigious phase and form of it to another.

—Henry James

i

Insofar as Dickens' art is seen as the attempt to find a balance between two contradictory impulses—the desire to dissolve limits and the desire to seek shelter from violation—it becomes clear that many of the failures in his novels occur when the balance breaks down and either desire emerges as dominant. For this very reason, in fact, Dickens has been alternately attacked by critics as too excessive and as too conservative. As we shall see in later chapters, Dickens does tentatively resolve these contradictory experiences in his heroes, in his endings, and, most successfully, in the purity of his writing style. But it is worthwhile taking a look first at failures in his work to fuse excess and restraint, as a way to broaden our sense of their fundamental importance in the novels. In this chapter, we will look at two of Dickens' most commonly conceded failures: the melodramatic form that dominates the plots of his novels and the overriding emotional climate of those melodramas, sentimentality.

To begin with the question of melodrama, the obvious point —but, nevertheless, one that circumvents a good deal of talk about the psychological vapidity of Dickens' characters—is that the purpose of his melodrama, rather than to impart psychological knowledge or insights, is to be itself a psychological act. Specifically, Dickens' morally simplified melodramatic form enables him to focus energy on the overcoming of a personified obstruction—a villain—in order to produce, for his characters and for the reader, an experience of radical expansion, freedom, release. So much critical effort has gone into oversubtilizing Dickens that it is useful to recall this most obvious, most appealing —if seemingly superficial—aspect of his form: Dickens' plot demands and delights in the destruction of the villain. If this were not so, why should the conclusion of *A Tale of Two Cities* require the killing of Madame Defarge? The death scene nearly distracts the reader from the more important development of Carton's strategy and his eventual death, and the plot could easily have gotten on without eliminating Madame Defarge. Again, why, in *Great Expectations*, should the death of Compeyson, who has so limited a physical presence in the novel, be featured in such a long and uncharacteristically nonreflective, purely descriptive passage in Pip's narrative? Obviously, if such characters were allowed to live and flourish, they would loom large in the mythopoeic space of the novels as threats of future restriction on the heroes, whereas their deaths, graphically realized in the action, produce a palpable sensation of release for the reader that transcends merely amicable resolution.

In the destruction of the villain and in the consequent liberation of the heroes, the reader participates—insofar as he identifies with the good characters, or at least dislikes the bad ones—in the kind of action that we have termed expenditure: a sudden, violent dissolution of restrictions that yields a sensation of limitlessness. The intensity of the restriction, followed by the violent liberation of the heroes, makes the principal action in melodrama an experience of "death" that does not disrupt life, since death and violence are made present and are experienced by both heroes and readers vicariously, as a condition of freedom, without actually extending to them or requiring their affirmation. The heroes' liberation alone would represent an experience of release analogous in spirit to the excessive release featured in violence, but their liberation carries with it a more profound association with violence because it is made to depend on the actual death of the villain. That is to say, both readers and heroes sustain a deeper sense of the significance of liberation because of this brush with violence, which links the heroes' freedom to the final release of death. Thus, at the heart of melodrama is a kind of willful, contained violence. And, in this context, one of the functions of the moral absolutism in Dickens, as in all melodrama, is to validate the expenditure, or even to induce the reader to will it, through the desirable destruction of the villain.

The simplified moral polarity of melodrama further allows the atmosphere of excess to spill over into its two rival camps,

though in different ways. On the one hand, because we do not
have to question seriously our identification with the villain, we
can comfortably enjoy his violent "excellencies." Clearly, villains
are interesting in themselves because of their infantile, unrepressed indulgence of illicit desires for violence and power, and
the Parisian audiences who renamed the Boulevard du Temple
the "Boulevard du Crime" knew that, despite the eventual triumph of virtue, the quintessence of melodrama lies in villainy—
that is, in the pleasures of melodramatic violence. It would be
difficult to argue that we do not enjoy the villainy of Quilp,
Squeers, and Carker, or the unrepressed violence in ambiguous
characters like Bucket and Jaggers. Dickens' own identification
with the criminal, the rebel, and the transgressor is legendary,
and although there have been recent attempts to compensate
for modern interest in the "dark" Dickens by denying the presence in Dickens of any love of crime for its own sake,[1] it seems
hard to believe that the tireless reader of Nancy's murder from
Oliver Twist—who actually hired a man at Leeds to stand up in
the audience and protest against the reading of such scabrous
material before ladies (the man was shouted down by the crowd,
of course)[2]—did not enjoy breaking taboos. Dickens frequently
compared himself to the murderer or the criminal not in his wanton moods, but in his most exalted, most oblivious states of creative productivity; upon completion of his Christmas fable, "The
Chimes," for instance, he wrote Forster, "I have not been able to
divest myself of the story—have suffered very much in my sleep
as a consequence—and am so shaken by such work . . . that I
am as nervous as a man who is dying of drink and as haggard as
a murderer."[3] No wonder, then, that Dickens' biographers have
often seen versions of his own personality in Quilp, in Jaggers,
and in Bill Sikes.

On the other hand, Dickens' heroes, absolved of evil through
the absolutism of the moral form, are charged by the violent atmosphere of melodrama in even subtler ways. Because the villain has polarized the fundamental ambiguity of unrepressed
emotion, heroes are allowed to spend themselves in legitimately

excessive emotion. Virtue asserts itself fully, brazenly in melodrama, with an unalloyed spirit we do not allow ourselves in real
life. The ecstacies and apostrophes of Dickens' good characters
—their relishing of emotion for its own sake—are made possible
largely because melodramatic form frees us of any suspicions
about such characters' innocence. Moreover, the emotional excess of good characters is often not just a question of exuberance; enthusiasm among Dickens' good characters often extends
to morally ambiguous behavior. It has been pointed out that
melodrama is the form in which anything can and must be said;[4]
because events turn on the direct expression of characters' intentions and feelings, characters may say things we do not allow
ourselves to say in real life for fear of outraging our own or others' sense of moral limits—Jarndyce's declaration to Esther of
his intentions about Rick and Ada, for instance, or his ingenuous
arrangement of Esther's marriage to Woodcourt. The emotional
relationships of good characters thus reverberate positively
with the plenitude of their excessive, unqualified feeling, even
in objectively troublesome areas; the love of Dr. Manette for his
daughter Lucie or the love of Kit for his mother take on an excessiveness of expression that would be inhibited in real life—as
our self-conscious response to melodrama shows—by Oedipal
apprehensions. Similarly, Florence and Walter's filial piety toward the broken Dombey is never felt as condescension, and
Lizzie Hexam's generous relationship to her brother is wholly
generous, in ways that their sibling relationship could never be
in real life. And although brothers and sisters might very well
love each other, none can do so as unreservedly and yet as innocently as Tom Pinch and Ruth, whether indirectly, through the
lover-like gallantry of Tom's defense of Ruth at the brass-and-
copper founder's (the only passion Tom exhibits in the entire
novel), or more explicitly, in their frequent declarations of famil-
ial love. Even the narrator contributes a mildly erotic view of
the Pinches; "The serious way in which she looked at Tom; the
way in which Tom looked at her; and the way in which she gradually broke into a merry laugh at her own expense; would have
enchanted you" (39).

When moral complexity is quelled, emotion is uninhibited. For Dickens' good characters, melodrama allows a complete spending of the self into emotion freed from its ambiguous status—a general victory over repression. And readers are allowed to identify with various kinds of emotional effusion that are prohibited in normal life despite their appeal. In this way, the good society in melodrama is always an attempt to represent a conservation of life and virtue based paradoxically in an atmosphere of excess.

Unfortunately, this synthesis is not a happy one—at least, for twentieth-century readers it is not. While the form of melodrama creates two camps—the camp of sin and the camp of salvation—that participate in a single act of contained violence, and while it even tries to infect both camps with the spirit of exceeded limits, the disturbing aspect of the genre is this very separation of factions. Too convenient and too naive, Dickens' moral polarization ultimately overvalues the good society and the importance of unviolated, conserved wholeness. In melodrama, the reader must finally identify with values that are fundamentally conservative, although they flirt with excess. The rigid moral structure strikes us as primary, and the excesses it contains seem trivialized by that contrivance.

A parallel with a related genre can be illuminating. As in tragedy, the crisis in melodrama is sacrifice; both stage violence as a vehicle for emotional release. The major difference between these two forms, however, is melodrama's desperate desire to embody in a pure, enduring form what the dramatic sacrifice or *agon* of tragedy achieves through destruction. In tragedy, feelings of loss and feelings of a compensatory wholeness brought about by new knowledge or new perception are fused in catharsis without resulting in a paradigm for such resolution. But, as Peter Brooks puts it, because of the degenerated state of cultural myths in nineteenth-century society, when the socially cohesive beliefs that alone can support the unprogrammatic catharsis of tragedy no longer bound audiences together, Victorian melodrama attempted to incorporate the energies released by sacrifice into a visible society of thoroughly good individuals, a society that has transcended ambivalence toward sacrifice and toward the energy that triumphs over repression.[5] The tragic catharsis is followed in melodrama by a recuperation of the transcendent energy that has been released; the good society is both emotionally limitless and morally untainted. In a world of disintegrating order, to end in death would be to confirm dissolution; for that reason, melodrama presents a battle of transcendent forces—Good and Evil—played out in the field of the ordinary, a battle in which the ordinary survives, electrified now by the combat. However, because the tragic hero, who has the audience's sympathy but who must be sacrificed in order to purify them of the dangerous qualities they share with him, is split in two in melodrama—into a hero and a villain—there is a consequent loss of dramatic tension. Whatever purity of expression is gained through an intensified approval of the villain's destruction is compromised by the villain's slighter relationship to more passive heroes, who remain untouched by actual violence, and by the fixity of the form; if we know that heroes will survive and that villains will be sacrificed, and that such an outcome is determined at the start, our overwhelming impression of melodrama as a form is of its conservative nature. As a result, the violence itself seems rigidly excessive. When the boundaries of the form become obvious, the intention to shock also becomes obvious and, therefore, impotent.

The most important aspect of this formal rigidity, this framing recuperation, is that the nature of the violence directed against villainy in Dickens' novels remains illicit and unacceptable through the careful distancing of any actual violence from the good characters. This emphatic illegitimacy is foreign to tragedy, which makes the hero's own transgressions seem at least partially justified. But in melodrama, the heroes are kept completely free of the final violence. Heroes never overcome a villain themselves, thus remaining clear of any attaching guilt. Quilp drowns as a result of his self-imposed isolation and because of the very decrepitude of the waterside conditions with which he had loved to torture others; Madame Defarge is killed

not by the principals, but by their servant, Miss Pross, who, despite the accidental nature of the killing, suffers deafness as a
chastisement nevertheless; Tulkinghorn is murdered by another
villain, Hortense, who in turn is pursued and captured by the
morally dubious Bucket; Compeyson is killed (unless he merely
drowns by himself—we never know for certain) by the already
culpable, doomed Magwitch. Purity from violence among the
good characters in these deaths is as necessary as blackness in
the villains for the reader to participate in the ritualized violence
with clean hands. Nevertheless, Dickens can never make explicit what we tend to suspect, that all these deaths are desired
by the heroes or, at least, by the exigencies of heroism. Alexander Welsh points out that many Dickens novels read like revenge tragedies; besides the villain, everyone who either does
not love the hero enough—Mrs. Copperfield, Dora, Mrs. Clennam—or who comes between the hero and a woman—Steerforth, Mr. Wickfield, Drummle—is punished with death.[6] The
form hinges on a complete release from impediments. But in
order for the surviving, good society to balance the violence
generated by villains, that society must be kept clear of violence
at the same time that violence works in its interests. Hence the
many half-formed symbolic reverberations in Dickens between
the hero and the villain: Orlick's insinuation that he only acts out
Pip's own wishes; Blandois' similar assertion to Arthur Clennam; even in an early novel like *Oliver Twist*, there is the
strange vindictiveness of Mr. Losberne, the shadowy implication that Harry takes part in the mob's pursuit of Bill Sikes as
"the man on horseback" (50), and the unsettling willingness of
good characters to use the very institutions of society that had
oppressed them against other social victims. The atmosphere of
guilt that surrounds many of Dickens' heroes, especially the
later ones—Arthur Clennam, Charles Darnay, Pip, Eugene
Wrayburn—lies precisely in their suspicion that their desires
for freedom somehow align them with villains—with Blandois,
the Marquis, Drummle, and Bradley Headstone. But the connections are never made explicit, and Dickens' heroes all receive

blanket pardons before the true nature of their crimes comes to light.

Because these relationships between hero and villain must remain shadowy in order for the melodramatic form to work, we are left with only vague sensations of universal guilt—which has given rise to the many Christian interpretations of Dickens —without fully recognizing the specific actions that incur guilt: desires for radical liberation, for the release of violence and death. As a result, the easiest response to Dickens' melodrama is to take it at face value, as a conflict between homogeneous Evil and homogeneous Good, between radical violence and radical conservation, a conflict in which conservation is ultimately predominant and in which violence is a tease. Even the limitlessness of the good characters' emotional lives is compromised by our sense that, for them, nothing is really at stake and nothing is really lost, since all complete loss is external to the surviving social group. The good characters never actually will loss, violence, or release; it simply happens all around them. Thus, the form of melodrama, though it is consistent with Dickens' desire to integrate excess and conservation, only forces them further apart for the reader who recognizes the hidden moral manipulations of the form. No wonder, then, that most contemporary readers share the response to Dickens expressed by one important early critic; "his bourgeois-humanitarian instincts protect him from all tendency toward the supernatural, the marvellous, the revolutionary, from all exaltation of passion."[7]

ii

Sentimentality—even more so than melodrama—is a deadly issue for the critic of Dickens. Nevertheless, it is an integral part of his work, and trying to approach Dickens without mentioning sentimentality is like analyzing the popularity of football without admitting the appeal of its violence. But at the same time, serious readers of Dickens, too well aware of contemporary pressures against sentimentality, are usually forced into ridiculous postures of defense. The two standard critical judgments about Dickens' sentimentality are: one, that it is our age that suffers by being deficient in feeling; and, two, that we must simply be tolerant of differences in cultural taste. The first argument condescends to us, the second usually condescends to the Victorians. And besides being hopelessly arbitrary, such arguments ultimately tell us nothing about the actual function of sentimentality in literature. I shall make no attempt to explain the phenomenon of sentimentality historically or to make it palatable; I only wish to show some of the aspects of its function in Dickens' novels that tie it to his larger literary concerns.

The first thing that can be said about sentimentality is that it implies a closed world. Sentimentality seems to stop short of tragic knowledge, short of grief, short of terror; it assumes that fundamentally everything is all right, or that it will be all right. Sentimentality is safe emotion, and it mourns loss only as the condition of a greater kind of security, since sentimentality usually implies the presence of a social group united in common recognition of loss. Loss can even, of itself, form the humanizing, fraternal bond within a social group; death, or some other radical kind of loss, permits the reconciliation of good characters with Mr. Dombey, Tom Gradgrind, Scrooge, or even Pip. The symptom of this larger, secure, closed context implied by Dickens' novels is the extraordinary bond of trust that must have subsisted between Dickens and his readers. Sentimentality can be sustained only if the reader does not suspect that he is being manipulated, and if he does not expect any shock that might oppose author and himself to one another in an analytical relation. Sentimentality is socialized, communal emotion; it reassures the self about the group. Frequently, too, we object to sentimentality for this very reason, because extravagances of trust make for a noncritical attitude, they foster illusions, and they are accompanied by complacency, which is the very assumption that the world is closed. Sentimentality thus expresses through its closure the essence of the wish to conserve.

But we also object to sentimentality on the opposite grounds, because it is excessive. We find sentimentality embarrassing because it seems to enjoy itself, which is to say that, on some level, it appears to desire the experience of loss. In this context, sentimentality is impure emotion masquerading as pure emotion; it embarrasses us because it seems to indulge tabooed impulses: the forbidden desire to witness excess, to witness death, to grieve loss. This transgressive quality in sentiment was noted even by some of Dickens' embarrassed contemporaries; Fitzjames Stephen wrote of Little Nell's death, "He gloats over the girl's death as if it delighted him; he looks at it . . . touches, tastes, smells and handles as if it was some savoury dainty which could not be too fully appreciated."[8] And the sentimental treatment of relationships like Tom and Ruth Pinch's, or even that of Esther and Jarndyce, can seem a way to entertain and cherish erotic desires without fully admitting to them. It is interesting to note, too, that Dickens was alternately praised by his age as pure and attacked as vulgar.[9] There is a delicate point, for example, at which his sentimental euphonies over female modesty become prurient. Jack Lindsay has provided us with a thorough, if tentative, analysis of the way Dickens' distress over his threatened heroines covered a deep sense of guilt associated with his forbidden desire for Mary Horgarth; unconsciously, Lindsay says, Dickens felt as if he had killed Mary by desiring her.[10] His sentimental portrait of a character like Nell, then, can be perceived as a defense against guilt that nevertheless signals unacknowledged erotic desires.

The presence of these contradictory aspects of sentimentality—the excess and the economy—are not merely parallel in Dickens; ideally, they function together as a dialectic, one heightening the other. One half of this dynamic has already been mentioned: the way in which loss is the basis of a recovered sense of community. This recovery through loss is thematized in the novels in a number of ways. First, sentimental renunciation is always made the basis of a greater gain—Esther's ability to renounce Woodcourt, for example, is the initiation rite that makes her worthy to be rewarded with him; the same can be said of Walter Gay's initial determination not to win Florence's love, or of Pip's claim to have overcome his desire for Estella. Second, death itself is often imaged in Dickens' novels not as a disruption, a violent end, but as the condition of a higher completion —characters like Little Nell and Paul Dombey are actually resolved to die and convinced that death produces a superior kind of integration; even characters like Jo and Richard in *Bleak House* die as part of a general movement toward recovery and completion, Jo among his first friends and with his first forgiveness, Richard expecting to "begin the world . . . that sets this right" (65). Dickens' sentimental style in describing these deaths, too, has the effect of stilling the event, turning it into a tableau that is circumscribed by its rococo imagery. Of Paul's death Forster wrote, "It is a fairy vision to a piece of actual suffering, a sorrow with heaven's hues upon it."[11] Here, style, by miniaturizing the scene, locates loss within an artificial context, thereby emphasizing its distance from the reader and its ability to be safely comprehended. The reader feels these deaths as experiences that are contained by the sentimental world of the fairy tale, which is always a reassuring—because a completed—world.

On the other hand, the sense of a stable, consoling community is a great incitement to an indulgence in feelings of grief. The principle is, in fact, the basis of many contemporary "release" psychotherapies. Charley and her brother express this dynamic in *Bleak House* when they tell their troubles—perhaps for the first time—to the sympathetic Jarndyce, Esther, Ada, and Richard: "The little orphan girl had spoken of their father, and their mother, as if all that sorrow were subdued by the necessity of taking courage. . . . But, now, when Tom cried; although she sat quite tranquil, looking quietly at us, and did not by any movement disturb a hair of the head of either of her little charges; I saw two silent tears fall down her face" (15). The awareness that our feelings of loss will be safely contained within a larger, untroubled context enhances our willingness to give way to them. "Taking courage," which represses emotion, is no longer so imperative; thus, Charley gives in to Tom's tears, rather than trying to contain them herself. Similarly, the solidarity of Dickens' readership could only have aided their willingness to give way to wrenching emotion. In these two ways, then, sentimentality is the staging of limit experience within and with the aid of a closed world.

But this balance is one that does not hold up over time. Because Dickens' sentimental scenes are so clearly staged, we are no longer able to take them seriously; like melodrama, they seem to be rigidly conservative frames in which Dickens merely flirts with excessive emotion. Unlike melodrama, which at least provides an image (even if it is overtly rejected) of unrecuperated violence through the villain, sentimentality never gives vent to emotion free of its place within a social context. Dickens' good characters, though they may suffer, always have each other; none of them is consumed by grief, which is one reason why—no matter who has died—the novels can always manage to end on an upbeat. And there is never any question about the limited, communal kind of emotion Dickens wants us as readers to feel. The modern reader, more sensitive to the compounded formulas of Dickens' novels, too easily perceives his sentimental scenes as occasions that call for socialized kinds of emotional excess. The collective nature of Dickens' sentimental moments— the ritual presence of the good society around the deathbed of a good character, for instance—makes the excesses of emotion he demands seem too clearly solicited as a mark of our loyalties. By contrast, the more extreme impulses we suspect beneath sentimentality—the latent eroticism, the latent relishing of loss —never actually surface and in fact seem alien to the moral righteousness of the good society. The excessive qualities in sentimentality thus seem furtive and dark, secretly desired. We suspect that Dickens harbors wells of repressed emotion that he could not express directly; hence, Dickens' sentimentality is often described as regressive. In general, the communal context for sentimentality prevents us from seeing the element of loss in these scenes as anything but a formula, a framework in which everything is designed and nothing is really at stake, or as an insipid screen for darker, socially illegitimate desires.

It would be difficult, if not impossible, to determine why melodrama and sentimentality worked for Victorian audiences.[12] Perhaps the crucial insight available to us is only this, that they did work; somehow, the balance between excess and restraint for Dickens' first readers was maintained. We have the proof of this in his almost universally sympathetic readership and in the unqualified praise—and the unrestrained tears—of critics like Lord Jeffrey. In both melodrama and sentimentality, however, clearly it is the dominantly conservative nature of novelistic actions and emotions that diffuse them today. We might identify with the desires for excess underlying melodrama and sentimentality, but it is impossible to sympathize with Dickens' formulaic indulgence of such desires. All we can know for certain, then, is that these two phenomena are governed to some degree by the mutability of conservative, social conventions, which, as the arbitrary limits by which a culture defines itself, are always in a state of flux. Bataille, for instance, claims that eroticism, which he defines broadly as the experience of violated limits, is an organized activity; hence, the relationship between permissible kinds of excess and social taboos is always being redefined.[13] While the desire for excess is constant in every age, the forms designed to invoke it change and seem empty once they have lost their ability to jar us. The important implication is that any cultural synthesis of excess and restraint, any moment of excess that is stopped short of death and converted into a form, is destined to lose its transparency and to acquire a conservative rigidity that will become obvious with time and with repetition. Fusions of excess and restraint always present new problems of limitation. It is this very law that Dickens himself dramatizes through his villains.

Chapter 3

Villains

The genius of the novel rises above the oppositions that stem from metaphysical desire. It tries to show us their illusory character. It transcends the rival caricatures of Good and Evil presented by the factions. . . . But it does not end in moral relativism. Evil exists. The tortures inflicted by the underground man on the young prostitute are not imaginary. The suffering of Vinteuil is only too real. . . . Evil is that negative pact of hatred to which so many men strictly adhere for their mutual destruction.

—René Girard, *Deceit, Desire, and the Novel*

Villainy is the focal point for the violent energies unleashed by Dickens' novels. In the figure of the villain, the problem of expenditure is raised explicitly and without reservation, since the form of melodrama enables us to resist identification with evil characters. Of course, this lack of identification between reader and villain means that we are never directly confronted with the great problem in expenditure, the simultaneity of our desire for and horror of it, but it does enable Dickens to unravel another danger in expenditure, a double one: the tendency of violent release to seek reincorporation within temporal forms that become merely other kinds of restriction, and, more disturbingly, the tendency of this recuperated expenditure to be used as a tool of power over others. On this level, villainy enables Dickens to present problems latent in the very goal of his novelistic project, the blending of release and restraint. In this chapter, we will approach problems of recuperation by noting, first, the actual quality of the violence defined by Dickens' villains, and, second, the way villains put violence in service of power. It will remain for the following chapter to apply the dialectic to problems facing Dickens' heroes.

The two alternatives to repression—pure expenditure and some kind of recuperated, constrained expenditure—are present in the very structure of Dickens' collection of villains. Despite the familiar assumption to the contrary, villainy does not make up a single category in Dickens. There are actually two very distinct species of villain and a very small range between them where they might be said to interbreed. Most critical commentary has defined the Dickensian villain in terms of only one of the two categories, concentrating on that class of Dickens' villains who are the money-grubbers, the individualistic, greedy bourgeois: Scrooge, Dombey, Pecksniff. These villainous, middle-class capitalists—along with their aristocratic counterparts, like Merdle—represent the politically satiric, polemical side of

Dickens' fiction, and the one most assimilable to social criticism, which is why they have received the most attention. However, while figures in this group certainly qualify as villains, being obstacles to the good characters that must eventually be overcome, they do not participate in the larger spheres of Dickensian evil. As a villain, the exploitative, purely economic capitalist is never awe-inspiring. Often, he is made endearingly ridiculous, like Pecksniff, or he is made pathetic, like Dombey. In either case, his energies are not taken seriously in themselves: he is simply misguided. Utimately, too, in keeping with their secondary status, these villains meet with mild punishments, if they are not actually converted to the side of the good characters—a conversion that, significantly, takes the form of a conversion to the side of expenditure; Dombey, Scrooge, and Gradgrind, for instance, all learn to violate the terms of their rigid conservatism and to expend themselves through generosity.

But there is a second class of villains who are less tied to Dickens' economic and political satire, and who are the real melodramatic antagonists. These villains threaten irrational, violent danger that does not have a narrowly economic motive; Quilp, Carker, Jonas Chuzzlewit, Madame Defarge, Bill Sikes, Tulkinghorn—these are the irredeemable, confirmed villains. The neat division of Dickens' villains into a class of economically conservative villains and a class of violent, self-expending villains is stressed by their frequent appearance in pairs: Sampson Brass and Quilp, Pecksniff and Chuzzlewit, Dombey and Carker, Fagin and Sikes; or, in less clearly villainous roles, Wemmick and Jaggers, Stryver and Carton. These two classes seem paired purely for the sake of the contrast, especially because the absolute and irrational evil of the excessive characters eventually dominates and ridicules the economic concerns of their petty, miserly counterparts.

Dickens' absolute villains, the ones who always attract criticism on the grounds that their seeming motivelessness makes them unfaithful to life, are deliberately made so in order to shift our attention away from the niggardly realm of middle-class greed toward a more magnificent kind of villainy rooted in limit experience—a kind of villainy more interested in violation for its own sake than in money, or in any other reducible, profit-seeking motive. If Dickens, who is almost always precise in his exposition of his characters' behavior, had intended us to comprehend completely the motives of these villains, he would never have tantalized the reader with passages like this one on Tulkinghorn.

Whether he be cold and cruel, whether immovable in what he has made his duty, whether absorbed in love of power, whether determined to have nothing hidden from him in ground where he has burrowed among secrets all his life, whether he in his heart despises the splendour of which he is a distant beam, whether he is always treasuring up slights and offenses in the affability of his gorgeous clients—whether he be any of this, or all of this, it may be that my Lady had better have five thousand pairs of fashionable eyes upon her, in distrustful vigilance, than the two eyes of this rusty lawyer. (29)

Flirtation with Tulkinghorn's possible motives is not just coyness on Dickens' part; this list of motives, all of them plausible, are trivialized almost to the point of irrelevance by the bland equivalence drawn among them by the narrator. The very clutter of this list of motives takes away their grandeur from the reader who thinks he has privately guessed what really motivates Tulkinghorn, and it emphasizes instead their inadequacy as explanations, which, of course, is attested to by the frequent complaints among Dickens' early readers that Tulkinghorn could not exist.[1]

Dickens' obscurity is well-founded; if we could psychologize these villains, if we could say, finally, that Tulkinghorn's motive is grounded in sexual repression, or that Quilp merely projects outward his contempt for his own dwarfishness—arguments that seem to confuse the symptoms with the disease—these figures would lose the malevolent hold they exercise over the reader. Unlike the bourgeois villain, the evil villain is defined only by his recklessness and his lack of restraint, even if his actions endanger his own life. And, since repression has often been defined as death fear,[2] the implication is that these villains desire death. The truly evil Dickensian villain will stop at nothing, and in his pursuit of violence he seems intent instead on actually proclaiming his freedom from normal human concerns for self-preservation. Carker, for example, throws over his lucrative and prestigious position in Dombey's firm for pure revenge; Tulkinghorn is willing to risk his position with Sir Leicester to bring down Lady Dedlock; Quilp seems oblivious to money and to physical comfort except as instruments for torturing others. This determined interest in violent expenditure ties the evil villains to the preoccupation of Dickens and his audience with the violence in melodramatic form—the freeing of censored drives toward excess for their own sake. For this reason, Dickens surrounds these villains with an atmosphere of transcendently inhuman violence that seems even larger than the villains themselves: the explosive energy of the train that kills Carker; the demonic intentions of the Clennam house that implodes upon Rigaud "as if every tumbling fragment were intent on burying the crushed wretch deeper" (2.31); the awesome isolation from humanity and the sense of their own insignificance felt by Bill Sikes and Jonas Chuzzlewit.

At the same time, this clear-cut distinction between the two sets of villains does not constitute a final break between them. Instead, it establishes a fluid, dialectical opposition between, on the one hand, characters who are willing to pursue without restraint their drives toward violence, and, on the other hand, characters who seek to reintegrate violence into permanent form, thus diverting the direction of violence away from death and toward usefulness. For instance, even an economically conservative character like Dombey thrives on violence, but he distances himself from it—he has Carker do it—so that he can possess in a safer, more static way the fruits of violence: aloofness from the common, slavish world; luxury; the freedoms expressed by power. Dombey's latent violence toward Florence erupts only when his economic world collapses. A similar rela-

tionship exists between Fagin and Sikes, the one consolidating
his "guiltless" power by delegating violence to the other. Even
though Fagin's violence is closer to the surface than the usual
conservative villain's—since Fagin inhabits the explosive world
of thieves—his circumspection and caution constantly stress his
economic concerns: his preoccupation with saving Number One,
his great fear of "peachers," his dependence on the thievery of
his boys and the violence of Sikes to keep him in supply. The essence of Dickens' bourgeois villains lies in their very attempt to
conceal the real violence of their activities in order to enjoy the
surpassing of limitation solely in terms of goods, or in terms of
prestige. Mainly through the bourgeois villain's hatchet-man—
like Carker or Pancks—Dickens reveals that middle-class capitalism is not merely a stable and conservative economy, but
that it hides an underlying drive toward reckless growth, expansion, and an overcoming of all barriers to itself, which requires the violation of others as its goal.

Within this dialectic between radical violence and restraining economy, there is a wide range of alternatives, a number of
different ways for villains to adjust the balance. We can delineate this range best, however, by examining in detail the second
class of Dickens' villains, the palpably evil ones, if only because,
in these villains, desires for violence are featured as primary,
and because the process by which these desires are diverted toward the more permanent forms of status is easier to trace.

ii

Quilp is perhaps the prime example of Dickens' fascination with
the "excellencies" of transgression. In his demonic exuberance,
Quilp is the closest of Dickens' villains to the violent pole of the
dialectic; he is the villain most given over to his drives to push
life toward death. And in Quilp, Dickens exhibits the raw enthusiasm and erotic vitality implied by those drives. The reader
who finds Quilp enjoyable is hardly alone; Mrs. Quilp herself tes-

tifies to the erotic attraction of Quilp's excessiveness. "Quilp has
such a way with him when he likes, that the best-looking woman
here couldn't refuse him if I was dead, and she was free, and he
chose to make love to her" (4). All of Dickens' villains have their
scenes, those moments when their glowing exercise of violent
energies against other despicable characters shows to their own
advantage: Madame Defarge, when she puts to rout the treach-
erous spy, Barsad; Jaggers, when he dances circles around the
pompous Wopsle; Hortense, when she hurls away Tulkinghorn's
blood money. Even Tulkinghorn himself is enjoyable when he
turns his chilling austerity on the ridiculous Guppy. "You are to
be congratulated, Mr. Guppy; you are a fortunate young man,
sir. . . . High friends, free admission to great houses, and access
to elegant ladies! Why, Mr. Guppy, there are people in London
who would give their ears to be you" (39). But no villain is so
consistently applaudable as Quilp. For one thing, Quilp's victories are plentiful because he is conveniently surrounded by
straight men who are either hateful—and therefore expendable
—or resilient like Punch's puppet-show victims: Sampson and
Sally Brass, Quilp's mother-in-law, Dick Swiveller. But the main
reason Quilp delights us is the sheer gratuitousness—partly because he is more purely physical than most of Dickens' villains—
of his hostility.

In general, Quilp never acts out of a consistent, calculated
motive. He seems instead to want only to expend energy recklessly through violence. He tortures a chained-up dog, he forces
Sampson Brass to smoke a pipe because it nauseates the lawyer,
and he plunges into a fight with Tom and Kit—all with an abandon so complete it makes these incidents seem equivalent to him
in importance. For that matter, even his pursuit of Nell never
seems to have any real priority despite his semifacetious sexual
proposal, and Quilp seems to take up and drop the chase at his
whim. Unlike Sampson, Quilp does not calculate in his villainy;
he leaves elaborate strategies like the betrayal of Kit to the lawyer. Alexander Welsh points out, too, that, like the Devil in stories from European folklore, Quilp cares for money only as a

means of destroying others through usury.[3] As motiveless as Punch in his violence, Quilp fulfills no purpose; in fact, he defies purpose. His exuberant inventiveness consistently surpasses our expectations of the reasonable, the gainful. For example, there is simply no reason for Quilp to torture Mrs. Nubbles, since she means nothing to him. Guided solely by his "taste for doing something fantastic and monkey-like" (9), Quilp's talent for creating new situations for unremunerative exercises of his malice constantly takes us by surprise because it defies the normal limits of human motives and energies; at the same time, the pressure of real violence keeps Quilp's antics from seeming merely frivolous.

In its profitlessness, its lack of economic purpose, Quilp's violent energy is echoed in lesser ways by the drives of all of Dickens' villains. Even when they have a restricted purpose in mind, the villains' capacity for violence exceeds that purpose and insists on its primacy as violence. Thus, Bill Sikes seems to have a limitless store of violence that he easily displaces from one object to another. For example, at one point, Sikes tries to strangle his dog for no apparent reason and, when someone opens the door to Sikes' room, providing the dog with an exit, the narrator tells us, "There must always be two parties to a quarrel, says the old adage. Mr. Sikes, being disappointed of the dog's participation, at once transferred his share in the quarrel to the newcomer" (15). Sikes' violent exploits in the novel are often unpremeditated, in contrast to the strategies of Fagin and the conniving of Monks; unlike the latter two, Sikes is a volcanic force seeking any outlet, which is why Fagin is able to set him against Nancy so easily. For Sikes, the energy of violence instinctively and without qualification overcomes the conservative claims of love. Similarly, Rigaud in *Little Dorrit* is driven by a motive no more specific than his hatred of good people. His random violence against society seems to settle arbitrarily on Mrs. Clennam, and—comically so—on Flintwich. Rigaud even declares that his only intent is "to make variety in my position, and to amuse myself" (2.28). And Rigaud explicitly states a freedom from economic concerns that we suspect in a character like Quilp. "I am a gentleman to whom mere mercenary trade-bargains are unknown, but to whom money is always acceptable as the means of pursuing his pleasures. . . . the satisfaction of my animosity is as acceptable to me as money" (2.30). Of course, these villains do have purposes, even deep-seated ones. Yet their purposes—Sikes' need to steal for a living, Rigaud's hostility against society—are made broad enough to license an orientation to random violence that transcends any narrow interest in goals or profits in favor of the less profitable satisfactions of vengeance. Both characters are more destructive than conniving, and their motives seem only a reflection of a general desire to violate wholeness that cannot be traced to specific psychological causes.

Carker in *Dombey and Son* is another good example of this surplus violence that transcends purpose. Early in the novel, he seems gratuitously cruel; why should he hate Walter and want to send him to sea? Why should he hate Cuttle? His malice toward Florence is even more enigmatic. Indeed, the very first time Florence meets Carker it is because he has sought her out, barely repressing his glee, to tell her that Walter is dead. And his ferocious attack on Rob the Grinder, though intended to scare the boy into his service, demonstrates the unsounded, purposeless depths of Carker's malevolence. Carker seems to leap outside of himself in this scene and to vent untold angers on the unsuspecting boy, who is meeting Carker for the first time. "The moment they were face to face alone, Mr. Carker, without a word of preparation, took him by the throat, and shook him until his head seemed loose upon his shoulders" (22). At one point, too, the narrator reveals Carker's limitless fantasies of violence; he was "a man who saw, in his fancy, a crowd of people slumbering on the ground at his feet, like the poor Native at his master's door; who picked his way among them: looking down, maliciously enough: but trod upon no upturned face—as yet" (26). Of course, we can assume that Carker is plotting to revenge himself very specifically against Dombey's power over

him and that all these private wars have their origin in his desire
to attack anything that approaches Dombey. Yet Carker ultimately surpasses this supposed purpose, demonstrating its
subordinate importance for him, when he runs away with Edith.
Edith herself points out the profitlessness of this course: "You
might have cajoled, and fawned, and played your traitor's part a
little longer, and grown richer" (54). But Carker exceeds the
confines of his strategy of revenge against Dombey simply because he becomes drawn to another kind of combat, one free of
any potential for revenge; Carker becomes intrigued with the
evil side, the purely and profitlessly defiant side, of Edith, and
wants to overcome her resistance to him at the expense of any
worldly gain. Riding home from Dombey's mansion, Carker is
fascinated by a mental image of Edith's hatred of him, with "her
pride, resentment, hatred, all as plain to him as her beauty;
with nothing plainer to him than her hatred of him" (46). This
image hauntingly "flit[s] about him on his ride, true to the reality, and obvious to him." Rather than seeking specific, profitable, or even personally vengeful goals, a villain like Carker
thrives on obstacles, no matter what kind. At the point when he
has conquered Dombey he freely shifts his attention to Edith—a
more formidable obstacle—with no thought to consolidate the
gains of his victory. The important point is just this: a preoccupation with gratuitous obstacles—what René Girard calls
"masochistic mediation"[4]—diverts these villains from an econ-
ony of purpose and reward, lifting them into a world of transcendentally profitless combat.

Even an obsessed villain like Bradley Headstone has a potential for violence that transcends his narrow pursuit of Lizzie
as a reward and reveals itself instead as a fascination with obstacles. Headstone's infatuation with Lizzie seems to blossom at
the moment he perceives Eugene to be an impediment. When he
first meets Lizzie, Headstone is "not at his ease," but the narrator tells us neutrally that "he never was, quite" (2.1). And
Headstone remains composed enough to insult Lizzie by telling
her "that the less [Charley's] attention is diverted from his work,

the better for his future." Only on the way home, when Charley
sees Eugene Wrayburn going to visit Lizzie, does the schoolmaster actively become interested. Immediately after Charley
recounts the contact Eugene has had with Lizzie, Headstone
says, "'I suppose—your sister—' with a curious break both before and after the words, 'has received hardly any teaching,
Hexam?'" And from this point on, Headstone devotes by far the
greater share of his attention to defeating Eugene, rather than
to courting Lizzie. In fact, Headstone's repression of his "animal" and "fiery" past as a "pauper lad" gives him a general manner of "lying in wait" (2.1), and the opportunity to test that
repressed energy against the obstacle he creates out of Eugene
—who has actually refused to court Lizzie himself—seems, in
one sense, an arbitrary exercise of this deep, frustrated violence. Because of the very arbitrariness of this violence, Headstone easily transfers all the weight of his desires for violent
release from Eugene to Riderhood, which is why Riderhood is
taken by surprise at how volcanic his tame schoolmaster can become. "Bradley stared at him so very suddenly that Riderhood,
not quite knowing how to take it, affected to be occupied with
the encircling smoke from his pipe" (4.15). And Headstone's suicide, girded to Riderhood, is a forceful image of his commitment
to destroying obstacles, rather than achieving specific goals.

The villain who most clearly displays this love of random
obstacles is Jonas Chuzzlewit. Even though Jonas is one of the
few Dickensian villains who does seem interested in money,
Jonas' satisfaction comes less from accumulating wealth than
from stealing it. His dependence on money as a medium for violation stems only from the overwhelmingly economic restrictions imposed on Jonas by his father. Thus, murdering Anthony
for his money is, in a larger sense, an attempt on Jonas' part to
revenge exclusions, to overcome restrictions, in the only medium he can recognize. The important point, though, is that at
the time of his death, Anthony represents not nearly as much of
an economic obstacle, since Jonas has no interest in spending his
money anyway, as Jonas imagines him to be. And the presence

of a general fascination with obstacles is signaled even more
strongly by Jonas' marriage. Rather than marrying Charity,
who openly courts him, Jonas flabbergasts everyone by marrying Mercy, who has resisted him and coyly displayed her contempt. For no apparent reason, too, Jonas imagines that Tom
Pinch is a threat to him and picks a fight with Tom. Even Jonas
seems surprised at his own impulsiveness; at one point, he wonders why he has tied himself "like a log" in marriage so soon
after gaining freedom from his father (28). For Jonas, neither
money nor freedom is the issue; Jonas seeks violent contact with
an arbitrarily chosen obstacle. In his violence against his father,
against Mercy, against Tom, and against Tigg, Jonas is driven,
not solely by a need for profit, but, more importantly, by a reflexive desire to experience violent release. When obstacles to
his freedom do not exist, Jonas will invent them as a pretext for
violence.

The gratuity of the villain's violence is only the first of its
noteworthy qualities. The second is the consistent tendency of
the villain's own violence to double back on himself. Quilp is
probably the purest and most enduring example of this principle. The constant blending of sadism and masochism in Quilp
seems to remove him even further from the pettiness of self-
gain and to lift him into a world of egoless destructive energy.
His self-violence usually manifests itself innocuously, as when
Quilp interrupts Mrs. Jiniwin's description of the flatness of his
nose. "'Aquiline!' cried Quilp, thrusting in his head, and striking
the feature with his fist. 'Aquiline, you hag. Do you see it? Do
you call this flat?'" (49). Earlier, Quilp hangs over the edge of a
moving coach "at the risk of his life" merely to make faces at
Mrs. Nubbles (48). And the clearest instance of this mixture of
sadism and masochism is Sampson's discovery of Quilp gleefully
beating a huge statue that he thinks resembles Kit; Sampson at
first supposes that the statue resembles Quilp himself.[5] The suggestion that Quilp punishes others out of self-hatred grounded
in his own deformity[6] seems plausible at first; he does, for example, punish Kit for calling him "a uglier dwarf than can be seen

anywheres for a penny" (6). But this motive appears to be too conventional, if only because Quilp exaggerates and exploits, rather than resists, his deformity, even turns deformity itself— an emblem of his distance and freedom from normal humanity— into pleasure. Quilp's initial response, then, when Tom tries to defend him against Kit's insult, is, "Do you mean to say, I'm not, you dog?" And at one point Quilp gloats over an overheard insult:

he often stopped . . . and stood listening for any conversation in the next room, of which he might be the theme.

"Ah!" he said after a short effort of attention, "it was not the towel over my ears, I thought it wasn't. I'm a little hunchy villain and a monster, am I, Mrs. Jiniwin? Oh!"

The pleasure of this discovery called up the old doglike smile in full force. When he had quite done with it, he shook himself in a very doglike manner, and rejoined the ladies. (5)

In the broadest sense, Quilp's masochism is rooted in his spontaneous, infantile contempt for restrictions. When Tom says that Quilp does not dare hit him again, Quilp replies childishly, "I won't do it again, because I've done it as often as I want" (5). Although violence transgresses all boundaries, the desire for release from boundaries always begins with the boundaries of the self, and violence directed outward is only a substitute for violence directed inward. As Norman O. Brown says, "Murder is misdirected suicide, to destroy part of oneself; murder is suicide with mistaken identity."[7] In this context, Bataille points out that violence against others releases the aggressor from his own self-restriction in at least three ways: the entrance into a world of violence proclaims a general lack of concern for human boundaries and for human survival; the penetration of the victim's limits produces an intimacy for the aggressor that disrupts his own isolation; and, finally, the aggressor is able to identify in imagination with the victim's violation or death and to experience them vicariously as his own.[8]

As we might expect, all violent figures in Dickens are also self-violent. Jaggers' probing, accusing forefinger is also the forefinger that he always bites; Hortense proclaims her freedom from Lady Dedlock by walking through wet grass barefoot, which, as Jarndyce notes later, is a good way to catch a killing cold; and, in *A Tale of Two Cities*, the narrator pauses at one point to generalize about the reversible direction of the mob's violence:

A species of fervour or intoxication, known, without doubt, to have led some persons to brave the guillotine unnecessarily, and to die by it, was not mere boastfulness, but a wild infection of the wildly shaken public mind. In seasons of pestilence, some of us will have a secret attraction to the disease—a terrible passing inclination to die of it. And all of us have like wonders hidden in our breasts, only needing circumstances to evoke them. (3.6)

Thus, too, Bill Sikes ignores Fagin's plea to "be crafty" (47) and murders Nancy with no thought of self-preservation, recklessly dooming his own life with hers. In *Dombey and Son*, after Carker loses Edith, what he learns is that the real goal of his fascination with Dombey and Edith is not revenge, but self-destruction. He realizes that he is "having a deadly quarrel with the whole world, but chiefly with himself" (55). In physical terms, he is "irresistably attracted" to the railroad; he walks along "the brink of the road"; and he waits for the train to come screaming by—then "for another, and for another." Rigaud enjoys playing at his own death, much as Quilp does; he conceives "the happy idea of disappearing" (2.28) and seems to relish how his death would please Flintwich and Mrs. Clennam. Bradley Headstone is probably the best example. Headstone's uncontrollable nosebleeds signal a self-rending that the schoolmaster willfully exacerbátes through his pursuit of Lizzie and Eugene. "He knew equally well that he fed his wrath and hatred, and that he accumulated provocation and self-justification, by being made the nightly sport of the reckless and insolent Eugene" (3.11). Headstone's beating his hand against the tombstone—his very name proclaims his desire—and his suicide betray what is finally the inward direction of his violence. Dickens cruelly underlines the perverse pleasure Headstone takes in his own degradation when

he has the schoolmaster tell Riderhood, "These are my holidays"
(4.1). No wonder, then, that many Dickensian villains—Quilp,
Headstone, Jonas Chuzzlewit, Bill Sikes, Carker—either deliberately or by some accident are responsible for their own
deaths.

Among the heroes, too, Pip wonderfully highlights the tendency of violence to turn inward when Estella first rejects him.
"As I cried, I kicked the wall, and took a hard twist at my hair;
so bitter were my feelings, and so sharp was the smart without
a name, that needed counteraction" (8). The pursuit of release is
always tied to self-hatred—not, of course, self-hatred in the
sense of psychological guilt, but self-hatred in the sense of contempt for the restrictions imposed by human identity. Quilp is
the clearest example. Quilp's career of violence—to others and
to himself—does seem to gain him just such a release, or transcendence, by achieving for him a state of demonic nonhumanity. His mother-in-law at one point "began to doubt if he were
really a human creature" (5). Significantly, too, Nell has a dream
in which Quilp's face merges with the faces of Mrs. Jarley's waxwork figures. It has been pointed out that our discomfort with
waxwork arises from our inability to resolve them either into
life or into nonlife; they irritate by defying the limitation of either form.[9] Quilp irritates in a similar way, being grotesquely
human and nonhuman at the same time.

Quilp may be the most enthusiastically evil villain in Dickens' work, but all of Dickens' excessive villains share Quilp's
motivelessness and his potential for self-annihilation. Even
characters who might only marginally qualify as villains share
these tendencies. It is worth considering, at this point, a particular class of Dickensian characters who appear morally ambiguous because they threaten gratuitous, self-destructive violence,
even though their violence can be harnessed for good purposes:
the agents of the law, particularly Bucket and Jaggers. As we
shall see in later chapters, Dickens tries to incorporate desires
for violation within legitimate society, and the ambiguity of
Bucket and Jaggers testifies to the presence within society of
tendencies that have the potential to emerge as evil but remain

uncomfortably ambivalent. More important, these characters' affinity with villainy is worth consideration because their slightly more restrained drives highlight in precise ways another direction taken by Dickensian violence; Bucket and Jaggers demonstrate most clearly how motiveless, self-destructive violence can be inscribed within conservative forms. That is to say, Bucket and Jaggers keep violence shy of actual self-destruction by turning it into a more economical exploitation of the relationship of villain to victim.

Bucket in *Bleak House* is not totally villainous, because his office institutionalizes his energy and neutralizes any harm he might cause; he is "angel and devil by turns" (54). But Bucket is clearly perceived by the reader—especially at first—as an undesirable, potentially villainous model of human action because of the motiveless and sometimes self-violent energy he shares with villains. Far from freeing him from the excesses of Quilpian energy, Bucket's office really increases the gratuity and the intensity of his pleasure in combativeness—that is, Bucket never lays claim to a self-serving motive, dissolving himself completely into the chase, into his "duty," instead. Bucket's attitude is childlike, as if his combats were just a game; for example, he tries to encourage the defeated Gridley by draining their opposition of any significance. "Don't go on in that way, Mr. Gridley. You are only a little low. We are all of us a little low, sometimes. *I* am. Hold up, hold up! You'll lose your temper with the whole round of 'em, again and again; and I shall take you on a score of warrants yet, if I have luck" (24). Bucket exists only to expend his energies in the chase, no matter whom he pursues, no matter for what reason. Though Bucket is certainly efficient, his freedom from a hierarchy of motives makes that efficiency, like Quilp's creative hostility, a means to no end. Because of this absence of priority, his arresting Gridley seems neither more nor less important than his taking of Hortense; or, at least, both seem to absorb him equally. And in large part, it is this very randomness that makes Bucket a threatening figure; the conservative claims of ethics have no authority over him.

Rather than physical violence, though, Bucket's conspicuous

means of self-annihilation is disguise and the playing of parts. In this way, he presents an alternative, conservative field for self-violence that at the same time does not compromise its transcendentally evil qualities. Through his acting, Bucket gives way to self-destructive desires and yet contains them in a more conservative set of relationships. Significantly, this particular method of release is one that is close to Dickens' own satisfaction in his readings; in a letter to Bulwer Lytton, Dickens wrote, "Assumption has charms for me—I hardly know for how many wild reasons—so delightful, that I feel a loss of, oh! I can't say what exquisite foolery, when I lose a chance of being someone in voice, etc., not at all like myself."[10] Like Dickens as reader and as writer, Bucket continually fascinates us because of the tremendous energy with which he disperses himself in his roles, some of which seem entirely unnecessary, such as, for example, his performance of affability at the Bagnets', which is completely defeated in its purpose—if it really has any—when they find him out later. Interestingly, this scene also has the effect of neutralizing Bucket's final kindnesses, when he sides with the good characters; his consideration for Esther during their pursuit of Lady Dedlock and his respect for Sir Leicester could very well be just another version of the same kind of theatrical exercise of proficiency. We never know, since, beneath all these disguises, there is never any real Bucket. The only instance in which Bucket ever says anything that we might take to be authentic occurs in Lady Dedlock's chambers when, alone, he catches sight of himself in a mirror and says out loud, "One might suppose I was a-moving in the fashionable circles, and getting myself up for Almack's" (56). Here again, though, Bucket's preoccupation is with his role, with his appearance in the mirror, and not with his own thoughts or feelings. "One might suppose" ties him to a relationship with an imaginary audience. As with Quilp, this fundamental hollowness of personality earns for Bucket a kind of transcendency that the other characters comment on. Hortense says to him, "you are very spiritual" (54), and Jo believes Bucket to possess a kind of Godlike omnipotence. Bucket's "motivelessness" and the totality of his self-expenditure through disguise are prerequisites for this apparent transcendency.

However, there is an important qualification to the release featured in Bucket's disguises. Though Dickens clearly enjoyed Bucket's facility with disguise, at the same time Dickens' ultimate dissatisfaction with disguise as a means of expenditure is evident toward the end of the novel, particularly when Bucket produces, as if in triumph, the final will—a will that proves to be just as meaningless and ineffectual as all the other wills. In this last exercise of his duty in the novel, Bucket approaches the mechanical in his commitment to the particular play in which he acts; his vitality seems to be rigidly circumscribed by his limited notion of duty. The fact that Bucket has an institution and a title with which to work of itself indicates that in some way he is closer to the world of conservative impulses than he is to Quilpian excess, but the proof of this ultimate conservation is that, for Bucket, a world of disguises is still a closed world, a world of limited forms. Bucket's energies are circumscribed by the very masks that free him. Bucket *must* exercise his "duty"; otherwise, he does not exist.

Ultimately, too, Bucket's private satisfactions are inseparable from the constraints of performance, the relationship of the role-player to his audience. Our discomfort with Bucket's insensitivity to Sir Leicester in the scene in which he takes Hortense —"Sir Leicester sits like a statue," we are told, "gazing at the cruel finger that is probing the life-blood of his heart" (54)—reminds us that this is a performance staged for an unwilling Sir Leicester. The inappropriateness of his performance underscores the fact that Bucket's love of role-playing is circumscribed by his need for an audience. Significantly, we rarely see Bucket actually investigating cases; we only see him performing the results of his investigations to others, as if Bucket comes into existence only while he is watched. Even in his pursuit of Lady Dedlock, in which we follow his movements carefully through Esther's eyes, we only glimpse the surface of his physical movements in and out of London, along with what Esther

calls his "watchfulness," without any access to his thoughts. He
never tells Esther his plans until they are well under way; for
example, as he rouses Esther with a cup of tea, Bucket says,
"You was what you may call stunned at first . . . and Lord! no
wonder. Don't speak loud, my dear. It's all right. She's on ahead"
(57). At the crucial moment of the chase, too, Bucket holds Esther and the reader in suspense when he gains knowledge that
he wants to save for a more appropriate moment. Bucket cannot
possibly want to soothe Esther here, as he claims, since he
causes her more anxiety by letting her think they are abandoning Lady Dedlock in the snow than he would have by letting her
in on his strategy. Like Cuttle in *Dombey and Son*, Bucket
seeks to absorb and to shock his audience. The importance of
Bucket's performance before others is also stressed at one point
by the narrator, who, in referring to Bucket as a gambler,
blends metaphors of risk and recognition. "From the expression
of his face, he might be a famous whist-player for a large stake
—say a hundred guineas certain—with the game in his hand,
but with a high reputation involved in his playing his hand out to
the last card, in a masterly way" (54). Here, and in his final production of the will—shown up as it is by Jarndyce's indifference
—Bucket is foolishly and rigidly a performer. In similar ways,
Dickens' readings were severely limited by their nature as public entertainments—despite his efforts to "create" and control
his audience—which may be one reason why Dickens kept pushing himself to make the readings more and more violent, until he
literally killed himself reading.

As for Bucket's pursuits themselves, even though his ascen-
dency is never meant to be permanent, which would spoil the
game, it is there momentarily nevertheless—an instant of limited form. Bucket asserts his transcendence of human identity
at the moment when he can place his forefinger on his opponent's
chest and say "that's what *you* are, you know" (22), reducing
his rival to a category. And Bucket does gain recognition of his
transcendence through his assertions of superior freedom, and,
hence, power. But the price of this recognition is Bucket's slav-

ery to his victims. Nowhere is this more clear than in the scene in which he apprehends Hortense; both sit tightly together, shoulder-to-shoulder, their wrists manacled to each other as they perform a kind of marriage ceremony.[11] "Now, my dear, put your arm a little further through mine, and hold it steady, and I sha'n't hurt you!" (54).

In one way or another, a potential enslavement of the villain to his victim ultimately binds many of Dickens' larger villains and dictates their embarrassments. Rigaud's ferocious embracing of Flintwich, though meant to torment the smaller man, also hints at the arbitrary confinement of Rigaud's energies to an insignificant victim. In Rigaud's case, this confinement, which signals the arbitrariness of his persecution of Mrs. Clennam, is eventually fatal. Similarly, Headstone's narrow, obsessive pursuit of release ties him to the humiliations of Eugene, and Edith Dombey teases Carker with the humiliation his constricting attachment to her has caused. "You have fallen on Sicilian days and sensual rest too soon. . . . You purchase your voluptuous retirement dear!" (54). Perhaps the villain most anguished by his imprisoning relationship to his victim is Jonas Chuzzlewit, who even complains to Mercy, "I hate myself for having been fool enough to strap a pack upon my back for the pleasure of treading on it" (28). All of Dickens' villains are trapped by the very "masochistic mediation" of arbitrary obstacles that serve to confine their motivelessness.

However, Bucket illustrates a kind of restriction that is more limiting than just a commitment to arbitrary obstacles. Rigaud, Headstone, Carker, and Chuzzlewit all achieve violence, even if in enslaved ways. Through role-playing, however, Bucket deliberately fashions an identity for himself that diverts outright violence into a merely symbolic annihilation of self, one that demands an audience. Bucket's violence is performed, rather than actual. As such, it arrives at no real consummation. Bucket's violent energies are thus condemned to repeat themselves in ways that appear foolish by the end of the novel.

This particular conservation of violent energies is one with disturbing implications even for some of Dickens' larger villains. But before we proceed to them, we should note more fully how the dangers in this fabricated kind of inhuman identity are spelled out by Jaggers. Because he performs a more restrained kind of role, Jaggers shows even more clearly than Bucket how the meaning of expenditure can be diverted into conservative, nonviolent forms. Like Bucket, Jaggers is not technically a villain—Jaggers defends as often as he prosecutes. But Jaggers' affinity with the criminal is clear. He is violently passionate; he is fascinated by criminals himself, even placing busts of two of them in his office; and he admires Bentley Drummle. Moreover, in Jaggers the absence of motive is clearly revealed as a deliberate self-expenditure, a willful annihilation of personality, since when Pip claims that Jaggers confuses him, Wemmick explains, "Tell him that, and he'll take it as a compliment. . . . He don't mean that you *should* know what to make of [him]" (24). In fact, the source of Jaggers' power over others is his ability to empty himself of any motive except the love of expending energy in conflict.

But Jaggers' method itself bears further study, since Jaggers articulates his transcendence indirectly, as an absence. To incorporate the potential for violence into the structure of a personality, Jaggers adopts a technique used by all of Dickens' role-playing villains, something that Girard, in a different context, calls *askesis*.[12] In a nonviolent way, the villain deliberately strips himself of desire, or motive, in order to occupy in the eyes of the other the transcendent space of the nonhuman—that which is beyond life and death. Jaggers himself represents his nonhumanity, his *askesis*, in a number of ways. He holds secrets about the desires and scandals of others without ever making admissions about himself, which emphasizes his distance from human culpability; his speech is frequently interrogative or imperative, rarely declarative, which focuses attention everywhere but on Jaggers' own motives and desires; he makes use of passive constructions to eliminate himself from statements, such as, "Put the case, Pip, that here was one pretty little child out of the heap, who could be saved" (51); he never initiates conversation, as Pip points out, but only extracts it from others; and he has no private life, even at home—unlike Wemmick. Jaggers' use of Wemmick, too, is significant; as Wemmick himself explains to Pip, Jaggers uses him as a go-between with his clients to help stress his distance from them. Furthermore, Wemmick is completely in charge of the money, which frees Jaggers from all petty association with the merely financial. In all of these cases, Jaggers does not "abandon" himself passionately, the way Quilp and even Bucket do; instead, he constructs in a calculated way a persona of indifference that he performs to others.

With Jaggers, actual expenditure is subordinated to a deliberate use of potential violence and implied expenditure as a means to power. In effect, Jaggers tries to privilege concrete identity by giving it a permanent status that includes violence. Unlike Quilp, Jaggers' propensity for release is less tied to the pure violence of self-expenditure than it is to its uses in his relationship with others. And this personal usefulness is even more apparent in Jaggers' behavior than it is in Bucket's relationship to his audience, since Bucket's self-effacements and his ability to switch sides dissolve him more completely in the masks of agency and distance him from any directly personal remuneration. Bucket, at least, does not blackmail others or keep them permanently under his thumb. By contrast, Jaggers' willingness to expose himself to violence, in addition to his love of conflict for its own sake, is a personal challenge to others, one meant to gain for him the indifferent status of the master. His dare to the criminals of London, in which he invites them all to rob him by advertising his perpetually unlocked doors, has such a function; Jaggers gains his mastery over others by proving that he is willing to risk more to destruction than they are. To borrow a set of terms from Hegel, Jaggers acquires mastery by proving his greater superiority to slavish, biological humanity, by proving his transcendence of instincts for mere self-preservation. The master, according to Hegel, is he who proves his devotion to higher values by his willingness to risk more in the way of common values—even life itself—than the slave.[13]

However, once he has proved his willingness to brave death,

the master enters into a stable, well-defined relationship to his
victims, a narrowly circumscribed identity—the mask of *askesis*. And Jaggers, in his complacent life-style and in his obsessive unwillingness to commit indiscretions with Pip, appears to
be a man resting on his laurels. With Jaggers, metaphysical
identity through power over others is a restricted identity.
Even more disturbing, it is a particularly cruel kind of restricted identity; the experience of expenditure, which is meant to
yield a transcendence of human identity, is inscribed within
identity only by entering into a structure of human relationships
in which transcendence is signified by power over others.

A dependence on *askesis* always characterizes villains in
Dickens who, like Bucket and Jaggers, adopt roles that advertise their impersonality and their potential for violence. In
particular, Rigaud and Carker display this tendency. These two
villains are much less free than Bucket and Jaggers—and more
patently evil—because their *askesis* clearly has a personal usefulness and is not diffused by their service of the law. In that
sense, their *askesis* is less complete and more of a mask; hence,
they are driven more strongly back toward real violence. Yet
the *askesis* is present in these characters, and it constitutes the
colder, more rigid cruelties of these two villains in comparison to
characters like Sikes or Chuzzlewit. Rigaud and Carker both
keep their violence in check by representing themselves as impersonal and inhuman, thus hoping to consolidate their power of
mastery over others.

Rigaud is never violent in *Little Dorrit*; he only implies a
willingness to commit violence. Ironically, this never-actualized
threat only makes his inhumanity seem all the more immense
because Rigaud's violence is withheld. In the first chapter,
Rigaud coolly describes the "suicide" of his rich wife, leaving
Cavalletto to assume that Rigaud actually murdered her without ever presenting him with an image of that violence. In that
first chapter, too, Rigaud is led away to what we assume is certain execution; when Rigaud surprises Cavalletto later at an
inn, Cavalletto is at first terrified by the apparition of a man he

thought dead. These early associations with death create an atmosphere of latent violence about Rigaud that is all the greater for their veiled quality; not only is this violence remote in terms of the action of the novel, but it seems unable to deter or form any impression at all on Rigaud, who is apparently beyond any sort of apprehensions about violence. And Rigaud frequently reinforces his intimate association with and indifference to death through his epithets: "death," "death of my soul," "death of my life." Then, too, though less flamboyant than Bucket, Rigaud is also an actor, which helps annihilate concrete identity in him; he has a constant "theatrical air" (1.1) and is able to falsify himself through performance. "He had a certain air of being a handsome man—which he was not; and a certain air of being a well-bred man—which he was not. . . . but in this particular, as in many others, blustering assertion goes for proof, half over the world." Rigaud's many aliases also insist on his shape-shifting abilities, as does his persistent claim that he hails from no particular country. And, like Jaggers and Carker, his possession of the scandalous secrets of others helps make him appear inhumanly motiveless by contrast. Finally, Rigaud's claim that he is a gentleman always takes the character of a denial of human needs for survival. "Have you ever thought of looking to me to do any kind of work?" (1.1), he asks Cavalletto. The suspicion of inhumanity other characters entertain of Rigaud—for all these reasons—easily makes him master over them; "it is my character to govern," he tells us many times, and other characters bow before the represented inhumanity of that character.

More like Bucket and Jaggers, Carker adopts a mask of *askesis* through agency. Carker empties himself not merely of motive but of all human personality through his relationship to Dombey. His deference to his employer thus serves him in the same way as Bucket's and Jaggers' indifference to personal gain; though Edith Dombey taunts Carker for what she claims is a "fawning" character, Carker is able to use his agent role to diffuse any personal motives and to project instead an impersonal, limitless potential for violence. For this reason, he ascribes his

insulting warnings about Edith's conduct and her feelings toward Dombey to "business" (37) and consistently professes his
"position of humility." Carker's impersonality is further signaled
by his skill at games. He plays them so well, in fact, that "the
Major was astonished" (26). And Dickens' incessant references
to Carker as a shark or a cat reinforce his awesome inhumanity,
as does Carker's ability to express himself "voicelessly." Certainly, Carker's relentless show of selflessness is precisely what
infuriates Edith. "As he bent forward, to be nearer, with the
utmost show of delicacy and respect, and with his teeth per-
suasively arrayed, in a self-depreciating smile, she felt as if she
could have struck him dead" (37). One suspects that if Edith
could define a personal motive in Carker at this point, she might
more easily be able to overcome him; in fact, when Carker openly displays his intentions toward Edith, stripping away the impersonal mask of *askesis*, Edith is able to humiliate him by
accusing him of lesser, sensual, merely human motives. Ultimately, though, like Rigaud—and unlike Bucket and Jaggers,
who more completely dissolve themselves into morally ambiguous agency through the law—Carker employs an inhuman mask
to root his violence in a conservative relationship of power over
others. In this way, Rigaud and Carker are less enjoyable than
the free-wheeling Quilp, less sympathetic than the disturbed,
reckless Chuzzlewit and Headstone. Even Bill Sikes' compas-
sionless fury is not as distasteful as the cruelty inherent in a
mastering *askesis*. As Dickens' villains attempt to consolidate
their violence in the useful, economic form of mastery, they dis-
tort sympathetic passions for expenditure into coldly inhuman
masks.

Perhaps the best example of a villain in which expenditure is
represented rather than experienced through violence is Tulkinghorn. Though an agent of the law, Tulkinghorn resembles
Carker more in his use of agency to mask violent desires that
are finally routed back into personal consolidations of power.
And Tulkinghorn is quite possibly the most inhuman creature in
Dickens—not even death moves him. "Mr. Tulkinghorn has

stood aloof by the old portmanteau, with his hands behind him, equally removed, to all appearances, from all three kinds of interest exhibited near the bed—from the young surgeon's professional interest in death . . . ; from the old man's unction; and the little crazy woman's awe" (11). Like Jaggers, Carker, and Rigaud, Tulkinghorn thrives on the contrast between the guilt of others and his own indifference; he pursues just such a contrast through Lady Dedlock. In opposition to her guilt, Tulkinghorn dissolves himself into his office; to make the point, he tells Lady Dedlock that "throughout our interview I have expressly stated my sole consideration to be Sir Leicester's feelings and honour, and the family reputation" (41). But this impassivity is not necessarily constitutional with Tulkinghorn. The reader knows that Tulkinghorn deliberately tries to empty himself of all human content for the sake of his appearance to others. Certainly, Tulkinghorn's *askesis* is transparent to the reader in his dealings with Lady Dedlock, which deeply engage him. His feigned indifference is also right on the surface at least one other time, in his first conference with George, for Tulkinghorn's "appearance of perfect indifference, as he looks over the papers on his table, and prepares to write a letter" (27) cannot affect what we know of his actual, eager interest in George.

Tulkinghorn's preoccupation with the effects of his behavior on others, and with their recognition of his transcendence, is dramatized in particular through his obsessive love of secrets— he refuses even to tell his own clerk where he goes and what he does. As "an Oyster of the old school, whom nobody can open" (10), Tulkinghorn tries to participate in transcendence through the desire of others for the secrets he possesses. He is referred to as "that high priest of noble mysteries" (42), and Volumnia calls him "such an immense being for knowing all sorts of things and never telling them" (40). But, although Tulkinghorn's power comes from his secrets, that power is not the power of being able to manipulate people and things through knowledge of their essences.[14] Tulkinghorn's power, like Quilp's violence, is purposeless; he earns from his secrets no more than the fascination of others. Tulkinghorn does not *want* anything from Lady Dedlock, nor does he manipulate her in any way, which would ultimately contradict the power he derives from his motivelessness; Tulkinghorn only relishes her recognition of him as an illimitable, inarticulated force, one not to be circumscribed by normal human intentions.

Nevertheless, Tulkinghorn is also the clearest example of a villain whose transcendent energies are trapped in the horizontal struggles of rivalry. At one point, the narrator comments directly on this reduction.

The time was once when men as knowing as Mr. Tulkinghorn would walk on turret-tops in the starlight, and look up into the sky to read their fortunes there. Hosts of stars are visible tonight, though their brilliancy is eclipsed by the splendour of the moon. If he be seeking his own star, as he methodically turns and turns upon the leads, it should be but a pale one to be so rustily represented below. If he be tracing out his destiny, that may be written in other characters nearer to his hand. (41)

Moments later, the moon is equated with Lady Dedlock—which is to say that Tulkinghorn himself is eclipsed by his own victim. Like Krook's cat, Tulkinghorn is jealous of the freedom of others, even jealous of Lady Dedlock's possible suicide; "a moment's observation of her figure as she stands in the window without any support, looking out at the stars—not up—reassures him." Consequently, Tulkinghorn's search for his own release takes the form of entrapping others—an illusory freedom. Most especially, he tries to make Lady Dedlock feel the full weight of her prison: "You [are] to be exactly what you were before" (48), he tells her. Then, too, he publishes her secret to Lady Dedlock's small aristocratic circle in the form of an allegory—not for his own advantage, but solely to make her experience the terror of being caught. Tulkinghorn's obstructionism, whatever image of transcendence it gives him, is ultimately limited to his relationship to others, and especially to Lady Dedlock. Thus, it is fitting that he should be killed on the night he threatens to destroy this relationship; since his blackmail has no goal and has totally consumed his project of expenditure, there can be no conceivable next step for Tulkinghorn. And on his walk home that night, Tulkinghorn is elaborately pictured amid the world of his secrets—a silent world that will not speak to him in warning, a world that culminates in the mute figure of Allegory. It is as if Tulkinghorn's own secrecy were burying him.

In *A Tale of Two Cities*, it is easiest to see how the opposition between expenditure and the recuperation of expenditure —a recuperation in which the affectation of inhumanity is deliberately represented to others to achieve mastery—is a dynamic opposition in Dickens, and not simply an arbitrary smorgasbord of choices. In Dickens, the two opposing poles are always in oscillation; violence is desirable as expenditure, but it leads disastrously to self-annihilation; *askesis* is a retreat from violence that attempts to retain its meaning by extorting recognition from others, but it can congeal into restrictive form and therefore require new violence. In *A Tale of Two Cities* the two dialectical alternatives are personified and set at war with each other.

The purity of self-violence clearly belongs to the lower classes, who "held life as if of no account, and [were] demented with a passionate readiness to sacrifice it" (2.21). Thus, the concrete effects of the revolutionaries' violence as an annihilation of their humanity are actualized before us; we witness the transformation of rational figures like the Defarge couple into maddened beasts during the storming of the Bastille. Furthermore, to emphasize the unnatural and nonhuman element in the revolutionaries' passion, Dickens made their spokesman a woman, since, in Dickens' world, the supreme disruption of normal expectations about human nature is an absence of tenderness in woman. In the Parisian violence, even La Guillotine is female. And to heighten this effect, Dickens sets Madame Defarge's knitting in service of violence in sharp contrast to Lucie Manette's "golden thread" of pacification and harmony, as well as to the "domestic arts" that Lucie had learned in Madame Defarge's France.

The liberating intentions behind the lower classes' violence, though, are only a response to the repressive image of nonhuman freedom and "represented" violence that define the power of the class of Monseigneur. Instead of seeking out overt acts of violence, members of the upper classes live lives that revolve around static representations of their nonhumanity. The Marquis' own nonhumanity marks itself in his freedom from emotion—the narrator at one point describes his appearance as being "a fine mask" (2.9), and his face is compared to the stone faces of his gargoyles. In his conversation with Charles, he annihilates feeling through the codified formality of manners; "the uncle made a graceful gesture of protest, which was so clearly a slight form of good breeding that it was not reassuring." Generally, the hallmark of status among the Marquis' class is this "leprosy of unreality" (2.7). The Fancy Ball, for example, is full of "Unbelieving Philosophers," who construct elaborately meaningless verbal structures, and "Unbelieving Chemists," who have their eyes on alchemy—both are in pursuit of the unnatural, through words or through metals. Good breeding itself "was at that remarkable time—and has been since—to be known by its fruits of indifference to every natural subject of human interest." Once again, too, the contrast is clearest in the image of the female; among the women of the Marquis' society, the chief distinction is an escape from maternity. It was "hard to discover among the angels of that sphere one solitary wife, who, in her manner and appearance, owned to being a Mother. . . . Peasant women kept the unfashionable babies close, and brought them up, and charming grandmammas of sixty dressed and supped as at twenty." This freedom from the limitations of pure biology as it expresses itself in human generation is an important requirement among all of Dickens' villains; few are married, and, of those who are, Quilp gleefully deserts his wife, proclaiming himself a bachelor; Rigaud murders Mrs. Rigaud; and Bucket absorbs his wife so completely into his own detective operations that she never even puts in an appearance in the novel—perhaps the only character in Dickens besides Mrs. Harris to be mentioned so much without being seen.

There is violence among the Marquis' class, of course, but it is colder and has a clear function as a representation; that is, violence is merely an occasional symbol of the mastery of the rich, since it proves their right to waste lives if they choose to—the lives of the lower orders.[15] When the Marquis asserts that running down children with his carriage is a right of his station, he takes no passionate satisfaction from the killing; he takes only a numbed confirmation of his status. Initially, when the rebels in *A Tale of Two Cities* kill, they kill in passion, while the rich kill as spectacle—as, for example, when the royal government executes the murderer of the Marquis and leaves him hanging forty feet in the air. The Marquis expresses this functionality of violence explicitly; when Charles complains that his family is hated in France for their cruelty, the Marquis answers, "Let us hope so. . . . Detestation of the high is the involuntary homage of the low" (2.9).

All of Dickens' villains, inasmuch as they necessarily stop short of self-annihilation, waver between both poles of the dialectic of expenditure and its recuperation—the phase of direct, transcending violence against self and others, and the phase in which villains substitute a more static recognition of their transcendence in place of the actual violence, extorting this recognition from their rivals by forcing them to confront images either of the villains' own inhumanity or of their violent potential. On the surface, these two phases are irreconcilable—self-violation is the opposite of a status, and experiences of release cannot take on form. But it is in the nature of expenditure to divert itself from death, toward usefulness. And through the recuperation of expenditure in a personality structure, the villain attempts to escape the infinity of self-annihilation by making the rivals' recognition of his power infinite.

In general, the more sympathetic villains in Dickens are those in whom expenditure is more complete, more pure, less tied to recognition—Quilp, Bradley Headstone, even Jonas Chuzzlewit. As expenditure slides over into deliberate *askesis* and the transparent attempt to fascinate others, the villain becomes more insidious—the Marquis, Tulkinghorn, Carker, Rigaud, or even Madame Defarge, as her violence gradually turns into calculated vengeance and earns for her a position of power among the insurgents. These villains are both more cruel in their use of expenditure as power to extort recognition, and more clearly circumscribed by these relationships. But in every case, what distances the reader from the villain more than the horror of his violence is the way in which violence and the struggle for recognition always merge, whatever the proportions of either. With the villain, the drive for expenditure, as it shies away from death, is always channeled into some form of competitive relationship with others—the very definition of villainy. In their search for transcendent expenditure, the villains in Dickens are always caught in the cold and illusory freedom of rivalry.

iii

It is worth considering at this point that the problem of rivalry as limiting form is not confined to the villain. The villain merely focuses the rivalry that permeates the atmosphere of Dickens' world. Any expenditure that stops short of death is implicated in represented release, which brings into play the question of audience, and such an audience is most easily created in the form of a rival. Villains are more successful and actually realize power in their rivalries; others merely trap themselves in the factional struggle. In all novels, characters try to make up for their sense of exclusion from metaphysical freedom by imitating real or invented oppressors and by setting themselves up as obstacles to the freedom of others, thus establishing cycles of rivalry.

This is the Hegelian horror of *A Tale of Two Cities*; at the point when the revolutionaries stop short of death and attempt to make their release permanent and meaningful in the form of a republic, they trap themselves in the reified form of diverted expenditure—the petty, mechanical, and cruel contortions of human rivalry. *A Tale of Two Cities*, more than any other Dickens novel, thereby stresses the imitative dimension of desires for expenditure that stop short. We lose sympathy with the rebels at the point when they lose sight of their limitless freedom— their own "pure" release—and imprison themselves in revenge, thus imitating their oppressors. The very name of Madame Defarge's companion is "The Vengeance," and Madame Defarge undercuts herself through an ironic imitation; she dedicates herself to destroying the Darnay family just as her own family was destroyed. More disturbingly, for Madame Defarge, as for the rest of the revolutionaries, passionate revenge gives way to the invention of spurious rivalry, the murder of innocent victims. The purely mechanical quality of this imitative violence is underscored by the ominous note of historical destiny in the novel: the continual references to the inevitability of things' "running their courses" and the metaphors of echoing footsteps and approaching thunderstorms. The revolutionaries' victory over repression leads only to their imprisonment in rivalry—just as Dr. Manette's liberation from imprisonment leads him directly into a rivalry with his own son-in-law, and just as Darnay's flight from France lands him squarely in a relationship of rivalry to Manette.

In other novels—especially in the later ones—the imitative, infectious atmosphere of rivalry is more subtly revealed. *Great Expectations*, instead of featuring a single villain—Compeyson and Orlick have only a marginal relationship to the main plot— has a number of menacing figures who are basically good, or at least reformable, but who are each turned into an "Avenger"— emblematically, the name of Pip's servant—as a result of their own victimization. Magwitch is such a victim/villain; when we first see him, he is a fellow sufferer of Pip's at the hands of an indifferent nature, "a man who had been soaked in water, and smothered in mud, and lamed by stones, and cut by flints, and stung by nettles, and torn by briars; who limped and shivered,

and glared and growled; and whose teeth chattered in his head
as he seized me by the chin" (1). Magwitch's abused condition
makes his aggressiveness seem an odd contrast; even stranger
is his subsequent suicidal battle with the other prisoner, in which
he gives himself up as a means of depriving another of freedom.
Magwitch is both pursuer and pursued. Miss Havisham, in a similar way, is turned into a villain—a defrauder of others—because
of her own injuries. Both of these characters also illustrate the
empty mechanism of rivalry through their relationship to Pip;
since neither has a specific enemy (Miss Havisham declares war
on the entire male sex, and Magwitch wants to avenge himself
against nameless persecutors—the blank faces of judge and jury,
and of his masters in Australia, who are not necessarily the same
blank faces that he wants to make envious of his "gentleman")
both settle on Pip arbitrarily, as either the victim or the agent of
their revenge, plugging him into their private formulas. But Pip
himself is a prime instance of a victim reflexively turned villain;
he is abused by others early in the novel, and then he simply reverses the polarity. He abuses Biddy and Joe indirectly,
through his indifference, and directly by trying to accuse Biddy
of envy; he plunges into an absurd rivalry with Drummle; and he
has Orlick and Trabb's boy dismissed. In more symbolic ways,
Pip's sin is the imitative reversing of the opposition between himself and his elders. Pumblechook gets the tar meant for Pip, and,
at the end, he gets a beating at the hands of Pip's rival, Orlick;[16]
then, too, Mrs. Joe is assaulted with Pip's file. All three of these
characters are trapped in imitative rivalry, which is what makes
their actions seem mechanical, frustrated. But rivalry is also the
vehicle that these characters have chosen for their rebellion
against specific restrictions: for Magwitch, the class structure
that insists on his innate limitations; for Miss Havisham, her
lover's rejection; and, for Pip, the collection of voices in his
world—Mrs. Joe, Pumblechook, and, finally, Estella—all of
whom tell him in one way or another that he is determined by his
class, by his occupation, and by his very sex. In all these cases,
rivalry as a mode of release that leaves the self unviolated becomes itself a restriction.

The list of imitative rivalries in *Great Expectations* goes on and includes almost every character in the novel. Miss Havisham's brother tries to reverse his exclusion from the love of his father by excluding his sister from romantic love; Pip's elders compensate for their own feelings of selfishness by projecting them into him. For example, when Mr. Wopsle holds forth that "Swine were the companions of the prodigal" and "The gluttony of Swine is put before us, as an example to the young," Pip comments, "I thought this pretty well in him who had been praising up the pork for being so plump and juicy" (4). Molly's crime is an act of revenge, and Mrs. Pocket spends her life berating an invented list of antagonists to the family name. Dominating the mood of the entire novel, in fact, is the parable of Abel and Cain, which is evoked through the battle of Abel Magwitch and Compeyson; the delusion all these characters share is the false hope that imposing one's own sense of exclusion on the rival yields up transcendence. In this way, the struggle in *Great Expectations* confirms Girard's notion of the mediator; the mediator imitates the structure of his own frustration by trying to become the obstacle to the freedom and the desires of others.[17]

As if to stress the automatic nature of rivalry, *Great Expectations* also presents us, in the early scenes, with a series of mysterious physical combats. Magwitch and Compeyson's battle seems odd because of the inexplicable, suicidal passion with which Magwitch sacrifices his own freedom to imprison another; Herbert's fight with Pip is nonsensical, although it seems to Herbert to be prescribed; and Joe and Orlick fight despite their lack of personal animosity—they split a pitcher of beer afterward—because the situation and matrimonial etiquette require it. These surreal, unaccountable combats are emblems of the fog that includes Pip and Estella's game of cards—"beggar my neighbor"—Wopsle's eagerness for competition with the local preacher, the rivalries among Miss Havisham's circle of heirs, and Pip's suggestion that, to his guardians, the taking of the convicts was a "terrible good sauce for a dinner" (5). Pip's great disillusion, in fact, can be formulated in terms of this ever-present web of rivalry; he finds himself fallen from a world where pure vertical

release seemed possible—where one might reach "the stars"—
into a world of horizontal entanglements, where the goal is not
freedom but revenge, along with the restriction and the frustration of others—what Magwitch calls being "low." These rivalries
in *Great Expectations* limit release within the very structures
through which characters had hoped to gain liberation.

In *Bleak House*, too, the drama of expenditure is generally
shifted away from direct violence toward the relational strategies of rivalry. In general, there is an absence of outright violence in this novel, in comparison with most Dickens novels.
Tulkinghorn, the principal villain, is cold and impassive, and he
even tells Grandfather Smallweed, "Violence will not do for me,
my friend" (27). Bucket, the most energetic of the characters,
satisfies himself with capturing his victims, and Boythorn is
unwilling to commit his brawling impulses to direct violence.
Hortense is the only murderous character in the novel, but Hortense's violence is as much a strategy of revenge as it is a matter
of pure physical release. The absence of the murder scene from
the narration—a great sacrifice for Dickens—deemphasizes its
violence and stresses instead its role in Hortense's calculated revenge against Lady Dedlock.

The prominence occupied by violent release in other novels
is here taken up by "secrets," which are always associated in
turn with rivalry. Rather than rebelling against specific kinds of
imprisonment—and in this context the necessarily suffocating
role of Chancery has been exaggerated, since only a few of the
characters actually struggle against or within it—characters
seem obsessed by their sense that they are oppressed by the unknown, the mysterious rival. The disease of secret, imagined rivalry is so widespread that it might be said to be the dominant
occupation of the novel; Miller, who isolates the chief concern of
the novel in "interpretation,"[18] neglects the fact that characters
are continually driven to interpret by the authority they project
into the unknown, and that the particular authority they imagine is always an obstructing one. Minor characters express this
disease quite clearly; Guppy, for instance, suspects

everybody who enters on the occupation of a stool in Kenge and Car-
boy's office, of entertaining, as a matter of course, sinister designs
upon him. He is clear that every such person wants to depose him. If
he be ever asked how, why, when, or wherefore, he shuts up one eye
and shakes his head. On the strength of these profound views, he in
the most ingenious manner takes infinite pains to counter-plot, when
there is no plot; and plays the deepest games of chess without any
adversary. (20)

In particular, Guppy pursues Krook, for no other reason than
that he "can't make him out." The Snagsbys are another example of this dread of the secret rival; Mr. Snagsby is gripped by a
holy awe at the apprehension that his life is dominated by some
dangerous, oppressive secret, and Mrs. Snagsby is convinced
that her husband's secret is the existence of her rival, the woman
she invents to be Snagsby's mistress.

On the subject of fabricated rivalry, Skimpole makes a tan-
talizing observation in the case of Gridley. "He could easily imagine that there Gridley was, years ago, wandering about in life
for something to expend his superfluous combativeness upon—a
sort of Young Love among the thorns—when the Court of Chancery came in his way, and accommodated him with the exact thing
he wanted. There they were, matched, ever afterwards! Otherwise he might have been a great general, blowing up all sorts of
towns" (15). The tone of Skimpole's observations is always disturbing, but their odd accuracy is fairly consistent, especially in a
case like this, where so many other characters seem gripped by
arbitrary rivalries. Even a benign character like Boythorn is absorbed—and, as the end of the novel shows, trapped against his
will—in a ridiculous rivalry with Sir Leicester. The conjunction
of secrecy and the unknown with deliberately sought-out or invented opposition reaches a peak in Richard, who supposes that
there is some hidden clause in the tangle of Chancery that ob-
structs him, or even that someone is actually holding him down;
ultimately, of course, Richard accuses Jarndyce of being his
rival. All of these characters are analogous, in their fixation on
rivals, to Mr. Badger, whose wife seems valuable to him only be-

cause of the existence of her three distinguished previous hus-
bands—his rivals. Mr. Badger remains totally fascinated by
these rivals, as if the quality of their opposition confers value on
his own success in replacing them.

In the world of *Bleak House*, characters do not search for a
pure release from restriction through radical acts of expenditure; instead, they are caught in a horizontal web of imagined
rivalry, which is associated with transcendence largely through
the mysterious aura surrounding secrets. In this world, characters who can take up the place of these supposed obstacles gain
for themselves the metaphysical aura attaching to them. Tulkinghorn, whose rivalry is rooted in his attempt to reverse his
relationship to Sir Leicester, is only the most obvious example,
trying as he does to exert a fascination on others through his
many secrets. There are innumerable echoes of this strategy;
Lady Dedlock, for example, cultivates an inscrutable facade as a
mark of her transcendence in relation to others. Esther comments, "She was as self-possessed, and as free to occupy herself
with her own thoughts, as if she had been alone" (18), and she
"had the air, I thought, of being able to attract and interest any
one, if she thought it worth her while." But Lady Dedlock's
askesis is only a tool for her. She uses it especially in her rivalry
with Tulkinghorn; in his presence she always "abstracts her attention." The more troublesome instance of secrecy as a means
to fascinate others, though, is presented by Esther, who keeps
secrets both from other characters and from the reader. Whether
voluntary or involuntary, and whether or not it is a function of
her humility, Esther's secrecy about herself and her desires is
one of the reasons that characters attribute to her a transcendent status.

Reflexive, rivalrous instincts plague characters in all of Dickens' novels, even if only in localized eruptions. In one of the
many seemingly random digressions of *The Old Curiosity Shop*,
Dickens toys with the petty rivalry of Miss Monflathers' two as-
sistants, who try to ingratiate themselves with Miss Monflathers by embarrassing each other. In *Dombey and Son*, the many

jealousies of Dombey are echoed in the rivalrous intrigues of Major Bagstock against Miss Tox. In *Hard Times*, Bitzer becomes obsessed with the circus and Sissy Jupe, thinking—apparently because Gradgrind plays him off against Sissy in the opening chapter—that the key to his success lies in frustrating the circus performers. Frequently, too, the problem of rivalry is expressed through the antagonistic pairing of literal or figurative brothers: Monks and Oliver, the two Carkers, David Copperfield and Steerforth, Edwin Drood and Jasper, Pip and Herbert. Rivalry may be most explicit in Dickens' villains, since their drives toward expenditure are more intense than other characters', and because they do not have other alternatives that are available to Dickens' heroes. But the dialectic that villains make explicit does not confine itself to them. In general, rivalry in Dickens is the great danger in the pursuit of expenditure. Through his villains, however, Dickens does bring the latent violence in rivalry back to the surface, and he does so through their very ability successfully to master and control their rivals.

iv

Among good or neutral characters, the problem of rivalry is always a matter of reinscription within a structured relationship to others. But Dickens reserves for his villains the possibilities for power in these relationships, and an even more disturbing aspect of rivalry: its tendency to reincorporate overt violence back into the static relationship of master to victim. Clearly, the austere identities fashioned by villains for themselves, the recognition by others of their transcendence, do not satisfy their desires for release; for the villain, that dissatisfaction promises a return to violence—but a return in a special way.

Tulkinghorn's pursuit of Lady Dedlock transforms the problem of rivalry understood only as a struggle for recognition. Tulkinghorn's satisfactions in this relationship cannot be said to

hinge simply on Lady Dedlock's awareness of his superior freedom from humanity, or even on the distance he allows himself to
feel between them—in other words, through the status brought
about by his successful rivalry. Instead, Tulkinghorn assumes a
rude intimacy with Lady Dedlock by penetrating her secret. His
very delicacy toward her is intended to torture Lady Dedlock
with the shamefulness and the degradation represented by his
knowledge. "You know—and I know—that you have not sent
[Rosa] away for the reasons you have assigned, but for the purpose of separating her as much as possible from—excuse my
mentioning it as a matter of business—any reproach and ex-
posure that impend over yourself" (48). What is most repellant
about Tulkinghorn, in fact, is the unstated lubricity in his violation of Lady Dedlock, not just the recognition he tries to take
from her. Lady Dedlock herself supplies the sexual terms that
Tulkinghorn never articulates.

> "I am to drag my present life on, holding its pains at your plea-
> sure . . . ?"
> "Yes, I am afraid so, Lady Dedlock."
> "It is necessary, you think, that I should be so tied to the stake?"
> "I am sure that what I recommend is necessary." (41)

In Tulkinghorn's case, trapping the victim in knowledge of
her limitation, her shameful humanity, is not merely a tool for
extorting recognition of his own freedom; it is a tactic designed
to increase the violence of his knowledge, to heighten the penetration of his victim's limits. Restriction is forced on Lady Dedlock to exacerbate her violation. In this way, the dialectical poles
of expenditure and form double back on each other again. With
Tulkinghorn, rivalry is not merely an alternative to violence; it
prepares the victim for psychological rape. It is only in this
sense that the malignantly evil villains in Dickens are finally different from the capitalistic villains; the capitalist is content with
his status and wants to deny the violence that underlies it, whereas the evil villain tries to use the dominant relationship that represented expenditure brings him as a vehicle for returning to

violence. Tulkinghorn aspires to a perpetual act of psychological violence against Lady Dedlock; that continual reinstitution of violence alone is able to free him from the professional ennui that had driven one of his close friends to suicide at the opening of the novel.

This dynamic—the reinstitution of violence within structures of rivalry—is not taken into account by most theories of desire. In Hegel's theory, and in those like Girard's which derive from it, expenditure, or violence, or the self-annihilation of *askesis* are all only tools for the gaining of a metaphysical status—either pure prestige or the possession of another's desire. Both Hegel and Girard discuss the eternal dissatisfaction of the master, or the mediator, on the grounds that proper recognition cannot come from a degraded object, whether degraded by an admission of biological instincts for survival, or by the presence of desire itself. But neither considers the possibility that recognition is unsatisfying simply because it is a status and, therefore, a new identity—a limited form. As a result, both these models have a similar problem; by stressing the functional, economic nature of the self-annihilation, they make it impossible to explain why anyone would pursue expenditure for its own sake—why, for example, anyone would risk his life without anyone to watch, which is the case with any teenager who has ever driven a car too fast, or why anyone might seek purely private relief from an unwanted desire, through alcohol, for instance. More importantly, these two theories do not account for the way the conquest or the possession of the rival can be the means to a psychological act of violence and, therefore, a more satisfying expenditure than the status of recognition.[19] In Dickens, as often as expenditure is diverted from release into rivalry, it uses rivalry to reenact psychological violence. The true villain is not satisfied with any concrete interpersonal form; he craves only making the potential for violence in that relationship real.

In Dickens' villains, then, it is difficult to separate the two dialectical phases of expenditure; they are not in the simple state of static opposition they appear to be in. Nor is one a weak substitute for the other; neither has priority, and their relationship is in a constant, dynamic flux. Ultimately, the villain's ideal position is to be poised momentarily between the two poles, doubly satisfied. For example, Tulkinghorn's public revelation of Lady Dedlock's story gives him a feeling of cold freedom—"He is sedately satisfied. Perhaps there is a rather increased sense of power upon him" (41)—but it also gives him the intense exhilaration of violating her resistance, an exhilaration close to lust—"And he thinks, with the interest of attentive curiosity, as he watches the struggle in her breast, 'The power and force of this woman are astonishing!'" Similarly, Bucket's satisfactions are located both in his cold, ascetic efficiency and, as his scene with Hortense shows, in a kind of sexual intimacy with the dominated victim. Hortense, after all, as Bucket's lodger, makes up a third triangle with Bucket and his wife, parodying the triangles of Sir Leicester–Lady Dedlock–Captain Hawdon and Jarndyce–Esther–Woodcourt. Bucket calls her "darling," while she calls him "my angel," and Hortense is often pictured in this scene as the damsel in distress, on the verge of violation. "He seems imperceptibly to establish a dreadful right of property in Mademoiselle . . . [and] the very atmosphere she breathes seems to narrow and contract about her, as if a close net, or a pall, were being drawn nearer and yet nearer around her breathless figure" (54). Only through the entrapping of the victim can Dickens' villains experience an orgiastic thrill through their rivalry; that is, the villain must create a strong sense of boundaries in his victim in order to produce the sexual shock of penetrating those boundaries with his knowledge. The villain actively combines in the victim both the suffocation of limits in contrast to the villain's own freedom—satisfying the conservative drive for recognition—and the purer degradation of violence.

Jaggers is perhaps the best example of this use of rivalry. Jaggers flaunts his own lack of concern for life or death in order to make his clients revere his freedom and to feel, by comparison, the full weight of their own instinctive fears. At the same time, though, he forces them to feel the threat to their lives posed by Jaggers' own recklessness.

"Then why," said Mr. Jaggers, "do you come here?"

"My Bill, sir?" the crying woman pleaded.

"Now I tell you what!" said Mr. Jaggers. "Once for all. If you don't know that your Bill's in good hands, I know it. And if you come here, bothering about your Bill, I'll make an example both of your Bill and you, and let him slip through my fingers. Have you paid Wemmick?"

"Oh, yes, sir! Every farden."

"Very well. Then you have done all you have to do. Say another word—one single word—and Wemmick shall give you your money back." (20)

Jaggers makes his clients feel guilty for the pettiness of wanting to survive. Simultaneously, he forces his own recklessness on them. In this way, Jaggers takes an almost sexual pleasure from his clients, a kind of rape; he exacerbates their fears for their vulnerability, making them that much more dependent on him, while at the same time he forces them to experience the agony of a loss of control they feel they cannot afford. Of course, Jaggers may also be said to take a kind of metaphysical recognition from his opponents by emphasizing his distance from them. But it would be wrong to underestimate the exhilaration he takes from staging this act of psychological violence. There is a phallic rape hidden in Jaggers' very name; Jaggers first appears in the chapter after Orlick, trying to make advances to Biddy, says to Pip, "I'm jiggered if I don't see you home!" and Pip explains:

He attached no definite meaning to the word that I am aware of, but used it, like his own pretended Christian name, to affront mankind, and convey an idea of something savagely damaging. When I was younger, I had had a general belief that if he had jiggered me personally, he would have done it with a sharp and twisted hook. (17)

Rigaud and Carker take a similar rapelike satisfaction out of violating what is deeply suppressed. Both force their victims to admit secret sins that Rigaud and Carker had gained knowledge of, and both find satisfaction in the tortures of the guilty, confessional release they provoke. Rigaud takes great delight in the wrenching confession he forces on Mrs. Clennam; he even takes Mrs. Clennam's hand to feel the palpitations in her pulse that his revelations cause. The eroticism of his penetration suffuses his oft-repeated "I love the sweet lady!" (2.30) and the "menace of affection" (2.28) he displays toward Flintwich. Mercilessly, he establishes the awful intimacy of his knowledge by deflecting Mrs. Clennam's attempts to extenuate her actions, thus forcing her to confront both his and her own violence. "Come, lady of purity, it must be! You can tell nothing I don't know." Rigaud resorts to the violating potential of narrative itself by telling her story to her face, and Mrs. Clennam's insistence on wresting the story away from him is an attempt to divert this narrative violence, if only by assuming its burden herself. Carker, too, knows Edith in "her worst colors" (37), and he presses his knowledge "upon her like the dregs of a sickening cup she could not own the loathing of, or turn away from." Like Tulkinghorn, too, in his use of Rosa, Carker traps Edith through a kind of blackmail, making her feel through her desire to save Florence the tension between Carker's violation and her desperate need to resist it for the sake of preserving another.

For all his raw physicality, Quilp is another good instance of this particular psychological violation. On the one hand, despite that physicality, Quilp—like all Dickens' villains—is interested in recognition. He uses his willingness to resort to violence, or to go further in outrageousness than anyone else, as a means to power. His pursuit of the good characters, for instance, seems to be a deliberate struggle for the recognition of characters who he knows will resist him. Then, too, his relationship with his boy, Tom, illustrates his need for solitary eminence through expenditure; Quilp refuses to let the boy stand on his head—a literal defiance of physical limitation—as if Quilp wants to keep to himself the province of expenditure as his claim to mastery.

But, on the other hand, within his relationships to others, Quilp cannot be said to take more satisfaction from his mastery than from violation. The recognition that Quilp takes is not cold; rather, Quilp forces his unwanted physicality on others. His principal method is to make others feel the restrictions of their bodies, while he imposes on them the freedoms of his own. For example, by intimidating his wife into staying up all night, Quilp augments the physical limitations of bodily fatigue in her, making her feel her own delicacy, only to outrage her the next morning with his boundless, untired energy, and with his demonic physicality.

He ate hard eggs, shell and all, devoured gigantic prawns with the heads and tails on, chewed tobacco and water-cresses at the same time and with extraordinary greediness, drank boiling tea without winking, bit his fork and spoon until they bent again. . . . At last, having gone through these proceedings and many others which were equally a part of his system, Mr. Quilp left [the ladies] reduced to a very obedient and humbled state. (5)

In a similar way, Quilp's Wilderness Retreat provides him with a way to establish and to violate the boundaries of others. When Sally and Sampson Brass have tea with Quilp there in the rain, Sally demonstrates the dynamic; while Quilp is already entertaining "a secret joy" (51) at their discomfort, Sally, who is at first uneasy, slowly comes to his turn of mind, eventually reaching an "amicable disregard of self" as she begins to notice her brother's misery. In this scene, Sally and Quilp enjoy a kind of psychological release that is not put to use in any way— certainly not for the sake of recognition, since they do not flaunt their release to Sampson. Instead, they bring out the narrow restrictions of Sampson's dignity through his groveling efforts to maintain it, to repress his bodily distress; at the same time those efforts to maintain his identity allow them the luxury of watching his dignity be violated. The expenditure takes place privately, but within a relationship of rivalry.

In the same way, Quilp's verbal tactics are attempts to make others feel the pull of their more conservative tendencies while they suffer the imposition of his brutality. Quilp's speech is a maddening parody of polite discourse that serves to draw attention to his underlying animality, and he tortures others with the contrast between their narrow world—the world his speech mirrors to them—and his unlimited because unstated willingness to violate it. Most especially, Quilp parodies terms of affection to his wife, heightening the contrast between her own anxious love for him and his willingness to annihilate the tenderness of love.

"Oh you nice creature!" were the words with which he broke silence; smacking his lips as if this were no figure of speech, and she were actually a sweetmeat. "Oh you precious darling! oh you de-licious charmer!"

Mrs. Quilp sobbed; and knowing the nature of her pleasant lord, appeared quite as much alarmed by these compliments, as she would have been by the most extreme demonstrations of violence:

"She's such," said the dwarf, with a ghastly grin—"such a jewel, such a diamond, such a pearl, such a ruby, such a golden casket set with gems of all sorts! She's such a treasure! I'm so fond of her!" (4)

Through ironies such as these, Quilp draws attention to his transcendence of the human world, certainly, and he masters Mrs. Quilp—but not in any austere way; his love of recognition is inseparable from his delight in the torture itself, the moment of psychological violation, which he makes possible only by exaggerating Mrs. Quilp's difference from himself and her dependence on conventional human needs. Beyond seeking to fascinate the other with his difference, Quilp also seeks the other's violation through means of that fascination. He would be less interesting without this tension—that is, if he simply dispensed blows.

Even in this second or conservative movement, then, the drama of expenditure tries to reimplement violence. When the two are fully distinct and are pursued each for its own sake, violence turns into mere brutality, as with Dennis in *Barnaby Rudge*, and the pursuit of recognition alone pales into the stereotype of the ineffectual egotist: Pecksniff, Heep, Chadband—all of whom seek only to flaunt their own supposed selflessness as a means to power over others. The hopelessly mixed condition of expenditure and restraint is a problem that Dickens expresses and condemns through his villains, and it is one he tries to untangle through his heroes.

Chapter 4

Heroes

Good and evil we know in the field of this world grew up together almost inseparably; and the knowledge of good is so involved and interwoven with the knowledge of evil, and in so many cunning resemblances hardly to be discerned, that those confused seeds which were imposed on Psyche as an incessant labor to cull out and sort asunder, were not more intermixed. It was from out of the rind of one apple tasted, that the knowledge of good and evil, as two twins cleaving together, leaped forth into the world. And perhaps this is the doom which Adam fell into of knowing good and evil, that is to say, of knowing good by evil.

—John Milton, *Areopagitica*

Dickens' novels always associate active rebellion against restrictions with transgression—so much so that Dickens is familiarly judged to be a conservative novelist, a moralist. The rigid association has prompted many to find a split in Dickens between good and evil that he could never heal;[1] it has caused readers to isolate passivity, withdrawal, and nostalgia as the final refuges in Dickens' novels for the heroes; and it has led even those who find the deeper challenge of a death wish in Dickens to concentrate on the peacefulness sought through death and, therefore, its nature as a regressive wish,[2] rather than on the active energy inherent in the heroes' desire for release.

But the goodness of Dickens' heroes becomes more interesting when it is placed in the same psychological framework as the villains' evil; just as the villains in Dickens' novels aspire to transcendence through an extreme violation of limits, so, too, the heroes achieve transcendence only through experiences of expenditure. Most important, the structure of these experiences—their twin components of violence and rivalry—remain the same for both sets of characters; Dickens does not attempt to ignore problems of violence and its recuperation when he turns to his heroes. Instead, through his heroes Dickens tries to build a positive attitude toward expenditure, even though heroes operate within the same essential psychological structures as villains. At the outset, we should understand that Dickens is never completely successful at resolving through his heroes the problems of violent release and rivalry we found in connection with villains; nevertheless, the affirmative versions of character he does present us with reflect new possibilities in his approach to those problems. In essence, Dickens does two things with his heroes: he either moderates the presence of violence and rivalry by altering slightly the quality of these impulses, or he directly affirms transgressive expenditures through his heroes in very careful, measured ways. In this second sense, it would be fair to say that Dickens' heroes employ both violence and rivalry in the manner of a *pharmakon*, the magic primitive drug that cures when taken in the right dosage and kills when taken in the wrong dosage or in the wrong circumstances.[3] Dickens never employs either course independently, though; both the moderation of violence and rivalry and their indirect affirmation proceed together.

Among the heroes, the problem of violence as a means of expenditure is moderated in two ways. First, as we have already noted, violence is indulged aesthetically through the overthrow of the villain, thereby freeing heroes of responsibility for the release they enjoy. By rooting violence in our expectations from plot, rather than in the expectations of good characters themselves, Dickens leaves his heroes' intentions guiltless. However, as we shall see, the violence heroes actually do exercise against their rivals can be affirmed precisely because it does not seem willfully desired. Second, much of what remains of the heroes' potential for violence is directed explicitly at the genuine goal of expenditure: the self. If they do not actually die—as do Nell, Sydney Carton, and Richard Carstone—Dickens' heroes willfully risk death for the sake of higher values—Dick Swiveller, Allan Woodcourt, Charles Darnay—or they actively annihilate their personalities—Esther Summerson and Pip. Outward violence is ritualized and distanced from the heroes; inward violence is made pure by being complete. Thus, Dickens' heroes manage to enact violence in a way the reader can affirm.

As we have also seen, however, violence is often redirected into rivalry; every self-expenditure short of death contains a reappropriation, a principle of economy; certain risks are taken only to acquire certain goals, which always implies the self-appropriation of recognition and mastery. And the problem of the good characters' rivalrous impulses is more difficult for Dickens to handle than it might appear. But Dickens is well aware of this problem in his heroes and in his happy endings, well aware that there is an inherent, compromising potential for selfish gain

in the limited self-sacrifices of good actions. In a satiric passage
of *Our Mutual Friend*, for example, Bradley Headstone's pupils
read about

the experiences of Thomas Twopence, who, having resolved not to rob
(under circumstances of uncommon atrocity) his particular friend and
benefactor, of eighteenpence, presently came into supernatural possession of three and sixpence, and lived a shining light ever afterwards. . . . Several swaggering sinners had written their own biogra-
phies in the same strain; it always appearing from the lessons of those
very boastful persons, that you were to do good, not because it *was*
good, but because you were to make a good thing of it. (2.1)

In Dickens' heroes, too, reappropriation through self-sacrifice is
always present in muted ways that qualify the heroes' expenditure—Esther's unavoidable egotism, for example, or Pip's tendency to manipulate through generosity.

As an attempt to mediate somewhat this potential for selfish
gain, however, Dickens frequently includes a member of the
good society who is not rewarded matrimonially, as if to build an
atmosphere of possible renunciation among his heroes—Tom
Pinch, Jarndyce, Pip. In a more positive way, though, Dickens
attempts to transform the problem of reappropriation by having
his heroes reappropriate mainly for the sake of others; that is,
Dickens' heroes do expend themselves for the sake of something
or someone that is conserved, but they locate the fruits of that
economy outside the self, in others. In Hegel's terms, Dickens'
heroes are like the Slave, who frees himself from his labor by
working for an Idea.[4] The instinct for survival is thus broken
from its association with repression and instead includes self-
release in the form of instincts to preserve something higher
than the self. Thus, work for the sake of others becomes an acceptable mode of release among Dickens' heroes. As we shall
see, the generosity of such work, though it is never absolutely
pure, is one of Dickens' crucial ways of resolving the dialectical
play of excess and restraint within his heroes. What these two
methods of moderation—the turning of violence completely

inward, and the deflection of conservative impulses outward toward others—accomplish, in fact, is a separation of the dialectical pulls of excess and restraint such that they do not meet within the self. In other words, the problem of recuperated status, and hence the problem of rivalry, is minimized if heroes are willing either to lose themselves completely or to make others the beneficiaries of their more restrained self-sacrifices.

To approach this kind of resolution, however, we should first consider just how Dickens' heroes are governed by the same psychological laws as his villains. In Dickens' novels, the most obvious sign that the world always structures gratification of desires for expenditure is the tendency of the heroes always to triumph, sometimes violently, within a well-defined structure of rivalry. Even in *Great Expectations*, a novel that clearly demystifies the will to transcend—revealing it to be caught up in struggles for power and recognition—Pip never leaves the cycle of revenge. Of course, there is no question that Pip has knowledge of the competitive structure of his desires and that he tries to escape that structure. Not only is he well aware of his entrapment in Magwitch's project of revenge, Pip also explicitly recognizes that he is caught in active struggles of his own for superiority, wanted or unwanted—his accusation that Biddy envies him, his involuntary humiliation of Joe, his feud with Bentley Drummle, and, most especially, his entire project to win Estella. Pip admits this entrapment to himself early in the novel, when he realizes that he cannot even tell Biddy whether he wants to win Estella over or wants to spite her. And Pip's problem in his repentance is, above all, how to extricate himself from these relationships of rivalry.

But the novel throws in doubt the very possibility of freedom from rivalry. Other heroes in the novel do manage to remain free of rivalry, but only at great cost. Herbert, for example, carries no grudge for having been displaced from Estella's favor by Pip; instead, he insists that there be "no restraints" between them. But Herbert's freedom from rivalry cannot be taken as a model, since Herbert is largely free only because he is unable, as Pip puts it, to distinguish between intention and execution. He has no concept of defeat, and, likewise, he does not try to act on his aggressive intentions. His purity is one of impotence rather than of desire. Instead of seeming an alternative, then, Herbert only seems helpless; his ability to get on in the world too clearly depends on Pip's protection. Matthew Pocket, too, is free from rivalry only because he has literally given up. And Joe is not caught in rivalry, either, but the problem with Joe—despite all of Dickens' reverence for him as an image of simple goodness— is this same passivity and inability to *act*; Joe deliberately chooses passive sufferance rather than venturing anything.

Given the range of choices here, Dickens does not seem content with simple refusals of rivalry. Accordingly, Pip's repentance differs from the virtue of other characters by being active. Pip does not finally renounce rivalry; instead, he functions within the structure of his relationships to others to achieve release. Specifically, Pip manages to overcome his two strongest rivals, Miss Havisham and Orlick. He is locked into his relationship with these two characters, significantly enough, in reciprocal ways. In the first case, Miss Havisham had been the obstacle between himself and a woman; in the second case, Pip had been the obstacle between Orlick and a woman—which is to say that Pip occupies both positions in the rivalry between victim and oppressor. And in both of these relationships, Pip ultimately emerges as a victor. In nearly back-to-back scenes, Pip confronts his two rivals in battle, against a violent backdrop of fire—Miss Havisham's burning bridal dress and Orlick's limekiln—only to emerge victorious.

With Miss Havisham, despite their mutual exchange of forgivenesses, Pip comes off as the dominant one through a laconically expressed self-righteousness that falls just short of being unkind.

"Believe this: when she first came to me, I meant to save her from misery like my own. At first I meant no more."
"Well, well!" said I. "I hope so."

"But as she grew, and promised to be very beautiful, I gradually did worse. . . . I stole her heart away and put ice in its place."

"Better," I could not help saying, "to have left her a natural heart, even to be bruised or broken."

With that, Miss Havisham looked distractedly at me for a while, and then burst out again, What had she done!

"If you knew all my story," she pleaded, "you would have some compassion for me and a better understanding of me."

"Miss Havisham," I answered, as delicately as I could, "I believe I may say that I do know your story." (49)

Then, after their parting, when Miss Havisham bursts upon him in flames, Pip plays the strange role of rescuer/aggressor. "We were on the ground struggling like desperate enemies, and . . . the closer I covered her, the more wildly she shrieked and tried to free herself. . . . I still held her forcibly down with all my strength, like a prisoner who might escape" (49). The sexual implication in this scene, when Miss Havisham's bridal dress burns off underneath Pip's cape, is picked up again in the last lines of the chapter. "I leaned over her and touched her lips with mine. . . . It was the first and the last time that I ever touched her in that way."[5] Pip's rescue of Miss Havisham is confusedly mixed with metaphors of violation and sexual conquest.

This odd battle scene does not involve Pip in aggressive motives; in fact, Pip nearly loses consciousness and does not clearly understand what he does. Pip does not willfully pursue self-gratification at Miss Havisham's expense. Still, in imagistic configurations, Pip is presented as the final victor in their long, unacknowledged battle. And there is no question that Pip's freedom from his former guilt is enhanced by this moral and physical victory over Miss Havisham; if he had not been able to shame her and then to overcome her, Miss Havisham's presence in the world of the novel would have been a nagging limitation on Pip's sense of his own independence and reformation.

In a similar way, Pip overcomes his former victim, Orlick. Again, the victory is not a purely aggressive one. Pip's triumph is in self-defense; it is even self-righteous. Nevertheless, Pip should logically accept some of the guilt that Orlick hurls at him after tying him up in the limekiln—and he does not. One of the reasons that commentators on this scene have fastened on the "allegorical" aspect of Orlick as an image of Pip's aggressive side is simply because of Pip's own refusal to acknowledge the connection, or to admit any affinity between them at all.[6] After all, Orlick's accusations—that Pip had gotten him dismissed from Miss Havisham's service, that Pip had come between himself and Biddy, and that Pip is involved somehow in the attack on his sister—are all just. But, because of Orlick's unctuousness, Pip's refusal to submit to him, rather than accepting his own guilt, is figured for the reader as a kind of liberation. In fact, Pip's resolution against Orlick is explicitly violent. "Above all things, I resolved that I would not entreat him, and that I would die making some last poor resistance to him. Softened as my thoughts of all the rest of men were in that dire extremity . . . still, if I could have killed him, even in dying, I would have done it" (53). Carrying all the reader's sympathy with him at this point, Pip successfully resists any guilt in his relationship to Orlick through this determination to free himself, however violently. Pip's self-righteousness thus has the effect of reaffirming his career of aggression against Orlick; it makes aggression—or at least self-assertion—seem the very condition for Pip's liberty and life, an indispensable, vital release. Pip's violent resolution certainly releases him from his own remorse in a way that simple acquiescence would not have done.

Dickens' intention in these two strange scenes—Pip's battles with Miss Havisham and Orlick—is definitely muted. But it seems clear that he felt it necessary to include scenes in which Pip actively overcomes his rivals in order to enhance Pip's freedom from guilt and, at the same time, to make a barely perceptible connection between liberation and transgression. Pip's stake in these physical struggles as a means to mastery is nil; he makes no attempt to consolidate the power of his victories, which is another reason why they do not associate directly with the personal appropriations of rivalry. Still, they are acts of vio-

lent release—in both scenes Pip swoons—that operate through
the structures of rivalry, even if those structures are imposed on
Pip against his will. In effect, the two scenes purify Pip's original impulses to find release through rivalry, elevating those impulses to the level of an involuntary, necessary assertion of
vitality. Both violence and the conquest of rivals are presented
here as acts the reader can approve because they are necessary
to the survival of virtue; as such, release through violence for
the heroes becomes a kind of *pharmakon*.

In one way or another, all of Dickens' heroes triumph in violence exercised against rivals, that is, over characters whose desires parallel their own. David Copperfield shares with Uriah
Heep a desire for Agnes and a more general ambition to rise in
the world from humble beginnings; when he strikes Uriah's
cheek, he enacts the violer
verting all the guilt of the
ferocious attack on Wegg a
rives from their mutual int
by Boffin. Pecksniff's physi
Chuzzlewit, which is so sev
sary because it fulfills the v
claim of young Martin Chu
and on Mary. In all these i
comes the forgiving—but,
ing—framework for the viol
failure of Dickens' heroes ev
is dramatized most fully in
Dickens does not simply sho
quate; he elaborately examir

Against the background of class rivalry in France, it is at
first a relief to find that the activity of the heroes is completely
devoted to suppressing the potentially violent rivalry inherent
in their own relationships. Faced with the dangers latent in the
relationship of Darnay to both Carton and Manette, the good
characters try in every way to prevent rivalry from surfacing.
Their virtue is entirely associated at first with repression, with

their attempt to preserve relationships by denying the violence that is latent in them.

Lucie Manette is the primary reconciler and preserver; Dickens' reference to her as a "golden thread" echoes her attempt to weave together factions and to inhibit the tendency of her men to displace each other. The other characters cooperate universally with Lucie in her strategy of repression. Manette enjoins Darnay not to tell him the secret of Darnay's own parentage; Darnay makes special efforts to conciliate Dr. Manette and to assure him that they are not competitors for Lucie's attentions; Carton vows to Lucie that he will not envy Darnay or pursue Lucie herself in any romantic way; and Darnay promises Lucie that he will hold no grudges against Carton. The minor character Miss Pross is perhaps the most concise example of a theme of suppression that the novel seems at first to affirm. "Mr. Lorry knew Miss Pross to be very jealous, but he also knew her by this time to be, beneath the surface of her eccentricity, one of those unselfish creatures—found only among women—who will, for pure love and admiration, bind themselves willing slaves, to youth when they have lost it, to beauty that they never had, to accomplishments that they were never fortunate enough to gain, to bright hopes that never shone upon their own somber lives" (2.6). Then, too, the final conflict of the novel itself has its origins in Darnay's initial act of suppression; he renounces his estate in France to escape being caught up in the rivalry of classes.

It is interesting to note, as a further emblem of the weight given to attempts to conserve rather than to violate or to rival, that *A Tale of Two Cities* actually features a businessman, Lorry, as one of its principal heroes—a rarity in Dickens. His conservative role as a banker even allows Lorry to travel safely between the two cities; he is a kind of international reconciler. Moreover, his functions in the plot are always rescue missions; his two dramatic messages—"recalled to life" and "acquitted"—as well as his three separate rescue operations in France are in sharp contrast to the operations of the only other business establishment in the novel, the Defarges' wine shop, and to the aggressive business ethic expressed by Stryver.

The disturbing contrast of the good characters' efforts to conserve life against the background of violence in France is reflected in a kind of overriding allegory represented by the two cities themselves. In the beginning of the novel, for all their ominous similarities, the two cities are given radically different tonal imperatives. In France, the effects of repressive order and repressive violence are so repellent that there is a clear need for some kind of revolt.

France, less favored on the whole as to matters spiritual than her sister of the shield and trident, rolled with exceeding smoothness down hill, making paper money and spending it. Under the guidance of her Christian pastors, she entertained herself, besides, with such humane achievements as sentencing a youth to have his hands cut off, his tongue torn out with pincers, and his body burned alive, because he had not kneeled down in the rain to do honour to a dirty procession of monks which passed within his view, at a distance of some fifty or sixty yards. (1.1)

In England, on the other hand, violence is miscellaneous, purely criminal, and seems to require a corresponding suppression and an affirmation of law and order.

In England, there was scarcely an amount of order and protection to justify much national boasting. Daring burglaries by armed men, and highway robberies, took place in the capital itself every night; families were publicly cautioned not to go out of town without removing their furniture to upholsterers' warehouses for security; the highwayman in the dark was a City tradesman in the light, and, being recognized and challenged by his fellow-tradesman whom he stopped in his character of "the Captain," gallantly shot him through the head and rode away. (1.1)

The tone of these passages seems to justify both revolt in France and suppressive order in England. This fundamental ambivalence is reflected in the novel as a whole by the image of the coach shuttling back and forth between the two cities—journeys that open and close the novel—an image that stresses a permanent irresolution of these two tendencies. What is most interesting, though, is the ultimate fragility and even the doubtful desirability of suppressive order in England. Even in England, the law itself indulges in conspicuous vengeance; "the hangman, ever busy and ever worse than useless, was in constant requisition; now, stringing up long rows of miscellaneous criminals . . . to-day, taking the life of an atrocious murderer, and to-morrow of a wretched pilferer who had robbed a farmer's boy of sixpence" (1.1). Order itself is accomplished through institutional violence. And Lorry, whose name is an ominous pun on the tumbrils in Paris, is a symbol of the underlying price paid for repression; Lorry repeatedly saves people only at the cost of abandoning others to violence—before the time of the novel, he rescues Lucie only by leaving Manette behind; at the end, he saves Darnay by leaving Carton to die.

These emblems of the fragile ability of order to contain violence signal the larger problem; in both of the crucial relationships among the good characters, inherent violence is only imperfectly suppressed and finally emerges—even against the good characters' wills—as rivalry. In the first conflict, Dr. Manette's voluntary suppression of his opposition to Darnay—which is both political, because the novel's germinal incident involves their two families in the war of classes, and sexual, because the two men are locked in a relationship of natural, generational rivalry—is itself dangerous. Often, it reduces him to the destructive oblivion of work as he tries to screen out his injury. Even Lorry wonders "whether it is good for Doctor Manette to have that suppression always shut up within him" (2.6). Even worse, though, despite all his attempts to overcome it, Manette's involuntary rivalry with Darnay is mercilessly actualized by events. Manette's very attempt to save Darnay through the revolutionary tribunal is compromised by a dangerous, potential one-upsmanship in his performance. "He was proud of his strength. 'You must not be weak, my darling,' he remonstrated; 'don't tremble so. I have saved him'" (3.6). This one-upsmanship is stressed by the doctor's dependence on the rivalrous mob, which is devoted to Darnay's death. And more significantly, the production of the document that recounts the story of the peasant family realizes Manette's rivalry in a deadly way. Of course, Manette is passive in the confrontation; only in a moment of weakness and desperate yearning for freedom did he curse the aristocratic family that he never supposed he would see again, and the production of the fatal document condemning Darnay is carried out here by others, against Manette's will. Still, on a symbolic level, the events enact an inevitable resurfacing of rivalry. Involuntarily, Manette is transformed from repressed victim to violent oppressor; he is identified with Madame Defarge and the rebels in their progress from one stage to the other.

In the second, more important rivalry, the one between Sydney Carton and Darnay, the conditions of the rivalry are again involuntary; the two characters simply look alike, which stings Carton with a sense of his inferiority. In Carton, too, this rivalry is explicitly associated with the metaphysical urges of expenditure, since Carton's greatest desire, he says to Darnay after the latter's brush with death at his trial, is to dissociate himself from "this terrestrial scheme" (2.4) and to escape what he calls "drudgery"—the competitiveness of Stryver's petty world. Carton's desire for escape—like the transcendent yearnings of a villain, like the desire of Manette for freedom, and like the desires of the lower class in this novel for liberation—is trapped in his envy of a rival, Darnay. Carton even selects his rival as the man who most completely displays a willingness to risk life and who receives recognition for it. "Is it worth being tried for one's life," he says, "to be the object of such sympathy and compassion, Mr. Darnay?" (2.4). As a consequence, Carton's general bitterness about the limitations of his life focus themselves in this competition with Darnay for the clearest claim to violent expenditure and selflessness.

What makes the second relationship more interesting than the first is that Carton is finally able to satisfy his drive for expenditure in a morally legitimate way precisely through the structure of rivalry. Carton's self-sacrifice, far from transcending structures of rivalry, actually operates within them. The will-to-power here is clear. Carton takes over Darnay's very handwriting and uses it to address an intimate message to Lucie, one that Darnay cannot understand or share; he refers to the unconscious Darnay as "me"; he envisions the surviving couple as "not more honored and held sacred in each other's soul, than I was in the souls of both" (3.15); and he pictures Darnay's own son named after him, along with a grandson also named after himself, who comes back to France solely for the purpose of hearing the Carton story. The crowning irony in Carton's violation of Darnay's identity and his claim to Lucie's admiration is that Carton is the one who projects the others' future in the last paragraphs of the novel, while both Manette and Darnay are lying in a coach, impotent and unconscious.

Through the vehicle of his rivalry with Darnay for the attentions of Lucie (who rides out of the novel looking backward toward Carton, not looking to her husband), Carton achieves a liberating victory over and displacement of his rival, Darnay. Rivalry with Darnay is necessarily present in Carton's death to give point to the expenditure, to give it significance. Through his death, Carton finds the same satisfaction that appeared aggressive in the beginning of the novel; the second time he saves Darnay's life, he displaces Darnay in Lucie's eyes as the man willing to sacrifice his life for the sake of others. Without the tension of this rivalry—as something that Carton both triumphs in and renounces at the same time—Carton's sacrifice would indeed seem a savage, suicidal waste.

At the same time, though, Carton does not appropriate for himself any undesirable associations with mastery because he makes his expenditure complete; he loses his life, annihilating self-interest. Moreover, besides the totality of Carton's loss, he further nullifies any conceivable appropriation of recognition by refusing to reveal his sacrifice to anyone while it is in preparation. Unlike Dr. Manette's ostentatious rescue of Darnay, Carton's proceeds in secret. He informs no one, not even Lorry, and he tells Lucie only in a note meant to be opened later, so that she would know that his life had not been "wantonly" thrown away. The awesome thing about Carton's death is just this, that he goes through it alone—he even dies under someone else's name (though recognition does come, innocuously, from a stranger on the scaffold, which implies that the reader's role in supplying necessary recognition that cannot come from within the world of the novel is crucial). Finally, while its rivalrous aspect is redeemed by the totality and the self-direction of the violence, the violent aspect of Carton's suicide is itself redeemed through the preservation of Darnay and his family. Restraint is exercised here only as the salvation of others, not as an economy of selfhood.

In Carton's death, Dickens frees himself, to some extent, from the good characters' initial constraint, their attempts to suppress rivalry. Instead, Dickens represents a release that operates through a relationship of rivalry at the same time that he dissociates it from motives of recognition and aggression. This tension is what makes Carton's death so enigmatic; it seems to be a romantic victory, both sensual and heroic—especially in light of the warm tone of the concluding paragraphs—and a chaste, virtuous renunciation at the same time, one which affirms the community of others as a cardinal value. The important point, though, is that Carton's death keeps these two satisfactions separate. Only the reader is allowed to integrate the thrill of Carton's self-abandonment with relief at Darnay's and Lucie's survival. The image of a doubled Carton—his imagined grandson—points toward this doubled satisfaction, placing a version of Carton in both worlds. In a similar way, Pip in *Great Expectations* participates in both a world of expenditure and a world of conservation at the end of the novel without ever allowing them to touch except through his "nephew," Biddy and Joe's child. On the one hand, Pip does achieve triumphs over Miss Havisham, Orlick, and Estella; on the other hand, Pip affirms the untroubled communality of Joe, Biddy, and Little Pip. But any direct relationship between the two is suppressed; hence, there must be two Pips.

This kind of separation of dialectically opposed desires for expenditure and for conservation is one way—ultimately, an inadequate way—for Dickens to moderate the presence of rivalry in his heroes. In this way Dickens manages to affirm separately both impulses as desires for transcendence, without allowing them to fuse completely in the satisfactions of rivalry. Through a figure like Carton, Dickens circumvents problems of rivalry by insuring that neither expenditure nor conservation seeks to become the condition for individual reward; both are expressed as the possibility of a total renunciation.

Although this bifurcation may present us with aesthetically satisfying alternatives to the problem of rivalry like that of *A Tale of Two Cities*, there remains something unsettling in Dickens' strategy. Since Carton must die for Darnay to survive, and since Pip must himself be denied any final satisfaction in order for expense and restraint to be reconciled outside of overt rivalry, we are left with no real model for action. In other novels, as the satisfactions of violent expense and more conservative, self-sacrificing forms of release are pushed further apart, prescriptive images of moral character become even less satisfying. Characters like Carton—Edith Dombey, Stephen Blackpool, Nancy in *Oliver Twist*—who sacrifice themselves completely for the sake of others are always morally compromised; their association with acts of transgression seems to require that they be sacrificed completely. But that atmosphere of moral compromise also helps taint their self-sacrifice, making them figures whose acts are conducive to awe but not imitation. Conversely, characters who commit themselves to work or other forms of renunciation in service of others are often trivialized because their satisfactions are so narrowed. Toots and Miss Tox in *Dombey and Son* negate themselves in service of other good characters, yet they seem to be miniaturized by their very modesty. Characters like Doyce and Peggotty suffer the same fate. And, in a novel like *The Old Curiosity Shop*, the separation of violent release and release through the self-sacrificing conservation of others jeopardizes the effectiveness of all of Dickens' heroes.

In *The Old Curiosity Shop*, Dickens' general unwillingness
to integrate the two extreme desires for the sake of purity manifests itself in his failure to resolve the problem of expenditure
and restraint even in the actions of any single character. Instead, release through violence is dissociated completely from
the surviving society, which, in turn, is freed from the burden of
repression and from rivalry through selfless work, or through
the rescue and preservation of others. Nell alone is allowed the
pure release of death, while the others, blocked from so total an
expenditure, free themselves by transforming the goals of their
economy; rather than trying to save themselves, the characters
dedicate themselves to saving someone else. Dick Swiveller
saves Kit from jail, then rescues the Marchioness from squalor;
Kit devotes himself to supporting his mother and Nancy, and—
futilely—to saving Nell; the single gentleman overcomes potential rivalry by trying to save his brother. In fact, in *The Old Curiosity Shop*, the pursuit of another's rescue becomes as successful a means of expenditure as self-violence; Dick nearly dies, and
Kit is nearly transported. But Dick's illness occurs before his
commitment to the Marchioness, and Kit is simply a victim of
Quilp's random hostility. Neither of these risks of life has any
necessary relationship to these characters' devotion to rescue
missions, which would involve questions of gratitude and, therefore, of recognition; they merely stress the latent presence of
self-abandon in these characters.

The fracturing of all relationship between the two dialectical
poles of expenditure and conservation is especially striking in
this early novel. On each side—the side of death and the side of
community—heroes are allowed to have both kinds of desire—
for expenditure and for conservation free of self-appropriation—but only by seeming to make each independent of the
other. Nell, on the one hand, is allowed to choose flight unconditionally, even to the point of death; yet at the same time her
flight is presented as a means of saving her grandfather, to keep
it from seeming "wanton," even though these two impulses
seem to have nothing to do with one another. Kit and Dick, on

the other hand, mix actual physical expenditures with their work, but without putting the two into any direct relationship. Both characters are like Quilp in their delight at excess or abandon. Kit is a ready fighter, who has a mysterious affinity with wild ponies, and he laughs with surprise to find his face covered with blood. Swiveller is a drunkard, and through absurd adaptations of dance-hall lyrics he continually refuses seriousness by transforming anxiety into the excessive, unreal world of play. Like them, the single gentleman is an excessive Quilpian figure. He seems dangerously aggressive at first, then simply unpredictable, and he has a love of the fantastic—as demonstrated by his miraculous machine, which simultaneously prepares coffee, fries steak, and boils eggs. All three characters' excessiveness is harmless, or even involuntary, unlike Quilp's, but what is more important, these violent expenditures of energy are harmless because they are fragmentary. They are completely dissociated from the characters' ability and willingness to do constructive work for others or to abandon themselves in attempted rescues.

This adjacency of expenditure and conservation is clearest in Kit's holiday. On the one hand, the narrator connects holidays specifically, if wistfully, to the death wish in expenditure. "To have drunk too much, to have had a great holiday, and to have fallen in love, are all one and the same thing in the next day's consequences. A sense of something lost and gone . . . such is the common dust into which these three great things of earth resolve themselves next day."[8] And on his holiday, Kit does a number of things that involve him in physical dissipation as it slides over into mastery; he hits a man on the head with a handkerchief of apples for getting in his mother's way, and he orders a waiter around, seeming to have earned the right because he spends money profusely on food. On the other hand, when Kit drags his mother out of church where she had gone in repentance the next day, he argues for the discontinuity between this dissipation and the rest of life, and hence for her freedom from guilt. "What was there in the little bit of pleasure you took last night that made it necessary for you to be low-spirited and sorrowful to-night?" (41). Rather than be mournful himself, Kit eagerly throws himself into the next day's project, which is, of course, saving Nell—a return to the spirit of conservation. This return is further linked to Kit's rigorous work ethic through the single gentleman's extraordinarily legitimate requisitioning of Kit's services from his employers, the Garlands. The entire holiday scene seems included for no other reason than to insist on the possibility of bracketing off expenditure from work and consigning it to holiday pleasures.

In this way, problems presented by Quilp—the necessary interrelation of expenditure and aggression against others—are diffused. The heroes vacillate between harmless physical excess and conservation dedicated to others, never integrating the two impulses. Instead, images of death and of survival are simply allowed to interpenetrate each other in undynamic ways. In the image of Nell's house, for example, "cunning architects" (45) have managed to combine reverence for death with the dignity of enduring art. This house is essentially no different from the original curiosity shop, in which wild grotesqueries signifying the nonhuman were represented and sold as cultural artifacts, except that the urgency has gone out of the opposition *because* it is perceived as an opposition; the paradoxes of the house have become objects for contemplation, rather than being forced together through use. Wistfully, the narrator stops the process blending life and death. Similarly, the image of Dick and the Marchioness gambling at cribbage together, along with Dick's project of making Sophronia a lady, is an exact repetition of the grandfather's initial gambling—which was a means to make Nell a lady—except that Dick does not found one project on the other. His gambling is a delight in risk as pure play, and it is separated from his project of making Sophronia a lady, which involves real benefits. The most concise image of this doubleness, though, is Kit's pony; the animal is so freely defiant that he is called "perverse" (20) even though he is completely obedient to Kit. Expenditure and service are yoked together, oxymoronically.

The radical distance between the desire for expenditure and

the desire for restraint in these three novels indicates, above all, Dickens' attempt to surmount problems of rivalry by isolating and exaggerating extreme impulses. This radical distance, because it is an image of what consciousness can imagine and not a description of reality, is also Dickens' greatest problem with his heroes. His attempt to separate the two extreme impulses is what gives his endings the meditative, stilled quality that critics have mistakenly seen as a wish for passivity. And the refusal of characters to accept recognition for their sacrifices continually runs the risk of appearing to be self-pity. The greatest danger, however, is that characters like Kit and Dick do not seem to be acceptable alternatives to the extremes represented by Nell and Quilp. They cannot bear the novel's burden of death; their very idiosyncracies, which make them so lovable, prevent them, in the reader's eyes, from assimilating the vast significance of the loss of Nell. In other words, the fragmentation of impulses to risk death and impulses to conserve life ultimately works against these characters by preventing them from achieving wholeness.

Dickens' efforts to segregate expenditure and restraint in his heroes ultimately do not satisfy him, and his later novels in particular aspire to the creation of more integrated images of human personality. Yet, in characters who do not die, there is simply no avoiding the lapsing of capacities for expenditure into a privileged selfhood, and Dickens was well aware that his heroes represent desires for release that can easily degenerate into mastery. In novels like *Bleak House*—or, as we have seen, in *Great Expectations*—Dickens tends to affirm the limited, *pharmakon*-like violence or rivalry of his characters without attempting to split the satisfactions of excess and restraint. Esther Summerson in *Bleak House* is perhaps Dickens' most successful attempt to link the transcendent good of expenditure to the good of self-sacrificing service in a single image of personality. And, as a direct result, Esther is the heroine who attracts the most suspicion.

More than any other Dickensian character, Esther demonstrates how the goal of moral selflessness, like the villains' pursuit of self-annihilation, is tied to a pursuit of release into the nonhuman. Like Tulkinghorn and like Bucket, Esther performs continual acts of *askesis*.[9] In other words, Esther's pursuit of a transcendent selflessness begins through a denial of her natural, instinctual human drives—most especially, through her engagement to Jarndyce, which is a nonmarriage, and through her denial of her love for Woodcourt. Esther even tells Woodcourt, "I have everything to be thankful for, and nothing in the world to desire" (45). Esther's humility, too, along with her continual refusal of knowledge—her great pains not to understand Mrs. Woodcourt, for example, or the supreme refusal of knowledge and *askesis* of losing her face—in its exaggerated form is another attempt to negate the human in herself. Most tellingly, like Jaggers, Bucket, and Tulkinghorn, Esther possesses everyone's secrets—or "confidences," as she calls them—without telling others, or the reader, the secrets of her own human desires, as if she had none. She takes in trust Jarndyce's confidence about his plans for Richard and Ada, Richard and Ada's confidences about their plans for themselves, and Caddy Jellyby's confidences about her marriage; Esther even remarks about the Pardiggle children that they seem driven instantly to want to confide in her. But perhaps the best illustration of Esther's attempt to purge herself of human motives and desires is the death wish she expresses in her feverish dream. "Dare I hint at that worse time when, strung together somewhere in great black space, there was a flaming necklace, or ring, or starry circle of some kind, of which *I* was one of the beads! And when my only prayer was to be taken off from the rest, and when it was such inexplicable agony and misery to be a part of the dreadful thing?" (35). In all these ways, Esther lives out Lady Dedlock's attempt to find an "escape . . . in death" (36).

Esther is, of course, only the most pronounced instance among Dickens' heroes of desires to negate the human and, hence, to approach death. Agnes in *David Copperfield* also achieves an *askesis* by being seemingly without desire; hence,

David's sense of her as an "angel." Most explicitly, Agnes is willing to negate herself completely in service of her father. "Papa
once free with honour, what could I wish for! I have always as-
pired, if I could have released him from the toils in which he was
held, to render back some little portion of the love and care I
owe him, and to devote my life to him" (54). A character like
Tom Pinch achieves an escape from desire into the nonhuman so
complete that he requires no real recompense in the novel to
achieve fulfillment. And perhaps the most completely nonhuman
of Dickens' heroes is Little Nell; her passivity is the key to her
unearthliness: "so shall we know the angels in their majesty"
(71). In general, the psychological vapidity of such characters is
a deliberate expression of their nonhuman status. Seen in this
light, the "blankness" of these characters as personalities is not
so much a sentimental exercise as it is a purification of a wish
that is fundamentally ambiguous. Dickens' heroes are deliberately blank psychologically, just as his villains are deliberately
motiveless, in order to express a more complete disruption of
normal selfhood.

As Esther's own *askesis* shows us, however, the purity of
these expressions of absolute innocence is always in question.
All these characters acquire positions of centrality similar to Esther's. Esther's selflessness does not have the combative component of rivalry we see in Tulkinghorn and Bucket, but there are
gentle hints that an aggressive motive is latent in the very form
of Esther's actions. Esther's power as narrator to transform the
world through her self-denial has been noted often,[10] but what is
more disturbing is the position of centrality she attains, willingly or unwillingly—we never know for certain, and perhaps it
makes no difference. Esther never blatantly extorts the recognition of others through her humility, but that humility brings it
to her nevertheless. She is always the center of attention, even
at the Miss Donnys'. And the most disturbing image of her sway
over others is the way she attracts Richard and Ada as her sat-
ellites; they "really seemed to have fallen in love with me, instead of one another; they were so confiding, and so trustful,

and so fond of me" (13). Whether we are finally suspicious of Esther, or whether we are reconciled to her, the important point is that a potential for the appropriation of others' recognition is structurally inseparable from the form of her self-denials.

Dickens does dilute Esther's appropriation somewhat. Like Tulkinghorn and Bucket, Esther diffuses the self-assertive potential of her selflessness by repeatedly ascribing it to "duty," accompanying the resolution with a jangle of her basket of keys. However, unlike Tulkinghorn and Bucket, Esther's sense of duty seems genuine; it is not a tool to achieve mastery, but an attempt to dissolve herself through the service of others. Although it is hard to imagine what she does around the house with her keys, Esther does help Caddy Jellyby, Charley, and Jo—the latter two to the extent that she is ready to die for them. More convincingly than Kit and Dick—because she is more completely self-negating—Esther finds a kind of expenditure through work for others. The importance of Esther's work as a kind of freedom is stressed in particular by Richard's failure to devote himself to work. A gambler and involuntarily lavish with money, Richard is lost in the direct pursuit of expenditure—the hope for a sudden, complete release—rather than committed to the pursuit of it through duty and work; Esther's duty itself contains such a willingness to lose everything. And unlike Guppy, who turns his convenient renunciation of Esther into a pretentious, heroic duty with which he tries to master Weevle and Small, and for which he expects remuneration at the end, Esther really does seem willing to give up Woodcourt, an act that impresses us more as a sacrifice—because of Esther's frequent tears over Woodcourt—than as a contrived show of power. When work as a form of self-abandonment is associated with these "blank" characters, it becomes a much more convincing expression of release than when it is associated with characters who have more limited personalities. Thus, like Esther, Agnes is willing to dissolve herself in duty. She is enthusiastic at the thought of supporting her father; she wants "to take our future on myself" (54). Tom Pinch achieves happiness in the "domestic economy" he establishes with his sister. And Little Dorrit cannot be happy unless she is dissolved in labor. Tasting freedom for the first time, Little Dorrit senses that her new life "is not real"; "to have no work to do was strange, but not half so strange as having glided into a corner where she had no one to think for, nothing to plan and contrive, no cares of others to load herself with" (2.3). For Little Dorrit, that disruption of her work involves a loss of the self-expending freedom she had found through her nurturing relationship to her father.

More subtly, perhaps, Esther abandons any hope of transcendent recognition from Ada. It is worthwhile taking a closer look at their relationship to see how Dickens frees Esther from association with the manipulated recognition of rivalry. At first, Dickens deliberately inflates the importance of Ada to Esther in a number of ways. Esther says "she is like the light to me" (35); she ends one of her chapters on the odd visionary note, "I think I see my darling" (37); and she arranges elaborately to leave Ada after her illness so as to orchestrate a private reunion. There, too, Ada acquires the special status of a nurturing mother for Esther. "O how happy I was, down upon the floor, with my sweet beautiful girl down upon the floor too, holding my scarred face to her lovely cheek, bathing it with tears and kisses, rocking me to and fro like a child, calling me every tender name that she could think of, and pressing me to her faithful heart" (36). Dickens' insistence on the importance of this relationship to Esther, because there is never any conventional explanation given for it—no shared past, no real interaction between them in the novel—can appear as either an instance of his sentimentality or as an instance of Esther's attempt to control others. On the other hand, though, it seems more likely that the dramatic pre-eminence of the relationship is deliberately constructed to intensify the crisis of Ada's elopement with Richard. Besides the fact that Ada conceals it from Esther, this elopement seems even more crucial for them because Dickens has Esther suppose that Ada's uneasiness about marrying Rick is really uneasiness about Esther's own denial of her love for Woodcourt. Repeatedly, Esther tries "to undeceive my dear" (50) by putting on a show of cheerfulness. Esther's subsequent discovery, then, that Ada was not concerned about *her* at all, but about Ada's own life, could produce a rupture between them if we supposed that Esther's interest in Ada was primarily a preoccupation with her own veneration. Instead, Esther accepts Ada's break from her—with sorrow, certainly, but not with any trace of bitterness, and with no attempt to intrude herself into Ada's and Richard's lives. The two women's entire relationship seems designed to give Esther a chance to free herself—at least in intention, if not in the consequences of her actions—from needs for recognition.

Early commentators criticized Esther for being a hypocrite,[11] for wanting recognition despite her seeming indifference; more recently, critics have defended her by seeing Esther as a victim of childhood psychological traumas that, though irritating, somehow do not interfere with her efforts to do good.[12] But Dickens' conception is infinitely more subtle. I should like to return to the first line of argument, but without the moral stigma of hypocrisy. Esther does try to deny drives for love and recognition that she actually has, but only because, in Dickens' world, any act of expenditure or any desire for selflessness—short of death itself—inevitably involves characters in a relocation of self in relation to others. Esther states the problem well enough herself.

I don't know how it is, I seem to be always writing about myself. I mean all the time to write about other people, and I try to think about myself as little as possible, and I am sure, when I find myself coming into the story again, I am really vexed and say, "Dear, dear, you tiresome little creature, I wish you wouldn't," but it is all of no use. I hope any one who may read what I write will understand that if these pages contain a great deal about me, I can only suppose it must be because I have really something to do with them, and can't be kept out. (9)

Even Esther's purifying sense of duty runs the risk of being a contrivance, rather than a pure loss of self; at one point, Richard makes the same claim about himself and ascribes his involve-

ment with Chancery to his sense of duty toward Ada. Though
her remunerations are minimized by the novel, they are minimized in such an ostentatious way that Dickens seems to be emphasizing the inseparability of release and aggression. Only the
magical, correct dosage of deliberate selflessness in Esther enables her to perform acts of goodness; she never escapes the entanglements of expenditure and rivalry.

Esther embodies the central dilemma among Dickens' heroes: the energy of selflessness is potentially also the energy of
appropriation; they cannot be fully separated. It is the purpose
of Dickens' narratives to sanctify such energy, largely through
the polarity of his good and evil characters; but Dickens is complex enough to show us that the purification of this energy is itself an aesthetic ritual—Esther's willingness to sacrifice herself
through duty is stressed more than the inherently selfish motive
in duty, that is, the seeking-out of a purely personal release,
along with the potential for sought-out recognition inherent in
every performance of duty. In a less analytical way, Dickens always reminds us that the assertion of good is still an assertion
by placing his most innocent characters in a position to harm
others—unwillingly and even unknowingly. Oliver Twist is only
the first innocent to devastate others simply by surviving. Esther herself becomes an unknowing threat to Lady Dedlock,
and, in a lesser way, Florence Dombey's love for Edith is used
by Carker as a tool to help destroy her.

Ultimately, in terms of his heroes, Dickens' most complete
resolution of liberating expenditure with moral restraint is the
most conventional one available to him: romantic love. In the
union of heroes and heroines that forms the core of Dickens'
novels—as well as that of most nineteenth-century English novels—Dickens finds a traditionally satisfying synthesis. Characters are allowed to surrender themselves up completely to
passion, and yet that passion is contained and made useful by
the conservative dimensions of romance: tenderness, dedication,
the care and nurturing of children. Particularly in the later novels, the male protagonists' search for meaningful discipline and

purpose—David Copperfield, Arthur Clennam, and Eugene
Wrayburn all come to mind—is merged with the emotional release of romantic love. David even dovetails what he calls his
"earnestness" with love for Agnes. And in the last paragraph of
Little Dorrit we are told that Arthur and Little Dorrit "went
down into a modest life of usefulness and happiness" (34). These
two sets of terms—signaling both conservation and bliss—reso-
nate in all of Dickens' romantic unions. Esther Summerson's
brief effusions over Allan—"what happiness was ours that day,
what joy, what rest, what hope, what gratitude, what bliss!"
(64)—are blended with a spirit of self-sacrificing work; "I do everything I do in life for his sake," Esther tells us, and Woodcourt
continues his "patient ministrations" to the sick (67). And yet,
because of the conventionality of this resolution and its proliferation as a guiding myth of Western culture, Dickens' resolution of expenditure and restraint in romantic love is finally less
interesting than his analysis of the many contortions his heroes
undergo in their progress toward synthesis. This particular solution—we shall soon see others—is less original and less convincing a treatment of human character than the inextricable
blending of transgression with morality Dickens emphasizes in
his heroes. It seems much more important to recognize the ambiguities in Esther's self-sacrificing sense of duty and in the
rivalrous freedoms achieved by characters like Pip than to test
the partial synthesis both find in romantic love.

In these nonromantic attempts of Dickens' heroes to synthesize excess and restraint within personality Dickens most
clearly reveals the complex relationship of good and evil in his
world. As a rule, practitioners of a morally absolute art are
probably the first to admit the similarity of the factions. And
Dickens would no doubt have agreed with Milton's remark that
we only know good by evil. The formulation implies more than it
might at first appear—Milton does not say that we can know
good once we have figured out what it is not; Milton says that
the knowledge of the two is one knowledge.

Chapter 5

Endings

All human happiness or misery takes the form of action; the end for which we live is a certain kind of activity, not a quality. . . . So it is that the action, i.e., the Fable or Plot—*that* is the end and purpose of the tragedy; and the end is everywhere the chief thing.

—Aristotle, *Poetics*

At this time my judgement is free and clear and no longer covered with a thick blanket of ignorance woven by my sad and constant reading of detestable books of chivalry. I recognize their extravagance and trickery. My only regret is that my disillusionment has come too late and that I do not have time to make up for my mistake by reading other books which would help enlighten my soul.

—Don Quixote

i

If Dickens' characters do not achieve a completely successful synthesis of excess and restraint on the level of personal psychology, it does not follow that these two desires cannot meet in the novels on the level of plot. By plot, I am not referring to what we usually understand as narrative sequence. Besides the literal progress involving characters and actions, there is another kind of plot in every novel, in which the development of a narrative symbolic logic changes the way characters and events can be perceived. It is to that level that I will turn in my discussion of Dickens' endings.

Before I proceed, however, there are larger questions about the possibilities open to the symbolic logic of novelistic conclusion that must be taken up. The symptom of the problem is simply this: conventionally, Dickens' endings are one of the least seriously considered aspects of his fiction. Seldom do they achieve critical attention at all; even a conservative stylistic critic like Garrett Stewart begins with the assumption that "the whole of a Dickens novel is seldom greater than the sum of its parts."[1] In general, recent critics have tended to ignore the movement of Dickens' novels toward significant conclusion, preferring instead to treat the novels as "organic" art, that is, as an art that is quintessentially Dickensian at discrete moments, and not at the level of a structured vision.

Partly, the problem is with Dickens; his plots and endings are superficially conventional. But, partly, there is a problem in recent criticism itself that makes special consideration of any work's ending a dubious proposition. Recently, there has been a movement away from notions about literature as crisis and a greater interest in literature as process; critics are inclined to see writing as an immediately self-fulfilling exercise, and not as a developing activity dependent on a deferred goal. One reason for this critical shift is the increasingly commonplace assumption that meaning is always "absent" from language, and that the best a text can finally give us is "demystification"; this assumption has helped draw attention away from the possibilities inherent in conclusiveness, which is conceived mostly as a dangerous lie, and toward a preference for meanings that a text can keep in play. It is important to remember, however, that fiction as a readerly experience is linear—although we have seen a few attempts to create nonlinear fiction—and that, even despite itself, it tends toward a goal, or toward a crisis. Although that crisis may be only a metaphor for the infinitely repeated crises of writing as process, it is still intended by the narrative as a moment, an event, an instant when conflicts are presented in unavoidable clarity.

Simple statements of position do not convince, however. As a consequence of this problem in contemporary theory, to know what is at stake in any specific concept of ending we must first reopen the question of literary closure in general, from the point of view of crisis. Later in this chapter, I will return to Dickens' novels to delineate the forces at work in his own endings, and I will argue that although these forces are articulated mainly through the heroes who were discussed in the previous chapter, they function more as symbolic, narrative readjustments than as psychological problems within character. Most important, through these symbolic adjustments, characters are able to perform liberating, excessive actions that the novels initially condemn as transgressive. The act remains the same in kind; our consciousness of it, however, is changed. Thus, I will be concentrating in this chapter mainly on actions that take place on the level of the symbolic plot and not on aspects of these characters that have already been discussed.

ii

There is no such thing as novelistic ending in the abstract; there are only different ways of ending, and different endings may support different theoretical assumptions about literature. It is as impossible to assimilate all endings to a formula as it is to say, once and for all, what writing is. Those who define novelistic endings as an embodiment of the arbitrary finality implicit in any formal organization, for example, can account for novels like *Finnegan's Wake*, a novel that deliberately sets out not to reach finality, only by classifying them as iconoclastic works that must nevertheless be understood through the conventions of finality they seek to violate.[2] But Joyce's work does have its own literal ending, which, in its circularity, affirms his vision of his work as self-referential and continuous rather than dramatic. His ending supports a full-bodied vision of human life as a special kind of texture; it does not merely seek to escape finality. Similarly, critics who take the opposite position and argue that an ending like Joyce's is the only epistemologically correct one have to resort to a classic-modern split to explain why all novels do not end that way. Usually, such a split implies that the classical novelists were naive, and the critic who resorts to it is obliged to discover in classical texts fledgling versions of nonfinality.[3]

Every concept of the end contains a particular attitude toward the goals of narrative structure. Frank Kermode, to take the most influential of recent writers on finality, sees endings as the expression of a human wish for order and centrality. Rather than merely describing the way novels end, though, Kermode demonstrates how his concept of ending as artificial order is implicated in all the major novelistic strategies—for example, in the strategy of a crisis, in the selective ordering of novelistic time, and in the performance of character as consistent identity. For Kermode, then, the goal of the novelist at every moment is the self-conscious imposition of order on the chaos of experience. At the same time, Kermode argues, because they are disturbed by the dangers of solipsism, novelists try to bring such order closer and closer to experiential chaos, which accounts for the novel's peripeteia—the occasional frustration of conventional expectations—and, historically, for the relentless evolution of the novel toward greater degrees of fragmentation. Nevertheless, for Kermode this flirtation with formlessness is always checked by a deeper desire for order, which triumphs inevitably in ending forms. Most importantly, in Kermode's view, this novelistic dynamic between form and formlessness, human order and chaotic experience, is more than just an aesthetic; it is a model for all human thought.[4]

Kermode's grounding of his concept of the end in a structure of human thought is paralleled by another critic, one with exactly opposite assumptions about the status of language and literature, Edward Said. The latter claims that novels end in "molestation"—the nagging awareness that novelist and characters have a spurious claim to independence and originality, which Said calls "authority." Rather than trying to impose a consciously made-up order on the chaos of experience—Kermode's view—the novelist fundamentally desires to escape the order of experience and to make a claim to a uniqueness of consciousness. However, he is always trapped in impersonal order, Said argues, because the novelist's bid for freedom only encounters its own form, its own textuality; that is, the novelist finds that experience is inevitably mediated by the structure of human thought and, ultimately, by the structure of language. For Said, chaos does not exist; it has no claim to ontological priority. Said can apply his sense of "molestation" to novelistic strategies even more thoroughly than Kermode applies his concept of endings, because Said bases his entire argument on a linguistic theory, one with structuralist roots.[5]

These two positions are convenient examples because they are at opposite poles of a modern debate in philosophy and literary criticism—the difference, to put it grossly, between phenomenology and structuralism: whether experience is infinitely particular, or whether it is infinitely ordered. Regardless of their opposition, though, by sharing a general belief that novelistic endings reflect the structure of human thought, Kermode and Said have a more important bias about novel-writing in common, one that is also shared by most modern critical theorists concerned for literature's place in a rational, scientific world. Both Kermode and Said assume that the task the novelist sets himself is to uncover the philosophical truth about our relationship to our experience, to fix once and for all the relative positions of human freedom and human necessity. In this way, they both see the novel as fundamentally epistemological. For both, although novels cannot be said to represent the world, they at least represent our way of understanding the world and accommodating ourselves to it.[6] Consequently, as part of an epistemological enterprise of one kind or another, an ending has impact chiefly through its clarity, its adequacy to describe a permanent state of affairs that is actually implicit in the organization of the work as a whole.[7]

For the reader, however, endings have an importance that is felt to be separate somehow from what goes before them—at least, sometimes they do. In some cases, the ending is the most important part of a novel; the entire work can seem only a backdrop to the conclusion, on which our judgment of the work hinges. But before we can know exactly how an ending matters dramatically, in order not to be trapped in dogmatism we have to admit that some endings are more important as endings than others. No one would disagree, I think, that the ending in *Middlemarch* or *The Red and the Black* or *The Sot-Weed Factor* is more important to the work than the ending in *Tristram Shandy*, *The Confidence Man*, or *The Castle*. Without drawing up precise categories, I wish to address in this section the question: what does it mean in general when an ending is crucial?

In a superficial comparison of any collection of books with crucial endings, the first observation that comes to mind is that those endings feature change. Although it is always qualified, some difference is introduced, either through action or through a decision that holds the potency of an action—even if that decision involves humility or renunciation. Emma throws over her egotism and marries; Marcel decides to write; Frédéric forgets Madame Arnoux; Hans Castrop goes to war. All of these are definite actions whose meaning lies in their radical departure from previous conflict. Of course, there is change in books like *Tristram Shandy*, but it is more or less effortless change, a flux.

Novels that end crucially, on the other hand, concentrate energy in the overcoming of a specific obstacle and, by ending, release that energy. The obstacle may vary from novel to novel, but it must be one that is overcome, or somehow put behind the ending moment.

Rather than dwelling exclusively on the finality, or the exhaustion, or the knowledge in endings, it is worth considering something more obvious: the activity that produces an ending, activity that is always linked with overcoming, with release, with the expenditure of energy that was tied up in conflict. In this sense, every crucial ending is a rupture of some kind, which, because of the infinite variations that novelists have explored, seems to be pursued for its own sake. This kind of rupture is not a beginning activity, which would imply some finite direction of development; it is activity that implies untested potential and thus has a dimension of limitlessness. What I have in mind is the same kind of activity that we have termed expenditure. Whenever an ending features action that breaks out of a limit—which is how I have defined "crucial" ending—in one of its aspects it is an attempt to fulfill a desire for release. This aspect of a crucial ending is not necessarily dominant, but, if only in the subtlest way, crucial endings always satisfy a deep desire to escape the pressure of our fundamental imprisonment in human life and to expend vital energy freely, without constraint.[8]

Of course, such expenditure—in novels or in human life—is not the same thing as liberation. *Don Quixote*, for example, ends with change that ominously suggests further repetition. Yet that there is a change for Don Quixote, an experience of release—however momentary—cannot be denied. The relationship here between total change and total repetition is left undefined, which means that *both* are felt by the reader in different ways.[9] On one important level, the meaning of Don Quixote's deathbed conversion is not the new book-reading he means to undertake, but the old book-reading he overcomes and allows us to overcome with him. The two are separate experiences linked only by the ineluctability of linear time, which Don Quixote's death—as the ultimate release—puts to an end. Similarly, in many novels the radical decision or action is not tested; the novel ends at the point of the rupture in an image of potency, not with the thorough implementation of new order. The image of a plausible rupture is the crucial experience.

Shifting the importance of crucial endings to their component of expenditure implies a shifting of aesthetic, a shift away from the epistemological. After all, for an ending to be experienced as a new action, or as a freeing of energy, it must resist being appropriated to any finite form; it will not produce a philosophy. As Kenneth Burke says, "Every philosophy is in some respect or other a *step away from* drama"[10]—by which he means that literature performs operations rather than defining them. It acts; it performs linguistic change. It is not objective, neutral. Most writers—there are obvious exceptions—are devoutly antiphilosophical in ways that place them on the side of the possible, not on the side of the actual, the limited, the knowable. John Barth puts the matter bluntly.

I don't know anything about philosophy. I've never even studied it, much less learned it. But ontology and cosmology are funny subjects to improvise. If you are a novelist of a certain type of temperament, then what you really want to do is re-invent the world. God wasn't too bad a novelist, except he was a Realist. . . . But a certain kind of sensibility can be made very uncomfortable by the arbitrariness of physical facts and the inability to accept their *finality*. . . . Robert Louis Stevenson could never get used to the fact that people had two ears, funny-looking things, and eye-balls in their heads; he said it's enough to make you scream.[11]

All writers, even the most professedly "representational" (since it is difficult to know exactly what is being "represented"—certainly not something that already exists in the world in a final, physical way) can be said to alter the world to some degree, or at least to add to it something that was not there before.[12] As Barth puts it, his motive is neither the overcoming of any particular obstacle—personal or social—nor the creation of specific new possibilities; his is a more general desire to put himself beyond the reach of worldly limitations.

Novelists are not alone with their interest in surpassing the given. The same need to exceed limits can be found in the most deterministic of critics, the structuralists. For example, once we believe Derrida when he tells us that we are locked in a self-referential, closed language system,[13] we are free—as he is, in his impacting of words like *differance*, or in his claim that he makes no claims, or in the very aspiration of a work like *Glas* to the idiosyncratically "authored" status of literature—to concentrate on what language *does* as a symbol system, or what it can be made to do. Derrida himself replaces the idea of "center" in Western metaphysics with the idea of "play,"[14] which is an attempt to reconcile the finality of conceptual systems with human needs to revolt against systems infinitely. This emphasis on the shattering of conceptual limits—the very dream of "deconstruction"—is, in fact, a constant theme of poststructuralist argument, stated perhaps no better than Roland Barthes does in an essay on narrative sequence: "The origin of a sequence is not the observation of reality, but the necessity to vary and to outgrow the first *form* that man ever came by, namely repetition: a sequence is essentially a whole within which nothing is repeated. Logic here takes on an emancipating value—and so does all the narrative, which rests on it."[15]

Language is, above all, an activity, not a static kind of knowledge or a description of things as they are. Equally important, as Barth and Barthes make clear, is the primacy, in such activity, of the desire to break with convention, repetition, form. Language, for them, is an act of pure excess; its virtue lies in how well it breaks with previous structures. According to Barthes at his most extreme, the need for such excessive activity is endless, since any repetition is constraining, and literary form, therefore, is not a clarification of content and meaning but is always at war with content and meaning. For Barthes, the task of the novelist is to unexpress what has already been expressed, to deliberately play havoc with what is undeniably and, therefore, frustratingly true.[16]

Both Barth and Barthes are flagrantly offensive to anyone who believes in meaning. Their view of the writer's project can seem futile and discouraging. Novelty by itself is not a very laudable goal; either it turns into mere fashion or its freedom is sterile, not usable—by definition not repeatable. I quote the writer and the critic not to prove that it is finally possible—or even desirable—to escape significance, but only to demonstrate, first, that for some writers the most compelling need is for release from repetition, and, second, that the need to experience such release, taken in its purest expression, is in some way threatening, a menace to more conservative but more useful order. We object to novelty not as an experience, but as a substitute for order.

Caught in this double bind between human needs for an expenditure that is total and needs for some relation to necessary or inevitable order, novelists try to mediate the two impulses most especially in their crucial endings, at the point where there is the greatest danger of either final limitation or complete dissolution. It is important to recognize, however, that the two impulses cannot be accommodated to each other in any finite way. The nature of expenditure, which has meaning only when loss is complete, forbids accommodation. In novelistic conclusion, though, both needs can be satisfied adjacently. So it is with most endings that we call "indeterminate" or "ironic." Emma's marriage is neither a complete surpassing of her egotism nor a fall into trivial social order—as an experience for the reader it is both. Dorothea Brooke's marriage to Will is both a break with Middlemarch's norm of stifled idealism and a lapse into conventional marriage. This is not to say that Emma's or Dorothea's marriage will not be affected by the double nature of the activity that produces it; expenditure and conservation have a mid-range where they modify each other in concrete ways. Still, their contradictory nature forbids complete integration, which inevitably leaves us with two separate attitudes toward the ending.

All novelists adjust the variable relationship between expenditure and conservation differently. But Dickens' endings are a striking instance of the critical nature of action in novelistic conclusion, if only because the dynamic of repetition and release is such a central problem for him. The role of crucial action may be the more striking here, too, because Dickens' endings are so commonly seen as expressions of a wish for stasis, for the permanence of passive withdrawal.[17]

It is true that Dickens' endings do attain a degree of rest. They push beyond mere chronicity into repletion. In *Bleak House*, for example, Esther's narrative jolts us at the end with its "Full seven happy years I have been the mistress of Bleak House" (67). The sudden passage of seven years reminds us that the mimetic temporal succession of the narrative is an aesthetic illusion—even for Esther—suspended as it is in a time sequence seven years beyond the time of the events she describes. Moreover, the apparent stability of those seven years—in contrast to the turmoil in the time of the novel—reinforces our feeling that time has ended or stretched out into a different kind of duration.

However much this may be stasis, though, it is a created stasis. It is helpful here to remember Burke's differentiation of two kinds of rest. "There is rest as the sheer cessation of motion . . . and there is rest as the end of action."[18] Or, to use a Burkean emphasis, there is rest as the end of *action*. Here, the achieved stasis is contingent on a certain kind of activity, namely, Esther's marriage to Woodcourt. The relevant action is not marriage in general, which only brings to mind all the clichéd meanings of domestic finality, but Esther's particular marriage, which, as we shall see later, releases her from a nagging conflict—her desire to be loved warring with her obsessive refusal of love—and implicates her in a specific movement, from Jarndyce's Bleak House to Woodcourt's Bleak House. That this timelessness is also a localized experience undergone by an individual, and not a new vapor of freedom descended on the world, is emphasized by the second narrative, which—like the real world—does not end. The point is, timelessness as a human wish for a given, illusory condition of stasis, passivity, and shelter is not the same thing as the sensation of timelessness produced by the act of surpassing a limit, whose metaphors more properly are eroticism, violence, and mystical experience.

Merely as a suggestion, these metaphorical equivalents for what Dickens' characters do in their endings sound either transgressive, or—at their weakest—embarrassingly absurd. In fact, any release from a constraint is potentially either a violation of a taboo or of common sense. What I hope to show is that the authorial activity in Dickens' novels solves this problem through its own break with symbolic limits; that is, narrative and symbolic values are shifted in such a way that the experience of release for characters becomes not only plausible but harmonious with more conservative values—a purely symbolic bridging of the gap between expenditure and conservation. Crucial endings never formalize a resolution between the two poles; they only allow them to merge momentarily in an image of action that has been redefined by the novel's metaphorical structure. All activity in Dickens has a problematic status, which is pointed up by those critics who find that characters who are superficially opposed on a moral level really operate with the same energies. But those critics often miss Dickens' alteration in the way certain kinds of activity are valued.[19] This symbolic readjustment of values is the real drama in Dickens; it is his authorial play with the limits of connotation in language, with the inescapably suasive nature of all discourse.[20]

iii

The most obvious question left unsettled by the ending of *Bleak House* is, how do we evaluate Esther's marriage, especially as it is conceived symbolically, through her transition to a second Bleak House? The question seems crucial in light of the ground-clearing tone to the end of the novel. Lady Dedlock and Richard Carstone, chief victims of the law, are dead; Tulkinghorn, its emanation, is dead; the Jarndyce suit is dead; all dangerous secrets are laid to rest. What, then, after this partial catharsis of the Chancery plot, is the concluding action in Esther's plot—is it a rebirth, a reenactment, or an evasion?

The more disturbing possibility is that this marriage is simply the way things happen to Esther, that is, that her marriage means something to her, and something else in our terms or in the terms of the third-person narrator. The question of the reliability of Esther's happiness in the ending reflects problems in our ability to evaluate her role in the novel all the way through. After all, not only do we know little about Esther's second house, but our judgment of her first is also clouded by ambiguities. Throughout the novel, there are ominous parallels between her world and the world of the third-person narrator. What is the difference, for example, between the chaos of Chancery and the "pleasant irregularity" of Esther's Bleak House? Certainly, too, Esther's mind is a labyrinth; it is difficult to estimate the emotional cost of her compulsive deference and self-denial. More seriously, as we saw in the last chapter, how much of that self-denial conceals a will-to-power? Esther's egotism has bothered many readers, but still more disturbing is the way Esther's control of others echoes Tulkinghorn's. Both are in everyone's confidence yet tell nothing about their own deeper intentions; both have a collection of keys and locks; both harp on their all-justifying sense of duty; both hold onto the fates of others by holding onto their letters—Tulkinghorn blackmails with Captain Hawdon's letters, and Esther keeps Jarndyce's letter proposing marriage for a month before she answers it. Of course, there is never any doubt whose side Dickens is on. Nevertheless, these strange, insistent resonances, by making Esther herself ambiguous, make it difficult to specify what kind of change—or what kind of repetition—is involved in the most prominent action of the ending, Esther's movement from one Bleak House to another.

Evidently, *Bleak House* would make Richard Carstones of us all. Rather than muddling through all these ambiguities, though, we can retreat to the most abstract level to make Esther's matrimonial pattern a little clearer. The most significant repetition of all is a repetition of sexual triangles that frames the entire novel. The triad of Sir Leicester, Lady Dedlock, and Captain Hawdon that is ultimately at the source of almost everything in the book—it even marks Esther's conception—is reworked in the sexual triangle at the end of the second plot, that of Jarndyce, Esther, and Woodcourt. The configurations are not readily apparent, but they mesh in interesting ways. For one thing, both triangles involve transitions between an older man and a younger one—Dickens' generational theme—and both involve transitions between a husband, or near-husband, and a lover—problems of adultery; for another, in both cases the forbidden lover is the more attractive: Lady Dedlock's affair with Captain Hawdon takes place against a background of social exhaustion and a dull marriage to a man old enough to be her father, while Esther's attraction to *her* sailor is placed against her betrothal to an aging father-figure, a cloying betrothal that "made no difference" (44). As denials of passionate love, though, we should note that both the Dedlock marriage and Esther's betrothal to Jarndyce also contain a kind of tender affection that positively stresses the value of conservative, as opposed to excessive, love. Sir Leicester, surprisingly, forgives Lady Dedlock in a gesture that actually foreshadows Jarndyce's own self-sacrifice.

What makes this repetition of triangles important is the obvious difference: the three characters of the first triangle are destroyed by social and moral constraints, while the second triangle works. It does not work as a *ménage à trois*, exactly, but it does feature a woman's sexual transition from one man to another, without doing violence to the first, more paternal relationship. The second triangle features a breakthrough, an expending of Esther's sexual energies beyond their confinement to Jarndyce, the same kind of surpassing of sexual boundaries that, in its original form, was the novel's great transgression. The inhibition and paralysis in the first triangle—defenses against transgression that are repeated in Esther's own obsessive self-denial, which is an indirect response to Lady Dedlock's excesses that keeps her from Woodcourt—are broken, however abstractly, by the successful, excessive action in the second triangle.

The kind of freedom Esther achieves is nonspecific and expansive, which makes it congruent with our previous notion of release, as a close look at the kind of action she and Lady Dedlock share will demonstrate. Lady Dedlock's sin, of course, is sexual, and the sexual act itself is an experience of an intense destruction of boundaries, a literal penetration of the limits of bodily identity. On another level, though, as we have seen, both Lady Dedlock's sin and Esther's marriage confuse problems of adultery and generational transition. There appears to be a failure on Dickens' part to be explicit, to spell out the nature of the sexual conflict—a vagueness which often makes Dickens subject to analyses like Françoise Basch's description of the Victorians' "systematic confusion of sexual roles" as a defense against female sexuality.[21] But in this instance Dickens' vagueness has a deeper purpose. Sex is not *the* issue in this novel. It is subsumed in a more general context of restlessness, constraint, limitation, and needs for release from boundaries.

To make the broader range of problems of boundaries clear, we need only cull other echoes from the novel, which are plentiful. Caddy Jellyby, for example, also struggles with the narrowly generational problem. Frustrated at home by parents who enslave her and who are incapable of receiving her love, Caddy escapes to a husband. That Prince Turveydrop brings in tow a father to whose nourishment Caddy dedicates herself is for her a compromise between excess and moral restraint, a mixture of sexual gratification and duty. George the Trooper is a more interesting case, though, in that George presents a problem of excessive, rebellious energy that is specifically nonsexual. Like so many other children in this novel—Caddy, Richard, the Pardiggle brood—George is unable to reconcile the restraints of his family circle with his restless drives. But George's desires have no sexual object; in fact, they have no object at all. Like Richard, George is pure restlessness. Feeling "smothered" is his favorite response to his problems. His presence in the novel suggests a primary need to vent rebellious energy; specifically, George has no particular dissatisfaction with the Rouncewell family; he simply *has to go*.

Seen in the light of primary restlessness, the polar opposition of social institutions and the individual—such a constant

theme of Dickens criticism—breaks down. In *Bleak House*,
both the individual and society are motivated by similar energies; the Jarndyce suit, for instance, is reckless growth, a blind,
expansive force, an appetite that breaks down and consumes all
obstacles to itself. Bucket, too, the arm of the institution, presents a similar problem of restless and unconstrained—because
sanctioned—energy. Critics who tend to oppose social systems
to the individual in Dickens also tend to see Bucket only as a
force for social order,[22] neglecting to see that Bucket thrives on
conflict and on overcoming others, not on regularity.

In a novel so saturated with the crushing weight of blackmail, repression, imprisonment, and legal dungeons, it is not
easy to see—except in characters like Bucket, George, Richard,
or Gridley—that there is also present a certain primary kind of
energy randomly seeking to break limits. Of course, if would be
nonsense to claim that the problem for Esther and for Lady
Dedlock is simply what to do with their excess energy, as if
there were not a spectrum of motives involved. Still, both are
driven by energies whose source it is difficult to locate as a response to anything: Lady Dedlock's social ambition, and Esther's obsession with her own saintliness. These drives have a
life of their own which is bent into more concrete motivations as
they encounter particular kinds of restraints. Lady Dedlock's
frigidity is her weapon against the Fashionable Intelligence; Esther's self-denial is the method she learns from her Calvinist up-
bringing and uses against its ethos of self-obliteration. Lady
Dedlock's and Esther's more important and more distinctly personal motives, though, arise only when they confront the fact
that drives for unqualified release—as figured in characters like
Bucket or Skimpole, or in themselves—threaten both their lives
and those of their loved ones. The problem for Esther, for Lady
Dedlock, for George, and for all the good characters, is how to
reconcile desires for expenditure with their resistance to the
cruelty and the violence of expenditure. They all must somehow
reconcile drives toward release with a conservative structure of
affection and love.

Lady Dedlock, of course, fails; so does Richard. But a char-

acter like George does gratify both his impulse to exceed his
family circle and his love for his family by the end of the novel in
a way that was not available to him in the beginning. Instead of
running away and sinking his energy into useless service in the
army, George again leaves his family—after getting their approval this time—and promptly binds himself to Sir Leicester.
This particular release and immediate binding of energy makes
more emotional sense to us than a career in the army does, now
that we have seen Sir Leicester's tender side. Significantly, too,
George insists on geographical separation from his family, yet he
remains near them. Seen in this light, George's compromise provides us with the key to the mystery of the two Bleak Houses
and the reason why Jarndyce's relationship to Esther and Woodcourt must be preserved: Esther and Woodcourt, too, remain
geographically separate, yet near Jarndyce, in a house that re-
peats his. The second Bleak House represents a movement out
of stability—an explicitly sexual movement—yet it retains its
tie to the first. It is imbalance-within-balance; excess is brought
in under cover of stability.

Before we consider whether Esther's marriage is a workable
strategy that resolves problems of release and restraint, however, it is important to see first how the narrative logic puts the
reader on the side of the expenditure, rather than against it. We
never question the logic of Esther's transition to Woodcourt; we
may doubt that the final arrangement is as completely happy
as Esther would have us believe, but there is no question that
Esther's transition is something to be approved as natural—
emotionally or in narrative terms. For this purpose, the narrative context carefully sets up conditions for plausibility. First,
the overwhelming atmosphere of mutual deference in *Bleak
House* makes the resolution seem appropriate for the characters, rather than either a merely fanciful, merely fairy-tale resolution, or an excessively violent change. None of the characters
involved contorts himself in any way—at least, given what we
know of them. On the contrary, they all seem to produce the resolution inevitably. In a strange way, Jarndyce's own system of

self-denial, which Esther has adulated and deferred to throughout the novel in precedent-setting ways, fittingly prevails again
over hers and seems to lead him logically to anticipate her needs.
At the same time, Jarndyce's own relationship to Esther is de-
sexualized well enough to minimize conflict between himself and
Woodcourt. Second, the reader is made to expect such a resolution because of the glaring "mistake" threatened by Esther's
quasi-incestuous betrothal to Jarndyce. We are made to hope
that Jarndyce will turn her over to Woodcourt and, when he
does, it seems both to relieve us and to confirm our expectations
rather than to play havoc with our sense of reality. Third, Jarndyce himself is not abandoned; rather, he is restored to his original, benign position by the introduction of Ada in her new
relationship to him as her "guardian." Finally, the only voice
of social opposition, Mrs. Woodcourt's, is made both harmless
enough and unpleasant enough for us to wish for her to be overcome. In short, because of the narrative logic and also because
there is a displacement in our awareness of conflict away from
the sexual problem toward the conflict in Esther's own internal
integration of desire and passivity—a conflict that does not play
any obvious role in Jarndyce's decision—it is easier to believe
that Esther's transition to Woodcourt is right for all three characters than to decide just what it is about any of it that bothers
us. This transition, which dissolves Esther's confinement to
Jarndyce, is possibly the greatest successful action in *Bleak
House*, and the reader experiences it as an unqualified, good
release.

Beyond the purely circumstantial framework for Esther's
transition, the marriage is also presented as an appropriate resolution because, like George's service of Sir Leicester or Caddy's
marriage, it is fused with symbolic terms for restraint. For one
thing, Esther's transition is acceptable because, despite her desire for it, she is capable of renouncing it. Release operates
through her, rather than involving her in the guilt of self-willed
freedom. More importantly, because we have been made to feel
that Esther's devotion to duty and her militantly organized self-

denial is too good and actually does her harm, it is refreshing to think that she can afford to lose some of that control. As for Jarndyce, his self-denial, which borders on being a new problem of limitation, is transfigured as an expenditure; he gives Esther to Woodcourt, and this act of deliberate loss affords him the kind of satisfaction he has been able to take through pure generosity all along. In this transition, then, the poles of limitation and release are combined symbolically in a way that resolves the initial problem.

At the same time, this "harmony" remains one of symbolic adjustment; it does not leave us with a prescription. Esther's marriage is felt as a success through the symbolic drama, but as an action it cannot be reduced to a formula for action. The addition of a Growlery for Jarndyce (and it is significant that it is a Growlery Jarndyce is consigned to) in the second house is not a worldly strategy; Sir Leicester, for example, would probably not have felt comfortable living with Lady Dedlock and Captain Hawdon in Krook's rag-and-bottle shop, even if they gave him his own room. The absurdity bears heavily on the possibility that Esther's marriage "solves" conflict; by shifting the two situations slightly, the novel never invites a direct comparison. The conditions of Esther's triangle are rearranged so that impediments can be reasonably overcome, and we accept the expansive movement of the second triangle without seeing it specifically as a redemption of the first. It is an act that makes logical sense, that resolves a symbolic dilemma, that provides a localized release from restrictions; it is not a solution.

Though elaborately idiosyncratic, Esther's successful sexual transition in *Bleak House* is not an isolated instance of this kind of resolution. Whenever Dickens uses sexual triangles, he always manages to permit a triumphant spilling over of erotic energies that remains enigmatically singular. In *David Copperfield*, we are explicitly warned against the transferability of love through Little Em'ly, who throws over Ham for Steerforth, and through Annie, who is almost lured away from Dr. Strong by the seducer Jack Maldon. Then, too, Mrs. Copperfield's second marriage becomes, in effect, a betrayal of David, and Betsey Trotwood is forced to remain single—in a celibate relationship to Mr. Dick—as if in punishment for her bad marriage. Romantic restlessness is also satirized through Micawber's comic insistences about his faithfulness to Mrs. Micawber. But through the narrative convenience of Dora's death, David becomes the single character who is able to correct the errors of his first choice and to find a new partner. Marrying Agnes is even made to seem a duty when David learns that their union was Dora's last wish. Though skewed slightly from problems presented by Em'ly, Annie, and the others, David's second marriage satisfies in an elliptic way desires for a liberation of romantic love that the entire novel seems to warn us against. Less strikingly, perhaps, in *Our Mutual Friend*, Eugene Wrayburn's ability to reject the girl forced on him by his father and to marry Lizzie instead is neutrally counterpointed by Bradley Headstone's disastrous attempt to forego Miss Peecher, who is eventually forced on him by Riderhood as well as by the conventions of class, for Lizzie. And, in the same novel, the balance between excessive or new love and conservative, older love is delicately maintained in a purely symbolic way by the novel's two love plots; while Eugene manages to escape a choice dictated by his father and finds a new mate, John Harmon does the reverse; he succeeds in first transforming and then marrying precisely the girl dictated by parental choice. These two love plots play off the rival satisfactions of excess and restraint in a fictional, nonusable resolution. Still another eccentric solution to the problem of sexual transition concludes *Little Dorrit*. The initial crime, the adultery of Arthur's father, is completed and legitimized in a symbolic way; like his father, Arthur defies his mother's repressive Calvinism by marrying the girl who—solely in terms of his father's will—*stands for* his sinning mother as the next surviving heir. Arthur's love for Little Dorrit thus resurrects the history of his father's adultery and seems to consummate it in a morally satisfying way while it shifts the burden of guilt in the novel to the repressive Mrs. Clennam. Thus, the rebellious liberation of his father's

erotic energy is fulfilled by Arthur's innocent love for Little
Dorrit and by the corresponding guilt of Mrs. Clennam, who
represents moral authority and restraint.

As these novels demonstrate, release and restraint are, in
their ultimate extension, adjacent values; there is no way to test
the ethical status of Dickens' successful triangles as integrated
acts that can be repeated. These triangles remain a kind of
stored potential, a delicate attitudinal disposition, an image, an
inclination. It is impossible to say whether the same kind of resolution is translatable outward. In *Bleak House*, for example,
the success of Esther's triangle does seem to be repeated in
George's retainership, and in the Turveydrops, and in Matthew
Bagnet's channeling of his martial spirit into "blasting away" at
his bassoon; but these secondary resolutions, imitating the main
one, border on being grotesque parodies. George's invisible iron
spurs, for instance, ominously echo Mr. Rouncewell's iron mills
(that one of these brothers should have only a first name, and
the other only a last name, is an emblem of permanent disloca-
tion); the factory, which combines progress and unrestrained energy with social use, is Dickens' most disturbing image in this
novel of safely reconciled expenditure and conservation. It goes
without saying, too, that George's role as retainer is mildly pathetic. In a more direct failure, the Turveydrops' marriage results in a stunted, deaf-mute child. Boythorn, too, is forever
divided against himself and against Sir Leicester in a burlesque
of violent energy linked to good intentions; he cannot escape
his split persona, even though he wants to. The inescapable fact
for Dickens in *Bleak House*—as in all his novels—is that any
synthesis of violence and order will be a contortion, a kind of
internal combustion. The form left over by compromise always
seems warped and can be as potentially dangerous as active
transgression. Symbolic resolutions, too—like the texture of
Esther's narrative, which reorganizes verbally the discordant
world of the third-person narrator—are always very delicate
and idiosyncratic.

Through such pressing insistence on instability and impossible opposition, the Dickens ending never really ends; *Bleak House* does not reconcile conflicts in any absolute way, not even in Esther's marriage. The instability of any permanent resolution is summed up in the last hanging, unresolved sentence. Do we take Woodcourt's flattery as a well-meaning matrimonial lie, but a lie nevertheless, one that conceals his disappointment with Esther's looks and, potentially, his failure to satisfy and contain his desires in her? Or do we take it as a complete release from any mortal interest in human beauty? As for Esther in this last scene, what of her final flirtation with egotism? The complex of mirror images in the book has suggested all along that Esther's continual destruction of her own selfish limitations is actually, in part, an economy of petty self-righteousness and self-aggrandizement.

Instability, madness even, is at the heart of this novel. But that Esther's life conceals—imperfectly—a radical instability is not to say that she is its victim. Through Esther, the novel builds a kind of attitudinal potency by developing a sexual transition that was hopelessly blocked in the beginning. Whatever the consequences, Esther has broken through the barrier of that sexual conflict in a very real way. Rather than merely repeating Lady Dedlock's muddle, she has broken with it and has made her life what her first chapter called it, "A Progress."

iv

In *Great Expectations*, the novel that is most un-Dickensian in its fusion of patterns of thought and action in a single consciousness—even David Copperfield's story is mostly about other people—the reworking of a previous failure is more direct for that very reason. Less disquieting but more poignant, perhaps, than in *Bleak House*, the reworking is also more clearly achieved by shifting the significance of key symbolic terms.

The problem in *Great Expectations* is one of boundaries, of progress and restriction. Pip's central discovery is that his proj-

ect of gaining autonomy has only forged him new chains; as the
novel develops several riddles about the grounds of Pip's identity, those grounds shift from seeming open and in the future—
somehow a reward for special merit—to seeming determined
from the past. Trapped by that past, Pip cannot rise to Estella's level because their histories determine a fundamental equal-
ity between them, even finding a common "father" for them in
Magwitch to belie their illusory, more free condition as orphans.
Rising above limitations is, in fact, an illusion, the illusion that
fosters dissatisfactions and the need to rise. Nevertheless, although the novel frames this pattern and seems to rest in disillusion, through its ending *Great Expectations* puts a kind of
distance on disillusion. Actually, the novel concludes on a note of
rejustified aspiration.

The debate over the two endings—whether Pip should be allowed to marry Estella or not—obscures a larger problem.
After all, whether Pip marries Estella (and the second ending is
much more ambiguous than is usually, perhaps wishfully, recognized[23]) is less interesting than why he still loves her at all. Loving Estella was Pip's big mistake; if he has learned anything,
how can he continue to love her? From beginning to end, Pip's
love for Estella is fused with the deeper meaning of "expectations." In this sense, the book seems to have been written from
a stable position of enlightenment that Pip loses at the end, especially in the second version, which, with its shift to a mood
that strains forward, toward desire, rather than resting in plac-
id affection, dangerously fuses Pip's confusion within mimetic
time with the writer's time, the past with the future.

Pip's confession to Biddy that "That poor dream . . . has all
gone by" (59) is betrayed even in the first ending, if only in the
prominence Pip gives Estella at the end of his narrative. But Pip
also betrays a final wish here, "that . . . [suffering] had given
her a heart to understand what my heart used to be" (59). Pip is
still imagining himself mystically completed outside himself. His
old dream had always been to find a center of being that was
displaced from himself and his situation in space and time. The

remoteness of that center, a distanced freedom and authenticity, was the very dream of "expectations." Now, Pip's dream persists in the ending through his desire to locate in Estella not even what he is, but what he was, which connects Estella to the entire project of Pip's narrative, his attempt to find his center in a displacement of himself into the past, into a narrative. If loving Estella was Pip's great mistake insofar as he made her a false emblem of his unrecognized merit, the ending puts him right back where he started. The second ending only makes this wish of Pip's more explicit than it had been in the first.

This idea of a center remains vague for Pip in the ending, as vague as his love for Estella. What Pip "expects" is always just something others must have that he does not have—a formula for expectation that René Girard calls "metaphysical desire."[24] Pip's motive is never to locate himself in some specific center; he revolts only against his sense of his own separateness, which is grounded in pure self-hatred. Estella herself, who represents freedom from these limitations, is never a person to him; she seems to inhabit the stars and the landscape—everything that is not Pip, a vagueness that reflects the crisis of separation between Pip and the world that begins the novel. In this way, Pip's desire to displace the self has the same significance sexuality has in *Bleak House*. Quite literally, it is a desire for expenditure; Pip's wish is to break down the claustrophobia of selfhood—not to be reincarnated in another specific form of selfhood, but to be released into the nonhuman sphere beyond selfhood in which Estella supposedly dwells. In this context, Pip's continued love for Estella at the end is disturbing not only because it leaves him in a confirmed search for a self-displacement that the novel seems to warn against, but also because it channels his desire for displacement into a single, inadequate form.

Still, the nearly universal reading of the book as a progress, a discovery, must have something to offer, especially because it is this aspect that Dickens emphasizes in the second ending. If nothing else, that critics would argue over whether Pip should get what he wants without questioning his desires, or that they should skirt the issue by calling it "real" love,[25] indicates that readers root for the boy who still wants something—even if they are enlightened and ironical and think that he should not get it—rather than for the boy who just resigns himself to reductive "self-knowledge." That desire is more interesting than moral resignation, perhaps because the act of reading itself involves "great expectations," or that desire can sneak in under cover of resignation as a reward is a good place to start.

As in *Bleak House*, there are symbolic adjustments that explain why Pip's return to Estella at the end is purged of its transgressive potential. In the first place, Estella comes to represent shelter for Pip, and not the radical violence of desire. After having been restored to the parental affections of Joe and Biddy, and having been given the chance to redeem himself by choosing them unconditionally—and, therefore, opting for conservative values—Pip is prevented from a complete reconciliation with his paternal and maternal figures by their marriage. Because of this disappointment, turning back to Estella is transfigured for Pip into seeking a refuge, not a release. Imagistically, too, finding Estella is turned around into finding a home; Estella saves the ruins of Satis House as a testament to her encounter there with Pip, and there is pressure on Pip to feel it, nostalgically, as his real native grounds—Estella identifies taking leave of Pip with "taking leave of this spot" (59). In the second place, Pip's exclusion from the lives of Biddy and Joe only points up the restrictions the world of the Forge has forced on Pip all along. For example, Pip's apprenticeship to Joe takes the form of a public imprisonment, as if to confirm his own claustrophobia; on the level of emblems, Joe is on the side of the soldiers and makes handcuffs to be used on convicts; but most important of all, Joe cannot empathize with Pip's struggle but can only dismiss it with a moralistic "lies is lies, Pip" (9). There are good reasons, then, for us to favor Pip's movement from Biddy to Estella, much as we favored Esther's movement from Jarndyce to Woodcourt. But we can take the problem of Pip's love for Estella further if we look at another kind of act transformed in the ending: the act of giving. Giving in *Great Expectations* is the real focus for drives toward displacement of the self; it is the principal means of expenditure in this novel, and the atmosphere of spending created by Pip's giving forcefully conditions our attitude toward his final love for Estella.

The novel has its genesis in a gift, since Pip's gift to Magwitch determines Magwitch's later, reciprocal gift of Pip's gentlemanly career. This first gift has an important metaphorical logic, that is, it is double-natured; Pip gives and takes at the same time, stealing from his sister to give to the convict. Taking—however unwillingly—and giving are merged here in the same action. However, there is something about the act that does not originate in either motive; Pip's only real intention is to save himself. His act is an act of survival that only secondarily implicates him in a structure of giving and taking. Moreover, because it is counterpoised against the cemetery and images of natural nullity, Pip's act does not have to be defended, despite its ominously ambiguous status. In similar ways, throughout the early part of the novel, Pip's actions have a forgivable double nature. We feel all too well the pressure of Pip's world, and we sympathize with Pip's resistance to it. But, unfortunately, this resistance naturally takes the form of denying the self-image imposed on him by Pumblechook and Mrs. Joe, who hate little boys indiscriminately, and of believing in a more justly deserved existence free of their pressure—the dream of displacement. Resistance compromised by displacement and giving compromised by taking are presented in the early part of the book in ways that make them seem natural and defensible, but vaguely disquieting.

The necessity of giving, however ambiguous it begins to appear, is further stressed early in the novel by the alternative presence of Joe, who cannot give. In a striking scene, at Christmas dinner when Pip is under fire from his sister and Pumblechook, all that Joe can offer Pip is gravy. Then, too, in his last conversation with Pip, Joe apologizes for his former inability to help him; he explains the problem in terms of his own fears that he would have engendered more harm than good by helping Pip—a significant philosophy, but hardly a consoling one. Joe's impotence in giving sends us toward generosity as a necessity, just as in the novel's first scene giving is felt to be an act of vitality, an overcoming of unjust pressures.

But the novel soon changes our attitude toward gifts, making the identity of giving and taking clearer and clearer. For example, the crushing blow for Pip is his discovery that his inheritance is not coincident with his own identity, that it is not a free gift, but that it has appropriated him in some way to the giver, Magwitch. In Magwitch, giving is defined as the attempt to live through another, to take revenge for the defeat of expectations by recreating desire and its fulfillment in someone else. Miss Havisham's benevolence to Estella has the same goal; it is an attempted creation of a remote selfhood of a kind that she feels was prohibited to her. These instances of gift-giving, which are forms of expenditure and displacement, realize the dangers that were only latent in Pip's first gift to Magwitch; in *Great Expectations*, characters repeatedly cannot separate satisfaction in their own generosity from the guilt of approbation, or manipulation. Giving is always congruent with taking.

Bataille's work on the primitive gift *potlatch* points up the conflict. No sacrifice is ever completely destroyed; it always achieves something for the giver, as long as sacrifice stops short of death. In Bataille's terms, it proves the giver's spiritual wealth by demonstrating how much actual wealth he is willing to do without.[26] The problem goes right to the heart of expenditure; short of death, all other expenditure is in some way a cheat. As Jarndyce finds to his distress in *Bleak House*, overcoming the conservative, hoarding limits of selfhood in acts of self-sacrifice always achieves something tangible again for the giver—the adulation of others—whether he wants it or not. Giving forces him to be a taker.

Against this background, Pip's actions after his enlightenment about the gifts he has received are a strange repetition. Pip's seemingly innocent decision to redeem his own failures by giving Herbert a share in a business that he had always wanted, and to let Herbert believe he had earned the position for himself, is suspect. The line between thankless self-sacrifice and the preservation of expectations in another breaks down here, especially since Pip and Herbert had been such twins in expectation. Wemmick underscores the difficulty when he comments to Pip, "This is devilish good of you" (37). Then, too, when Pip catches a glimpse of Herbert's joy, he cries secret "tears of triumph," which vaguely suggests the satisfaction of revenge. What most points up the problem, though, is that the gift to Herbert comes right on the heels of Pip's offer of money to Biddy, an offer that is awkward and condescending, and one that Biddy quickly, almost indignantly, refuses. Biddy wants to make her own way, free from ambiguous gifts, and Herbert had often claimed proudly that he did, too. Pip himself makes the connection between giving and manipulation only metaphorically, when he realizes with shame that he has helped Herbert with Magwitch's tainted money.

The narrative sets up conditions, though, that "forgive" this gift-giving of Pip's, just as Esther's overcoming of her relationship to Jarndyce is "forgiven." Not only do we feel that Herbert deserves his gift, that he gets what he wants, and that what he wants is modest, we also sense that the taint is exorcized symbolically by the diffusion of responsibility, rather than by the retraction of the gift. Pip gets Miss Havisham to make half the purchase of Herbert's share in the business; Miss Havisham, too, because her death negates any possible self-interest, is allowed more directly to atone for giving gifts to Estella by giving gifts to Herbert and Matthew Pocket, whose names certify them as receptacles; and Herbert helps further dissolve the guilt when he reciprocally secures a place in the business for Pip. In another kind of symbolic, ritual purgation, guilt is carried away by Orlick; the scene in the limekiln, as we have already noted, is less a punishment of Pip than it is a further scapegoating of Orlick, who, once he has attacked Pip, is left with all of Pip's guilt himself. The point is that guilt is ritually, aesthetically carried off, not redeemed by the reclamation of any gifts. The necessity for this exclusively symbolic readjustment of guilt both confirms its presence in Pip's gifts and supports our earlier feeling that generosity, with its potential as a resistance to suffocation, must be defended.

Defense comes easily, though, because of the new element of restraint that is fused with Pip's generosity. In the first place, Pip does not give enthusiastically but, rather, out of an inner moral compulsion, in order to atone for greater wrongs. Like Esther in *Bleak House*, Pip expends himself passively. In the second place, Pip's desires for some recognition of his release from limits by others—so important in his original love for Estella, which demanded, as a prerequisite, wealth as a social sign of freedom—are held in check by his final gifts. Pip never willingly appropriates recognition; he never intends to reveal to Herbert the source of Herbert's fulfilled expectations. In other instances of his generosity, this self-effacement is equally stressed; Pip hides his and Estella's actual unhappiness from the dying Magwitch, giving him instead a white lie about the possibility of their eventual marriage to preserve Magwitch's hopes even to the end of his life; and he conceals his desire for Biddy, along with his pain at the loss of her, from Biddy and Joe, in order to give them an unspoiled marital happiness. In each case, Pip eschews recognition of his generosity, at the same time defining himself, in the first two cases, against characters who still need the solace of "expectations." He thus fuses his more problematic generosity with humility and restraint. Moreover, the element of restraint does not compromise the nature of Pip's gifts as expenditures; rather, it helps make the expenditure more profound. Pip's gifts are complete sacrifices, total expenditures, thanks to his refusal of recognition. Because Pip's understanding of his acts is displaced outside the world's sense of him, his goodness seems unlimited, infinitely resonant. As readers, we confer a special, "released" identity on Pip *because* his gifts go unrecognized by the world, *because* he tells no one—not noticing, perhaps, that he does tell us, that the entire project of the narrative is to tell us. It is the reader who absorbs the appropriative dimension of sought-out recognition and who finally confirms in Pip a successful displacement.

Through giving, Pip frees himself from the narrow hopelessness of an identity burdened by guilt. But because Pip's "justified" generosity has to take him outside the world's recognition to avoid destructive appropriation, the symbolic resolution of release and restraint, once again, is not a real resolution; it is still qualified, in its nature as expenditure, by the solitariness that results from it. If Pip's virtue at the end is measured by the extent to which his generosity exceeds the recognition of the world, it is to that same extent that he suffers. Expenditure, even as moral action, leaves the world—and human companionship—behind; its function is not to conserve relationships, but to break free, to separate. Expenditure and reconciliation exclude each other.

Pip's relationship to Estella can now be understood in similar terms. Pip's love for Estella and his gift-giving obviously have in common the desire to expend the self, to create distance from the sensation of being trapped. And in a telling passage, Pip calls Estella "the innermost life of my life" immediately after identifying her with "those ill-regulated aspirations that had first made me ashamed of home and Joe" (29). As Estella joins them, Pip's sense of himself *is* his aspiration out of himself. This split is not healed by the ending; instead, it is made to work for Pip. Aspiration fuses with self-knowledge and humility; expenditure fuses with restraint. Just as Pip is spared a choice between giving and impotence, so, too, Pip does not have to choose between Estella and bachelorhood in the ending as if he were choosing between a lapse into illusion and resigned self-knowledge. What Pip does instead is to shift the terms of the opposition; he posits resigned self-knowledge *in* Estella. No longer a figure of spite and amorality, Estella has also learned resignation. She has learned it better than Pip, in fact, which is the way with enigmatic images of completion. In their final scene, Pip is the one who asks the naive questions; Estella gives the wise, poignant answers.

"I little thought," said Estella, "that I should take leave of you in taking leave of this spot. I am very glad to do so."

"Glad to part again, Estella? To me, parting is a painful thing. To me, the remembrance of our last parting has been ever mournful and painful."

"But you said to me," returned Estella, very earnestly, "'God bless you, God forgive you.' And if you could say that to me then, you will not hesitate to say that to me now." (59)

Pip plays a subordinate role in this last dialogue, as he has always played a subordinate role to Estella, but the stakes are different now. Estella represents a more painfully and more completely achieved selflessness (her suffering at the hands of Drummle outdoes Pip's at her hands) than Pip himself can claim. For Pip, Estella embodies in a more mystified way his own history of discovery and self-acceptance. By locating the qualities of self-knowledge and self-denial outside of himself, in Estella, Pip can desire them erotically as a displacement, instead of desiring success or revenge. Rather than representing an open future, as she had early in the novel, Estella now offers the same field for self-displacement by representing the wound in the past held out as a failure, but also as a promise of total compassion—something Estella seems to possess, in which Pip may possibly lose himself. Pip expends himself, paradoxically, in the more conservative direction of humility.

Validated by narrative and symbolic redefinition, Pip's love for Estella contains a continuing process of self-dissociation as a way of overcoming the dangers of resignation; the rhythms of humility are fused with a rhythm of progress, rather than one of impotence. By making the humbled knowledge of his guilt and failure the object of his final love for Estella, Pip combines expenditure and restraint in a double-pronged attitude that eliminates both helpless passivity and deliberate vengeance as motives. The effect of Pip's final love, read together with the re-justification of gift-giving, is to emphasize the necessity of realizing satisfaction, goodness, and identity *outside* the limits of the self in a movement of displacement, expenditure.

We should note that Dickens' symbolic merger of humility with expenditure in a novel like *Great Expectations* is broadly

Victorian; though traditionally perceived as novelists of moral restraint, Dickens, Eliot, the Brontës, Hardy, and their contemporaries all share a desire to use ethics and social commitment as a field for the exercise of energies that would be transgressive if not legitimated by moral codes. The self-sacrificing heroine of George Eliot's novels typically finds passionate love—despite the crimes of self-interest Eliot associates with passionate love through her Hetty Sorrels and Rosamond Vincys—by merging the self-dissolutions of love with the self-abnegations of social duty. Jane Eyre finds a way to mediate between the passion of Rochester and the strict self-denials of St. John by transforming her final relationship to Rochester into one of both sexual love and self-sacrificing devotion. Hardy's Gabriel Oak is one of the clearest instances of a Victorian hero who socializes passionate love—Bathsheeba's—by containing it within an ethical commitment so strong he is even prepared to forego such love. The point is simply that Dickens' tenuous solutions, though they manipulate dialectically opposed values into seemingly unique and nonrepeatable harmonies, reflect a widespread Victorian attitude toward the possibility of resolving the authenticating release of eroticism within an ethical, conservative community. The fictional adjustments of expenditure and restraint these novels represent are not self-contained fictions; they indicate a specific attitude toward the possibilities of social action.

At the end of *Great Expectations*, however, Dickens reminds us that the gap between expenditure and restraint is never completely healed; the loneliness of Pip's displacement through gift-giving is the final condition that makes his renewed love for Estella seem a forgivable consolation. And Pip's loneliness parallels Estella's own ruined status as a love object, a force for communion, that is, the ending never completely absolves Estella of her banishment from the world of innocence. While she may relieve some of Pip's loneliness, Estella's presence stresses the gap between her world and Biddy and Joe's. The two worlds—the one representing expenditure now linked

to passive self-sacrifice; the other representing a more conservative, more socialized community of love—remain adjacent; they
are never fully integrated. While Pip's final love for Estella and
his rejustified gift-giving insist on the necessity of realizing satisfaction through actions that dissolve the self in the expenditure of giving and of love rather than resting in a program of
simple resignation, and in the static meaning of "self-acceptance," for that very reason, sadly, these actions can accommodate Pip in only the most fragile and symbolic of ways to the
more tender, deferential, sheltering world of restrained self-
knowledge—Biddy and Joe's world—that activity necessarily
overcomes.

V

All of Dickens' novels in some way manipulate the symbolic
value attached to potentially transgressive actions, eventually
permitting an expenditure that had been blocked. But besides
the kinds of conservative adjustment to desire mentioned in
connection with *Great Expectations*, there is another, crucially
important ingredient in this shift: the hero's contact with death,
which helps purge the hero symbolically of the merely personal
in his or her desires. Pip's new-found humility, for example, is
partly signaled by his near-fatal sickness. In his delirium, Pip
tells us that he "confounded impossible existences with my own
identity; that I was a brick in the house wall, and yet entreating
to be released from the giddy place where the builders had set
me; that I was a steel beam of a vast engine, clashing and whirling over a gulf, and yet that I implored in my own person to
have the engine stopped, and my part in it hammered off" (57).
This extreme suffering, along with his expression of desires for
self-negation, helps purify Pip of any selfish intent when he
emerges on the other side of this crisis—on the other side of
death—and it helps make his love for Estella seem more disinterested than it had been before. The mere suggestion of death

as a new atmosphere associated with Pip's narrative purifies his motives. But that suggestion is nonetheless important; Esther's near-fatal sickness in *Bleak House* functions in a similarly important way for her, helping (if only by blighting her face and thus depriving her of value as a romantic object) to make her love for Woodcourt seem anything but opportunistic.

Many of Dickens' novels use his characters' openness to death in similar ways. In *Our Mutual Friend*, for example, both John Harmon and Eugene Wrayburn seek liberation from the imprisoning roles dictated by their stations in life, and in both cases near-drowning prevents such liberation from taking on an assertive quality. Harmon improves on his near-death by effacing himself in the role of John Rokesmith and actually putting that self-effacement to work for him as an instrument of freedom; Wrayburn's brush with death transforms him in the reader's eyes into a victim rather than a moodily arrogant cynic, and it prepares the reader to see his marriage to Lizzie as a debt he owes her for saving his life rather than as his taking advantage of a defenseless pauper. In a more complicated way, *Dombey and Son* symbolically sanctifies Florence and Walter's marriage through a form of self-effacement that the novel previously identified with death: banishment to a life at sea. When Carker mercilessly accuses Captain Cuttle of self-interest for having hoped that Walter might be intended for Florence, we might at first side with the childlike Cuttle. "You belong to an artful and audacious set of people," Carker tells the captain unreasonably, "You hatch nice little plots, and hold nice little councils, and make nice little appointments, and receive nice little visitors, too, Captain, hey?" (32). But Walter's fairy-tale dreams of marrying a girl like Florence are nevertheless potentially aggressive, so much so that Walter must repeatedly check himself early in the novel from giving way too completely to his fantasies; on his return, moreover, Walter is very careful to claim no right to Florence. The danger Walter threatens is actually similar to that threatened by Carker; he aspires to steal away one of Dombey's women. What Walter must do, then, is turn his land fairy tale—the tale of Dick Whittington his Uncle Sol and Captain Cuttle have nourished him on, the dream of property— into a sea fairy tale, one that cannot but remind us of Paul's vision of death in the waves and Walter's earlier shipwreck. By following in Paul's footsteps, toward dissolution into the sea, Walter seems less intent on claiming Florence for himself than he is on returning her to her mother and brother, who wait beyond the waves.

These novels demonstrate how death can be an important symbolic term legitimizing final acts of release. In a number of Dickens' novels, however, the role of death in the ending is much stronger. Rather than using death simply as a signal of selflessness that permits kinds of release that might otherwise seem aggressive and self-interested, Dickens often makes death itself the action permitted by his endings. Even the melancholy ending of *Great Expectations*, in fact, points to a deeper kind of satisfaction possible in some of Dickens' endings, a kind of satisfaction that thrives more completely on the element of loss in expenditure rather than on the discovery of new objects for love. To examine how Dickens symbolically alters the context of profound loss to affirm it in his endings through death, we should turn to that novel that ends most violently.

A Tale of Two Cities is the clearest instance in all of Dickens' work of the connection between a permitted, concluding action and the radical expenditure of death. In its ending, *A Tale of Two Cities* purifies general needs for a victory over repression, which the novel embodies as a desire for violence. The revolutionaries' problematical desires for freedom are translated into acceptable terms by the good characters in their own struggles for freedom, and they are focused finally in the pure self-violence of Sydney Carton, which liberates him from self-hatred. In an abstract sense, what this means finally is that the novel's symbolic logic affirms Carton's initial tendencies toward an internal kind of violence—his dissipation—under the guise of his later, moral conversion.

Before we turn to Carton's role, however, we should note

Endings # Endings   169

that the very texture of Dickens' novel is dominated by a non-specific, primary desire for a radical release from limits. The famous opening paragraphs of the novel launch this movement toward release, articulating frustrated desires for extremity by parodying the desire of the historical imagination to erupt beyond the limits of conventional significance. Mixing the historian's typical desire to claim the extremity of his own elected period with undermining hints about the fundamental sameness of all ages, Dickens' much-quoted, much-sentimentalized opening catalogues the extremes of 1775 in a series of superlatives that cancel each other out. "It was the best of times, it was the worst of times, it was the age of wisdom, it was the age of foolishness, it was the epoch of belief, it was the epoch of incredulity" (1.1). Despite themselves, these terms fail to produce a difference in meaning; instead, each term merely tends to produce its opposite and to be bounded by it.[27] In this way, the opening catalogue of extremes comments more on the needs of the historical imagination—and on those of the novelist—than on the actual tenor of any particular age. It emphasizes desires for extremity at the same time that it frustrates them. As he levels extremes, the narrator even claims that his own chosen epoch is not actually different from the present one—giving greater emphasis to his debunking satire—but that in short, "the period was so far like the present period, that some of its noisiest authorities insisted on its being received, for good or for evil, in the superlative degree of comparison only." Far from being extreme, the age is actually in the grip of a repetitive sameness in its very desire to be excessive, a desire which is trapped in conventional, competitive self-aggrandizements. And, on the level of political reality, the weighty repetition of desires for extremity is undisguised. "In both countries it was clearer than crystal to the lords of the State preserves of loaves and fishes, that things in general were settled for ever." Covertly, the belief that some kind of extremity has been reached becomes only the basis for dominance, as well as for repetition.

The pathetic desire for extremity within history introduces

more successful desires for upheaval on the part of characters. In the beginning, for example, Sydney Carton's dissipation is presented as the result of a metaphysical crisis over limitations and not as the vulgarity of the idle bum; Carton feels imprisoned by the banality of economic survival. Referring to himself as a "drudge," Carton, through his indifferently valued but very real skills and through his ostentatious rejection of preferment, deliberately affronts the acquisitive business world of Stryver. With sardonic pride, Carton flaunts his lack of economic sense. "Bless you, *I* have no business" (2.4), he tells Lorry. In keeping with this violation of the code of self-interest, Carton had always instinctively done work for others rather than for himself in school; professionally, he does all his work so that Stryver, and not himself, may claim the credit and prosper. Carton's utter intellectual competence to lead a successful, if ordinary, life gives point to his rejection of self-concern and defines it as a choice, however unconscious he may be of his own motives and however much such a choice is painful, bringing along with it the anonymity of self-abandonment. And, if Stryver and Lorry are examples of what success means, then Carton's comparative genuineness—his freedom from both aggression and repression—depends on his refusal to value worldly success. It is interesting to note, too, that Jerry Cruncher later stresses the unreality of the business world by claiming that much normal business represses the final reality of death; defending his grave-robbing to Lorry on the grounds that the business world depends on death, Cruncher observes, "There might be medical doctors at the present hour, a picking up their guineas where a honest tradesman don't pick up his fardens. . . . [H]ow can you rightly have one without t'other? Then, wot with undertakers, and wot with parish clerks, and what with sextons, and what with private watchmen (all avaricious and all in it), a man wouldn't get much by it, even if it was so" (3.9). In the context of the novel's sense that the business world is artificial and that it actively conceals the profounder reality of death, Carton's dissipation is a rejection of the world of petty survival on the broadest of philosophical grounds.

Despite the disapproval of other characters, and despite our own sense that Carton's dissipation is not right morally, we may find Carton's carelessness and his reckless honesty refreshing. Carton's dissipation is somehow pure precisely because it is free of self-interest. From the very beginning, Dickens forces the reader to discriminate between the popular judgment about Carton's degeneracy and the possibility of his possessing hidden merits, often by putting his condemnations of Carton into the wrong mouths. It is the ugly mob, feasting like flies on Darnay's trial, that finds Carton's appearance disreputable, and it is Jerry Cruncher, after his vulgarity has been established, who observes, "I'd hold half a guinea that *he* don't get no law-work to do. Don't look like the sort of one to get any, do he?" (2.3). But Carton's superiority to the crowd very soon emerges in the form of his intensified powers of perception. "Yet, this Mr. Carton took in more of the details of the scene than he appeared to take in; for now, when Miss Manette's head dropped upon her father's breast, he was the first to see it, and to say audibly: 'Officer! look to that young lady. Help the gentleman to take her out. Don't you see she will fall!'" The mark of Carton's genius is this very ability to penetrate to the most important, the most essential levels—to see beyond the limited vision of others, or to say what others dare not say. In other words, Carton appeals to us through his freedom from convention and from constraint. Thus, his success at Darnay's trial is a single, bold, imaginative stroke, one that Stryver calls "a rare point" (2.5). His facility for "extracting the essence from a heap of statements" shows to advantage against Stryver's plodding determination, and his frankness shines out against Mr. Lorry's restraint—at Lorry's expense, Carton observes, "If you knew what a conflict goes on in the business mind, when the business mind is divided between good-natured impulse and business appearances, you would be amused, Mr. Darnay" (2.4). Lorry's exasperated reply defines the difference between himself and Carton explicitly. "Business is a very good thing, and a very respectable thing. And, sir, if business imposes its restraints and its silences and impediments, Mr. Darnay as a young gentleman of generosity knows how to make allowances for that circumstance." But to confirm the imposing dimensions of Carton's position, the narrator tells us that Lorry was "perhaps a little angry with himself, as well as with the barrister." In contrast, then, to the other good characters, whose lives are ruled by restraints of one kind or another, and despite our sense that we must disapprove of him, Carton stands out as the most vividly authentic character in the novel. Even in the love plot, Carton confides in Lucie more honestly than the others. Darnay conceals from Lucie his intended trip to France, and Manette tries to conceal from her his instinctual jealousy of Darnay. In the reader's eyes, Carton momentarily has a more intimate relationship with Lucie than either Darnay or Manette, for the reader sees Carton "open his heart" to her in the pivotal confession scene, the only scene in which a man expresses himself passionately to Lucie.

More importantly, Carton's desire to release himself from constraints in dissipation, however much it is treated with repugnance by the good characters, is in fact not so far removed from their own desires, which, by contrast, remain frustrated. Darnay, who flees his own terrestrial scheme—France—is opposed to his uncle the Marquis in much the same way that Carton is opposed to Stryver (Stryver and the Marquis are linked later in the novel, when the lawyer gathers among the disinherited French aristocracy at Tellson's and joins in their contempt for the French rebels and for the anonymous son of the Marquis). From the perspective of French aristocratic values, Darnay's teaching school in England is an unmentionable degradation, one that is essentially as demeaning as Carton's lack of professionalism in England. And Darnay is eventually punished for this very desertion of France, a punishment that implies allegorically—since it is difficult for us to understand how running from a French inheritance could be a crime—that there is some kind of moral transgression implicit in any release from normal human bonds. For Dr. Manette, too, release from prison is figured as a release from restrictive labor, which is represented by his obsessive shoe-making. His return home, which could conceivably be perceived as a triumph of simple concerns for survival, is emphasized imagistically as a release from the conservative claims of survival largely because it frees him from the evasive narrowness of mind represented by his prison work-world. Though no longer functional, this work-world is an image of Dr. Manette's repression—his willingness to put on blinders and merely to endure, like all oblivious workmen. In its rigidly economic resonance, Manette's cobbling echoes Lorry's business-imposed restraint. However, the shadowy, disquieting destruction of Manette's workbench by Lorry and Miss Pross points to the guilt that inheres in the structure of such release; their destructive act is oddly congruent with the revolutionary destruction of the French mob. Darnay and Manette, like Sydney Carton, sin against an obscure moral law when they seek release from their respective imprisonments, no matter how much their freedom is approved by the reader.

Our ambivalent attitude toward Carton, then, is only an index of the generally problematic structure of violated limits. By being political, generational, sexual, and vaguely misanthropic, desires for release in this novel acquire a kind of generality that transcends their local manifestations; such desires seem fundamentally human and, at the same time, ultimately threatening. The novel makes clear that, while a desire for the destruction of psychological and social limitations may be profoundly human, it is always related to a desire for the destruction of restrictive personal identity in violence and in death.

As a way to approach the complex relationship between release from restrictions and death, we should note that the confluence of desires for violent release with potential transgressions implied by such release dominates the background action. On the one hand, in the initial stages of the revolution in France, it is difficult not to sympathize with the laboring class's pursuit of freedom through violence. Occasionally, Dickens dwells on the mob's achievement of "human fellowship" through their uprising and stresses the sympathetic unity of the oppressed people.

Not before dark night did the men and women come back to the children, wailing and breadless. Then, the miserable bakers' shops were beset by long files of them, patiently waiting to buy bad bread, and while they waited with stomachs faint and empty, they beguiled the time by embracing one another on the triumphs of the day, and achieving them again in gossip. Gradually, these strings of ragged people shortened and frayed away; and then poor lights began to shine in high windows, and slender fires were made in the streets, at which neighbors cooked in common, afterwards supping at their doors. (2.22)

Then, too, the bursting wine cask scene, which mingles the sympathetic energy of a well-deserved holiday with ominous hints about the ultimate form of excessive holiday energy—the desire for blood, a word that Gaspard writes ominously into the wall in wine—also has the effect of linking the mob's exuberant expenditure of energy with Carton's drunkenness, as does the code name of the insurgents, the Jacques, link them with Carton and his sobriquet, the Jackal. And at this point, early in the novel, both forms of energy—Carton's sottishness and the mob's—seem harmless and infinitely preferable to the alternative world of work that lies before both of them. Like Carton's, too, the insurgents' drives for extremity have a metaphysical cast—though they do not deliberately articulate it—in their collective willingness to risk life for something more valuable even than life: undefined, limitless freedom. The excessiveness of this risk of life, the way in which it breaks the mob loose from the repressive world of work, accounts for the ensuing eroticism—the mob's discovery that outside of the limits of self-concern is an idyllic world of plenitude and union. "Fathers and mothers who had had their full share in the worst of the day, played gently with their meagre children; and lovers, with such a world around them and before them, loved and hoped" (2.22). Something of this plenitude of sexual arousal is also conveyed by the "Carmagnole," the dance of the rebels, which combines excessive violence with a polymorphous, eroticized fellow-feeling.

Men and women danced together, women danced together, men danced together, as hazard had brought them together. At first, they were a mere storm of coarse red caps and coarse woolen rags; but, as they filled the place, and stopped to dance about Lucie, some ghastly apparition of a dance-figure gone raving mad arose among them. They advanced, retreated, struck at one another's hands, clutched at one another's heads, spun round alone, caught one another and spun round in pairs, until many of them dropped. (3.5)

On the other hand, of course, the meaning of rebellion in France soon sours. Our reaction to the "Carmagnole" cannot be the same as our reaction to the crowd that had dammed up flowing wine in the cobblestones. The scenes of violence are carefully built up to repel us gradually, and it is difficult to specify at what particular point we lose sympathy with the rebels. But it soon becomes clear that the mob's struggle for justice is totally outstripped by its brute satisfaction in the violence of dominance. Hence, although the mob's struggle has its roots in oppression and therefore takes our sympathy, the novel jolts us into a recognition of the form taken by the mob's desire for liberation—its inevitable tendency to congeal in cruelty and to project what was once a pure, disinterested violence outward against others. So, too, our original dissatisfaction with Carton derives partly from his projection of his bitterness outward against others.

However, while naked drives toward expenditure are repudiated through the mob, we have already seen how repression taints the efforts of the good characters to suppress their own violence. This enforced restraint makes for an almost bleak, numbed atmosphere of good will among the group of heroes, instead of the generous flow of spirits necessary to Dickens' vision of a closely knit, good society in his other novels. The atmosphere of repression in the good characters' world is one reason for the notorious want of humor in this novel, and it also echoes the narrator's complaint, in the beginning of the novel, against the isolation of the individual within the narrow limits of personal identity. "A wonderful fact to reflect upon, that every human creature is constituted to be that profound secret and mystery to every other. . . . Something of the awfulness, even of Death itself, is referable to this" (1.3). The "golden thread" foursome, though it obviously has Dickens' sympathy, participates in this gloomy fact of secrecy and repression. However sobering violence may be, then, Dickens is ultimately on the side of change, and on the side of excess. The tone of the novel, as well as the awkward tension created by the proliferation of lovers of Lucie, speeds the novel toward some kind of rupture. And it is finally through Sydney Carton that Dickens shifts the valuation of expenditure and dramatizes, if not a solution to the problem of human relationships, then an emotional release from that problem which occurs, for both characters and readers, on the level of experience. Through the concluding action, Carton continues and concludes logically his career of dissipation in death, thus fulfilling the novel's ever-present drive toward extremity.

While Carton's self-sacrificial final expenditure is more radical in an aggressive sense, it is also paradoxically more pure than his earlier dissipation. By losing his life, Carton annihilates in himself all self-interest and cruelty. At the same time, his martyrdom is moral because it has a conservative purpose, the salvation of others. This moral purpose absolves him of the transgression of suicide. As an action, then, Carton's death is the only expenditure or displacement in the novel that can claim the readers' unqualified assent, since even actions like Dr. Manette's liberation from jail or Darnay's liberation from his English trial immediately cause new, unavoidable problems of rivalry. Carton's death blends perfectly, almost ritualistically, the two adjacent values of loss and survival, realizing through narrative an impossible wish. Like Miss Pross, who changes the meaning of murder by losing her own hearing (as if in penance) and by saving the rest of the good characters when she kills Madame Defarge, Sydney Carton, by choosing death, changes the meaning of self-destruction. He carries out his earlier desires for dissipation free from the abyss of meaninglessness implied by such annihilation. His death is sanctified through its ability to preserve the Darnay family. And finally, Carton helps to elevate the

reader's fascination with expenditure; rather than watching his
death pruriently as the vulgar mob had watched Darnay's trial,
we share in the condemned woman's religious awe.

vi

Dickens' use of death at the climax of his novels as an event that
can reconcile, by symbolic adjustment, extreme expenditure
with the conservative harmonies of a social group is not an un-
usual solution to such problems. Though it reflects a delicate,
perhaps impossible balance, Dickens' symbolic socialization of desires for death reflects an important Victorian perception about
culture, and a Victorian desire to found culture on the contradictory—but creative—claims of death and violence. Like Dickens
in A Tale of Two Cities, the Victorians generally sought to bring
culture into a close, highly ritualized relationship to death. The
Victorians made the etiquette of mourning and burial into an
elaborate catechism. They invented the public—as opposed to
the church—cemetery, mourning stores, and burial clubs; they
staged theatrical public funerals, often graced with mutes and
glass hearses, that reached an apotheosis in that sublime grotesquerie, the Duke of Wellington's funeral, which brought a
million and a half mourners from all over England to London.
And the Victorians cherished the arts of spiritualism that claimed
to make contact with the dead—hypnotism, mesmerism, clair-
voyance. They consciously made death the most important
event of an individual lifetime. Old Sally in Oliver Twist is an
accurate portrait of the poorhouse pauper who saved up money
for a good funeral.[28] All this enthusiasm might be considered
purely an interest in social display, a means for the middle class
to prove both wealth and gentility, were it not for the spilling
over of the phenomenon into literary taste. The popularity of
Victorian works often rode on the immediacy of their presentation of death. The tremendous appeal of Dickens' deathbed
scenes is paralleled most significantly by Tennyson's catapult to

fame with *In Memoriam*, by the success of Andersen's morbid tales, and less directly by the Victorians' love of genres like melodrama, the detective story, and crime literature, all of which revolve in some way around death. The Victorians' inability to recognize this obsession with death in themselves suggests its compelling character; a writer like Dickens could satirize funereal posturing at the same time that he appealed to funereal emotion.

Statistics documenting foul urban conditions and a high early death rate have tended to make us see this Victorian preoccupation as either a concession to or a defense (through sentimentality) against grim fact. Often, too, the Victorian fascination with death is seen simply as a vehicle for stylized postromantic indulgences in emotion.[29] But the Victorians threw themselves into their love of death with a specificity of emotion (weddings were not nearly so important[30]) that signals some greater significance. It would be more accurate to say that, because conventions of social display, the physical immediacy of death, and romantic literary influences all helped lift normal taboos against death-related interest, the Victorians could actually relish death for its own sake. The Victorians were able to value, as an initiation into a kind of transcendent genuineness, their contact with the abyss of negativity represented by death and they were able to express this genuineness in a way that was more than just culturally acceptable. Because of its transcendent dimensions, death imaginatively legitimated society for the Victorians, insofar as society recognized death as its originating event. In this sense, the Victorians affirmed death. They affirmed it, not as passivity, withdrawal, or repose, but as transcendent violence, as the final rupturing and negating of restrictive, inauthentic human limits. The Victorians sanctioned this negation by grounding it in culture, making culture, in turn, transcendent through its reverence for death.

Seen in this context, Dickens' symbolic adjustment of death and social harmony in certain of his endings is not merely an aesthetic one; it echoes an intention toward culture that the Victorians attempted to actualize in a number of ways. *The Old*

Curiosity Shop, which sent most of literate England into mourning, is perhaps the greatest instance of the social dynamics of the Victorian preoccupation with death. In fact, Little Nell became more than just a fictional character; she was a Victorian sacrament, in large part because through her Dickens manages to associate death with transcendent violation and to affirm them both in social terms. That is to say, in a novel like *The Old Curiosity Shop* Dickens demonstrates that, rather than merely defending us against death, society provides a necessary way for us to internalize and to live the experience of death, while at the same time it mediates death's horrors. This project is fundamental to all of Dickens' novels, but the dependence of society on death is clearest here, perhaps because *The Old Curiosity Shop* seems to have been Dickens' most complete personal expression of grief. There is a clear symbolic movement in the novel culminating in Nell's death that ultimately produces an unconventional, affirmative significance in the violation represented by death.

Before we examine this symbolic logic, though, we should note that in Dickens' early novels, major action is frequently displaced outside of character, which makes it more difficult to draw connections between inhibited action and successful action. At the same time, however, the resultant diffusion of motive permits a subtler gratification of desires for death than was possible for Dickens in a novel like *A Tale of Two Cities*. By gratifying Sidney Carton's explicitly stated desires for dissolution, Dickens presents a fulfillment that is perhaps too neat. A persistent criticism of the novel, in fact, has it that Carton's sacrifice is trivialized because he has nothing to live for.[31] The problem is simply that a conjunction of desires for actual death and commitments to conservation is a balance too delicate to be projected in a single character. In other novels, however, particularly the early ones, Dickens is able to synthesize these opposing drives in a more satisfying way since problems of energy and restraint are diffused on a broad plane in the early novels, not focused in direct conflicts.

In *Barnaby Rudge*, for example, the problem of rebellion is never ambiguous for any one collection of characters. Instead, the revolting mob goes berserk in the absence of the two heroes, who are themselves both potentially rebels against fathers in their desires for freedom and for love. Because they oppose the excessiveness of the mob's violence against those same fathers, though, the heroes' return—their own transgressive aspirations still intact—is perceived by the fathers as a restoration rather than as further rebellion. The heroes' desires to overturn obstacles are thus fulfilled under the aegis of conservation. Similarly, *Oliver Twist* fulfills Oliver's rebellion, but only by shifting the object of his rebellion away from the workhouse and toward Fagin's gang of thieves. Thus, Oliver overcomes his oppressors, but only by retiring to the sheltered life of the countryside, while the violence inherent in social rebellion is diverted to Fagin and Sikes. Even in a later novel like *Hard Times*, the dialectic of excess and restraint is resolved outside of any single character. Those who rebel against social repression or the Gradgrind philosophy—Louisa, Tom, and Stephen Blackpool, whom Dickens cannot forgive for desiring his wife's death and for loving Rachel—are crushed; a successful liberation of energies is achieved only in a dissociated way by Sleary's circus, which has no apparent connection to the restrictions other characters labor against. The circus even manages to reconcile excess and restraint by devising a "lawful" escape for Tom Gradgrind, but the force of this transgression is diminished by Sleary's lack of personal interest in Tom, who is disowned as a mere thief.

Because the connections between similar kinds of action must be drawn across characters, or groups of characters, or clusters of events, a discussion of endings in the early novels must take into account these broader symbolic patterns. In *The Old Curiosity Shop*, the inhibited action carried out by the ending is, quite simply, the death of Nell. Inhibition is not focused in Nell; rather, it is the normal world—our world and the world of Kit, Dick, and the single gentleman—that collectively and instinctively resists death. Still, the possibility of affirming Nell's death is the very goal of *The Old Curiosity Shop*, one that necessitates a gradual transformation of our attitude toward death. When it is considered in its broadest symbolic dimensions, the threat of Nell's death—as the pun in her name implies—is not a separate element, a tear-jerking addition to the plot; it is at the core of the novel and it is developed symbolically in a way that courts our united approval.

The initial problem in *The Old Curiosity Shop* is, quite simply, death's gruesome aspect. At first, it is the mechanical regularity of death that is disturbing. Nell looks out her window and periodically sees "a man passing with a coffin on his back, and two or three others silently following him to a house where somebody lay dead" (9); Master Humphrey imagines noises from the "stream of life" falling on the ears of a man "condemned to lie, dead but conscious, in a noisy churchyard" (1); and the city is described as having "one dead uniform repose" (15). The novel abounds in similar images, which make death a grim reality that seems merely to confirm the unimportance and the futility of human lives buried in the struggle for economic survival. Early in the novel, there seems to be no difference between the restrictive sterility of life and that of death.

But, in *The Old Curiosity Shop*, it is that very sense of restrictiveness—in both life and death—that creates the pressure to violate the limits of normal, enduring selfhood. Despite the initial negativity of death, the claustrophobia induced by teeming, sheerly biological life creates an even more overwhelming atmosphere of suffocation in this novel. That claustrophobic feeling makes the much-discussed polarity of country and city less important to the thematic structure of the novel than the corresponding, subsuming polarity of freedom and work. For instance, at various points in their travels, Nell and her grandfather stop to contemplate the monotonous urban squalor of commerce and business, of people earning their livings. At dawn in London, they see the shattering of the city's nocturnal "repose."

Some straggling carts and coaches rumbling by, first broke the charm, then others came, then others yet more active, then a crowd. The wonder was, at first, to see a tradesman's window open, but it was a rare thing soon to see one closed; then, smoke rose slowly from the chimneys, and sashes were thrown up to let in air, and doors were opened, and servant girls, looking lazily in all directions but their brooms, scattered brown clouds of dust into the eyes of shrinking passengers, or listened disconsolately to milkmen who spoke of country fairs. (15)

Nell and her grandfather do not feel free until they have left these scenes behind. Later, when Nell takes her grandfather away from Mrs. Jarley's, they enter a small town, and Nell observes the working inhabitants in restrictive, self-involved terms.

Some frowned, some smiled, some muttered to themselves, some made slight gestures, as if anticipating the conversation in which they would shortly be engaged, some wore the cunning look of bargaining and plotting, some were anxious and eager, some slow and dull; in some countenances were written gain; in others loss. . . . In the public walks and lounges of a town, people go to see and be seen, and there the same expression, with little variety, is repeated a hundred times. The working-day faces come nearer to the truth, and let it out more plainly. (44)

What is disturbing in these scenes, and in others like them, is not simply the poverty; Nell's grandfather at one point even calls the great financial quarter of London a region of "ruin and self-murder" (15). What is disturbing is the claustrophobic sense we have of human energy buried in work or in the narrow maintenance of trivialized life. It is no coincidence that, although he championed work as a moral value, Dickens seldom celebrated it as an experience. His heroes and heroines—like all Victorian heroes and heroines who share the middle-class dream of a competence—are ultimately granted economic freedom and what Alexander Welsh calls a "radiant idleness."[32] Interestingly, a dichotomy between freedom and work is explicitly made the basis of class distinction by Miss Monflathers, who plays Dr. Watts' children's songs off against the *Alice in Wonderland* parody, claiming that genteel children find satisfaction "In books, or work, or healthful play" but that the poor can only be satisfied "In work, work, work" (31). We feel both the hypocrisy and the oppression of Miss Monflathers' reproach to Nell: "Don't you know that the harder you are at work, the happier you are?" No wonder, then, with the reality of work and economic survival pressing in from all sides, that "restlessness" is the "dominant sensation" Philip Rogers finds in this novel.[33]

The meagerness of economic survival is summed up best in Nell's grandfather; the greatest evil Nell flees is not Quilp but her grandfather's dream of making her a lady. This project, which in some sense is meant to satirize the roots of social ambition, is clearly a neurotic defense against the contingency of death. Nell's grandfather is also linked with economic conservation in the way he attempts to deny death through his business; in his old shop he hoards wasted fragments of culture, from which he hopes to piece together cultural protection. Not only the shop but also the old man's fascination with money itself and his feverish addiction to gambling are expressions of a wish that his will might be fused with the will of a larger destiny that will protect Nell from death. It is clear that we are meant to feel that Nell must be released from her grandfather's world, which is rigidly economic both in its concern for money and in its larger attempt to eliminate loss. Consequently, before they leave London Nell tells her grandfather, "Let us walk through country places, and sleep in fields and under trees, and never think of money again" (9). And later she pleads, "Let me persuade you . . . to think no more of gains or losses, and to try no fortune but the fortune we pursue together" (31).

It is crucial to recognize that only in its freedom from economic constriction is the countryside celebrated in this novel. Work in the uncorrupted countryside figures through the schoolmaster, who is free to walk about country roads lost in the pages of a book, and through various forms of socialized play—by circus performers, by the races, and by Mrs. Jarley's waxworks show, where Nell is employed at work that is "light and genteel" (27). Significantly, too, Mrs. Jarley, though less pretentious than

Miss Monflathers, emphasizes her distance from the work world; when Nell asks Mrs. Jarley how far the nearest town is, "The reply—which the stout lady did not come to, until she had thoroughly explained that she went to the races on the first day in a gig, and as an expedition of pleasure, and that her presence there had no connexion with any matters of business or profit— was, that the town was eight miles off" (26). In the countryside, the very idea of work dissolves before the invitations of nature; "even the bees were diving deep down into the cups of flowers and stopping there, as if they had made up their minds to retire from business and be manufacturers of honey no more" (25). So it is, too, that the countryside is destroyed in this novel by the "strange engines" of industry, which bury the vital energies of nature under oppressive forms of work. The sentimentalized opposition of nature and culture in *Oliver Twist*, a sentimentality that Dickens was later to satirize brutally through Mrs. Skewton and Harold Skimpole, is reconceived in this novel as an economic opposition.

But Dickens is not so puerile as to conclude that the liberating alternative to work in the world of *The Old Curiosity Shop* is idleness. Swiveller, who is idle, may be more humane than other characters, but his idleness is at first self-serving.[34] For instance, Dickens tells us explicitly that Swiveller's "high opinion of his own merits" (23) prevents him from recognizing the cruelty in his projected marriage to Nell. As long as freedom from work leaves the boundaries of the self intact, it is a restrictive freedom. Monflathers and her self-serving, elitist ideology amply prove this principle. It is not work per se that Dickens hates but the restricted condition of mind that it represents.

What Dickens does, then, is to give an affirmative meaning to death by dramatizing death as the deeply felt loss of something that has a commonly recognized value. The principle is a key one; loss fascinates us only when what is lost somehow matters. Perceived in this way, death becomes a surrender that, for all its terror, is profoundly more real, more pointed, more authentic than (and ontologically prior to) what we most wish to conserve in life. More important, as I shall argue later, the violation of death, by virtue of its contrast with the conservative, inviolate image of purity, becomes erotic and therefore desirable. Through Nell, Dickens makes death present as a vivid, painful event, not as a confirmation of meaninglessness or as a philosophical abstraction.

The narrative forces working toward a conjunction of value and its loss in Nell bear closer study, especially because critics who look at Nell in isolation from the pressure of the narrative find her curiously bland and cannot understand why her death should occasion any grief. Dickens' novel affected readers as it did because, whatever Nell's virtues, her existence is inseparable from the idea of its loss. It is impossible to conceive of an unthreatened Nell. Our earliest glimpses of her, in fact, are repeatedly cast in terms of her vulnerability. For example, in the opening scene, when Master Humphrey sees Nell wandering the streets, he ponders all the potential dangers to the "scantily attired" child. It is significant that his first words to her, when Nell asks him to show her the way home, are a perfectly gratuitous threat. "And what made you ask it of me? Suppose I should tell you wrong?" Master Humphrey then tells us that what strikes him about Nell—what makes her seem virtuous— is that she confides in him, a stranger, with total trust. In scenes like this, much of Nell's virtue is intended only to exacerbate her vulnerability. It is not the personality of Nell that compels interest, it is the conjunction of violence and purity within her as a character.

Master Humphrey's jesting threat is only the first in a series of threats posed by benefactors. In the opening scene, Nell is on a mission that "was a great secret—a secret which she does not even know, herself." When Master Humphrey asks her, "Who has sent you so far by yourself?" she replies, "Somebody who is very kind to me." But this secret, we find out later, is the secret of her grandfather's gambling affairs, which are the greatest of threats to them both. In this very first scene, then, Nell unknowingly carries about with her the seeds of her own destruction in the form of her protector's efforts to save her. The image of the parental, sheltering figure as a veiled threat appears throughout the book—not only in the grandfather, who robs Nell in a nighttime scene that has the emotional impact of rape, but also in her brother, Fred, who nearly pimps her to a drunk; in Codlin and Short, who, while protesting their friendship, want to turn Nell in for a reward; and even in Mrs. Quilp, who poses as a friend when forced to extract information from Nell for Quilp. Given this complex of benefactors-as-threat, it is no accident that Nell is pursued by both her friends and her enemies and that she can be freed from one group only by being freed from the other—in death. Indeed, the good characters are made to feel at one point that, because of Quilp's proximity, their own interest in Nell is a threat to her.

It is enlightening to note that Dickens remembered "Little Red Riding Hood" as his favorite childhood fairy tale and admitted that he had always wanted to marry Little Red Riding Hood when he grew up.[35] The image of the wolf in grandmother's bedclothes threatening innocent beauty is the same benefactor-as-threat image that dominates *The Old Curiosity Shop* and, as Dickens' childhood wish shows, the image is fundamentally erotic. The experience of release from limitations through death is concentrated on the erotic edge formed by Nell's trust and her imminent violation. Trust, like beauty, increases the value and insists on the wholeness and purity of what is threatened. The benefactor-as-threat image works to produce this erotic seam between trust and violation and to create in our conception of Nell a constant, vivid, erotically desired awareness of violation and loss. Most descriptions of eroticism focus on the role played by such radical contrasts. Bataille, for example, has written that the beauty-and-the-beast motif in literature is never a feature merely of interest in innocence; rather, the conjunction of purity and monstrosity gives point to the brutality of the degradation, making it a more intense violation.[36] Roland Barthes writes, "Neither culture nor its destruction is erotic; it is the seam between them, the fault, the flaw, which becomes so."[37]

It would be inappropriate to claim that our interest in Nell's violation is purely sexual and that we are all voyeurs at heart.[38] Certainly, the violation of purity and innocence is erotic, but

sexuality is ultimately not so important to this novel as the eroti-
cizing of death. Fundamentally, it is death, not Quilp, that hovers
over Nell. Dickens extends his erotic conjunction of purity and
brutality even to the prose of the death scene itself; repeatedly,
he dwells dreamily on Nell's tranquility only to puncture the portrait with an abrupt "She was dead," and he shifts back and forth,
seemingly without relief, from Nell's beauty to death's finality
(71). Moreover, Dickens' care in preparing the reader for the consummation of Nell's death testifies to the deliberateness of his
staging death as an erotic violation. By recounting Swiveller's
recovery, Kit's rescue, the death of Quilp, the bringing to justice
of the Brasses, and Nell's implied inheritance of the single gentleman's wealth, Dickens prepares his readers for a conservative,
happy ending, eliciting their trust and their desires for wholeness, even against their better knowledge, before he violates
them with Nell's death.[39]

The conjunction of purity and brutality that eroticizes the
reader's experience of imminent violation is also at the heart of
the "idyll" in *The Old Curiosity Shop*. The tension between
value and its loss is what makes the countryside in this novel so
poignant; nature is both precious and self-destructive. The country schoolmaster strides the gulf by valuing study and work,
discipline and economy, yet releasing his students into nature on
a half-holiday. He is upbraided later by the parents for undermining their rural economy, and they punish him by deducting
the holiday from his pay. The same tension is reflected in the
bachelor's remarks on the schoolmaster's students.

"This first boy, schoolmaster," said the bachelor, "is John Owen; a lad
of good parts, sir, and frank, honest temper; but too thoughtless, too
playful, too light-headed by far. That boy, my good sir, would break his
neck with pleasure, and deprive his parents of their chief comfort—
and between ourselves, when you come to see him at hare and hounds,
taking the fence and ditch by the finger-post, and sliding down the face
of the little quarry, you'll never forget it. It's beautiful!" (52)

The risk of death itself accounts for the boy's exuberance, and it
is this quandary between love of risk and love of life that creates

the contradiction in the bachelor's attitude. The edge between the desire to risk and the desire to conserve what is precious— the possibility that absolute loss can cohabit with life—makes *The Old Curiosity Shop* an idyll; that poignance is not merely the product of an atmosphere of "peaceful repose."[40] Only the conjunction of value and loss permits Dickens to evoke in us the sensation of a painful but genuine nakedness before death and, hence, an inarticulable sense of living beyond the limits of the self.

Death may be the only absolute way for Dickens to imagine authenticity, but in *The Old Curiosity Shop* the consciousness of death, and thus the interpenetration of life and death, can be generated in other ways. For instance, by making intense physicality seem a kind of freedom from the slavery of the work world, Dickens transforms our attitude toward bodiliness. Despite Nell's ethereality, which symbolically removes her from association with the physical and with decay, her flight to the more immediately physical country is connected to a general reaffirmation of physicality—physicality as a kind of flirtation with the fact of death. In a book filled with dwarfs and grotesques, with violations of the human body, it is strange that the only repellent characters are Sampson and Sally Brass, the two most socially proper and conservative characters. Physicality actually becomes affirmative in the good characters. Swiveller's playful drunkenness and Kit's cheerful awkwardness—their spontaneous, frank physicality—are refreshing when they are opposed to the cynical business mind of a Chuckster. But what most transforms the image of the physical in the novel is Nell herself. Rather than participating in her own rescue, Nell is on the side of nature; she leads her grandfather away from the city and from rescue into the country. It is her orientation toward nature that permits Nell to view her grotesque companions without revulsion. Her sympathy with the deformed factory worker, with the circus freaks, and with crippled Master Humphrey indicates an ease with physical violation that is often overlooked by critics. This ease helps Nell find the schoolmaster's house "a place to live and learn to die in" (52). Dickens is careful to dissociate Nell's own acquiescence in death from the grotesque, but, partly because she herself is never tainted by monstrosity, our sense of Nell's genuineness comes largely from her willingness to throw off shelter and to confront physical existence in a patient, naked way. The important point about Nell, as a character whose psychological depth expresses a positive impulse, is not that she feels terror or love of death but that her openness to the fact of death contrasts sharply with her grandfather's denial of it.

Considered in this light, Nell and Quilp become parallel characters, rather than opposites. Quilp, too, tries to strip away culture in every way. His principal delight is in forcing others to admit to the discomforts and awkwardnesses of their bodies. He, too, leaves the city and takes up residence in what he calls his "wilderness retreat," although his country house stresses only the other side of nature, refuse and decay. The difference between them is precisely this: Quilp takes on himself the desperate violence that is a potential of physical expenditure. In Quilp, we see violence as self-hatred consistently projected outward in an indiscriminate need to shatter the boundaries of others. In this way, Quilp is Nell's scapegoat, not only in that he absorbs the more brutal aspects of expenditure, but also because he occupies the dangerous territory of a compromise; to avoid the final self-expenditure of death, Quilp directs his violence outward into rivalry. By fleeing both culture, as protection against death, and Quilp, an image of insufficient expenditure, Nell is able to purify complete expenditure for us; we can participate in the eroticism of her loss because it is figured as a salvation as well as a release.

At the same time, too, the context of Nell's death recuperates for us the meaning of her death—its ability to turn the experience of violation into an earthly, conserved kind of union and interpenetration. In the novel itself, not only does Nell's death afford a lesson in accepting, or even celebrating death (she allows her grandfather to relax his apprehensiveness and to follow her humbly to the grave), but the ending also sketches in what

is recovered through Nell's death. Her great-uncle collects all
the people she had known in her travels and "remembers" them,
no doubt materially; Kit makes of her a story—like Dickens'
story—that he uses to educate his own children in the sharing of
loss. In this way, Nell's death, though it fulfills an erotic movement toward death, becomes exactly what death would seem to
strip away; her death is a cultural symbol of sheltering and fraternity. And only through this change in our way of valuing
death can we overcome the novel's initially bleak attitude toward it, which was symptomatic of its larger obsession with the
suffocating restrictiveness of human life.

Despite its relegation to obscurity, *The Old Curiosity Shop*
is perhaps the clearest revelation of a dynamic of permitted loss
that drives many of Dickens' novels. Though *The Old Curiosity
Shop* explores unlimited loss through death, more modest kinds
of loss form the solutions to many of Dickens' endings, which
then seek to realign loss with a sensitized but surviving group.
That socialization of loss accounts for the unstable blend of elegy
and uplift that concludes many late Dickens novels. In *David
Copperfield*, for example, one of the reasons why marrying
Agnes is so attractive a resolution for David is simply that he
has missed her for so long. Dickens emphasizes the importance
of Agnes as an image of loss at the point when, long after Dora's
death, David remembers his early attachment to Agnes. "In my
wayward boyhood, I had thrown away the treasure of her love.
I believe I may have heard some whisper of that distant thought,
in the old unhappy loss or want of something never to be realized,
of which I had been sensible" (58). David further stresses the
element of loss in this recognition by adding, "But the thought
came into my mind as a new reproach and new regret, when I
was left so sad and lonely in the world." By possessing Agnes,
finally, David manages to achieve both a measure of reclamation
and at the same time to possess a woman who reminds him in-
tensely of his earlier wasted opportunities. But Agnes embodies
more kinds of loss than simply David's earlier neglect; David
tells us that "out of [Agnes'] eyes . . . the spirit of my child-wife
looked upon me" (62). Agnes' ability to incarnate David's mourn-

ing for Dora is stressed elegantly when Agnes tells David she had promised Dora that she would "occupy this vacant place." Significantly, too, Agnes consistently manages to remind David of his mother. In all these ways, she succeeds in focusing attention on what has been lost at the same time that she redeems loss through marriage and the prospect of a family for David.

David Copperfield's mnemonic journey is itself a relentless, deliberate evocation of loss that also contains loss within the safety of a reassured, shared, narrative present. David's story even begins with an experience of loss; at his birth, he loses part of himself by way of his caul, the sale of which leaves him "uncomfortable and confused, at a part of myself being disposed of in that way" (1). At birth, too, David's father is already dead, and before the second chapter is over David tells us that his mother will soon die. Yet, the phrasing of this last revelation is important. "Can I say of her face—altered as I have reason to remember it, perished as I know it is—that it is gone, when here it comes before me at this instant, as distinct as any face that I may choose to look on in a crowded street?" David's memory is a way for him to evoke the profound feelings of loss that tie his life to the transcendent authenticity of death at the same time that it permits him to stabilize loss through narrative memory, which attempts to share loss and to make it the basis for a greater intimacy with others. Finally, though, it is the presence of Agnes at the end of the novel that personifies the way David's sense of loss can be shared and therefore freely felt. Thus, at the end of the novel, David turns the nostalgia of repeated loss, which has been painful through much of the book, toward a glorious vision of his own death. "I look back, once more—for the last time" (64), he tells us, and he concludes the final chapter by surrendering his death to the care of Agnes. "Oh Agnes, Oh my soul, so may thy face be by me when I close my life indeed." Agnes functions here for David as a way to contain loss and to make it the basis for new life; "so may I, when realities are melting from me like the shadows which I now dismiss, still find thee near me, pointing upward!"

In a very similar way, the ending of *Little Dorrit* merges

feelings of intense loss with a spirit of blissful union made more
intense through those very feelings of loss. Little Dorrit is Clennam's Agnes; in addition to all his other disappointments in life,
Little Dorrit is someone Clennam has "missed." The reader perceives their inability to admit their love for each other as a
tragic waste, and even the melancholy of Little Dorrit's blasted
life in prison together with Clennam's painful confinement there
at the end seem to blend finally with the two lovers' inability to
realize an opportunity for mutual happiness in love. In a novel
obsessed with the way various kinds of efforts to achieve freedom only proliferate states of imprisonment—William Dorrit's
release from prison, for example, leaves him more powerless and
repressed than he had been in the Marshalsea, and characters
like Miss Wade, Gowan, or Mrs. Clennam, who rebel against various kinds of restriction, are finally restricted by their own desires
for revenge—the only real escape for Clennam and Little Dorrit
lies in cherishing their purifying sense of loss, balanced against
the security that comes of sharing such loss. The novel extends
this tension between their proximity and their simultaneous
willingness to lose each other forever until the very last chapter.
Then, just before they confess their love, Clennam listens to
Little Dorrit read and he feels in a profound way the pangs of
loss through memory; "in the tones of the voice that read to him,
there were memories of an old feeling of such things, and echoes
of every merciful and loving whisper that had ever stolen to him
in his life." And, significantly, only when Little Dorrit tells Clennam that she has lost her entire fortune, along with Fanny's and
William's, does their marriage become possible. "I have nothing
in the world," she tells Clennam and then turns the fact of loss
into the bounty of shared loss: "Are you quite sure you will not
share my fortune with me now?" The double valence of the word
"fortune" stresses this shift; the plenitude of money, once lost,
becomes another, richer kind of plenitude—the fullness of time
and fate. In this way, Clennam's imprisoning sense of loss, which
has oppressed him throughout the novel, is converted into a
kind of loss that can be freely and extravagantly indulged.

These novels never end univocally either in tragedy or in happiness. Instead, they seem to build an atmosphere of hopeful community on the basis of a common experience of suffering. Like *Great Expectations*, they seem poignantly, wistfully poised between profound loss and a recovery of shelter and love. *The Old Curiosity Shop* is ultimately the model for such resolutions, yet because the emotional enormity of Nell's death swamps the small, eccentric society she leaves behind, these later novels seem a more perfect blend. The ambiguous emotional tonality of such endings can be better understood, though, if we see in them the preoccupations of that early novel: the deliberate seeking out of loss as contact with death, lending authenticity to those who survive together in triumphant mourning.

vii

In "A Preliminary Word" to *Household Words*, Dickens claims (in a formula he was pleased with to the extent that he later repeated it in the preface to *Bleak House*) that he wants to "show to all, that in all familiar things, even those which are repellant on the surface, there is Romance enough."[41] What Dickens meant by "Romance," from the countless number of *Household Words* sketches of English industriousness, public and private, would seem to be, quite simply, energy. In his magazines and in his novels, Dickens always evaluates social organizations more than anything else according to how well they circulate human energies. This prominence of romance and energy, of course, cuts right to the heart of the novel, which has never quite succeeded, despite its continual efforts, to distinguish itself from the romance. Ortega, for instance, claims that "although the realistic novel was born in opposition to the so-called novel of fantasy, it carries adventure enclosed within its body."[42] And Ortega's sense of adventure—like Dickens' sense of romance—includes everything that breaks the plane of reality, which is suffocating even to realistic novelists.

More than most novelists, perhaps, Dickens was willing to encounter the novel's inherent potential for romance, energy, and adventure head on. At the root of Dickens' novels is a continual expansion of the dimensions of the perceived world. Dickens' novels clearly intend to open up gaps in the world and in our symbolic apprehension of it that will let vital energies flow. Rather than ending his novels in a moral dictionary of palliatives for specific discontents, then, Dickens, in his endings, realigns the surfaces of human activity with their underlying romance—their basis in acts of expenditure—without hiding the fact that such expenditures are actions, not states or principles, and that the ultimate desire behind acts of expenditure can never be accommodated to definite forms, but demands a totality of loss. Finally, this resolution can be figured by the novelist only through a symbolic adjustment in the way potentially transgressive actions are re-presented as liberations. Yet, as the recurrence in Victorian culture of similar symbolic adjustments shows, Dickens' resolutions are more than just impossible, romantic wishes; they reveal the motives underlying Victorian attitudes toward both the dangers and the possibilities of their culture.

Chapter 6

Mechanical Style

The machinery of my novel is of a species by itself; two contrary motions are introduced into it, and reconciled, which were thought to be at variance with each other. In a word, my work is digressive, and progressive too,—and at the same time. . . . For which reason, from the beginning of this, you see, I have constructed the main work and the adventitious parts of it with intersections, and have so complicated and involved the digressive and progressive movement, one wheel within another, that the whole machine, in general, had been kept a-going.

—Tristram Shandy

Satire is a lesson, parody is a game.

—Vladimir Nabokov

i

In the last chapter, I discussed how Dickens' novels achieve a kind of cooperation between expenditure and restraint outside of the mimetic level, through broadly symbolic movements. In this chapter, I would like to extend the range of that cooperation to certain constant aspects of Dickens' narrative style. Through style, Dickens makes a form of radical release present for the reader, not as a single moment but as an experience repeated endlessly by the writing. Both because of this pervasiveness within the novels and because it is the aspect of Dickens' work that most preserves for us today the synthesis of expenditure and restraint his fiction tries to maintain, Dickens' style is perhaps the most satisfying aspect of his work.

I have no intention of examining all of Dickens' style; my attention will be focused only on a certain, salient quality that can be illuminated by the kind of discussion I have already opened. Even so, many of the issues I shall need to discuss in this chapter—questions of caricature, of irony, of authorial freedom—have been studied before by critics of Dickensian style. But it may prove useful to consider those well-known stylistic issues again in terms of excess and economy, expenditure and restraint, since Dickens' narrative does things with these drives that his characters and his plots cannot do. Most important, narrative enables Dickens to stage limit experience by emphasizing the restricted channels of human economy, rather than by challenging them. In other words, there is a way in which mechanicalness—as opposed to violence, or other impulsive liberations of energy—becomes a stylistic avenue toward excess in Dickens, one that circumvents the moral and psychological problems involved in a more direct access to expenditure. In a paradoxical way, Dickens' narrative style allows him covertly to achieve a kind of excess by extravagantly pursuing the mechanical qualities of human beings, and of language.

ii

On first consideration, any statement of the homeopathic qualities of mechanism in Dickens must sound inappropriate. Nothing seems further from the spirit of Dickens. Critics have long
ago defined Dickens' hatred of what is inorganic in human nature and of what society does to dehumanize the individual. Who
else but an enemy of rigidity and routine could have written the
Christmas stories? And this study in particular has been scrupulously antagonistic to any and all sources of self-limitation,
isolation, fragmentation, and solipsism in Dickens. In fact, we
have seen how the pressure of psychological and physical restriction in Dickens' world is what demands an orientation toward excess. *Hard Times*, which polarizes fancy and fact, the
imaginative energy of the circus and the devastating engines of
Coketown, is only the most explicit statement of Dickens' attitude toward mechanism; the robotlike qualities of Flora Finching, Mrs. Smallweed, Podsnap, Pecksniff, and an endless series
of obsessive Dickensian characters, who define and reinforce
their solitude through their adherence to personal themes of one
kind or another, through their grotesquely regular physical ticks,
and through the monstrous singleness of their desires—all point
to an author driven by his perception of the way human beings
circulate their energies in rigidly self-contained repetitions.

The problem becomes even more ominous when we put it in
a larger, historical context. Dickens was not the only Victorian
to have had strong feelings about the machine age. Though we
tend to think of alienation from technology as a twentieth-century crisis, it was a problem to which the Victorians were particularly sensitive. In "Signs of the Times," Carlyle summed up the
fearful dominance of machinery in his age unequivocally. "Were
we to characterize this Age of ours by any single epithet, we
should be tempted to call it, not an Heroical, Devotional, Philosophical, or Moral Age, but, above all others, the Mechanical
Age. It is the Age of Machinery, in every outward and inward

sense of that word."[1] Of course, the Industrial Revolution has its roots far back in English history, but an important acceleration seems to have taken place in the early nineteenth century, as Carlyle's reference to the "outward and inward" sense of the word "machinery" indicates. Lewis Mumford even locates the beginning of a new technological era, one which he calls the "neotechnic," at the beginning of the nineteenth century; this era, characterized materially by an eventual transition from coal and iron to electricity and metallurgy, is characterized philosophically, Mumford claims, by a new scientific conception of man himself, as exemplified by the work of Darwin, Bain, Herbert, and Spencer. "The concepts of science, hitherto associated with the cosmic, the inorganic, the 'mechanical,' were now applied to every phase of human experience and every manifestation of life."[2] Most important, science in the nineteenth century took as its field of knowledge not just the mechanical laws of matter but, rather, the unchanging laws of energy.[3] And energy, viewed as a province of science, bridges the gap between the organic and the inorganic. For Herbert Sussman, one manifestation of this change is the popular Victorian fascination with the locomotive, which surpassed any previous popular interest in machinery. Sussman attributes this new fascination to the fully automated, self-regulating, and therefore seemingly independent life of energy in the locomotive.[4] For the Victorians, the concepts of machine and of life began to merge.

Another way of putting this change in attitudes toward mechanism might be: lacking the Enlightenment's abstract faith in a transcendent Machine—a god who was the quintessence of rational mechanism—the Victorians had instead a much more concrete, unredeemed image of what a mechanical universe meant: the factory. For the Victorians generally—and for Dickens in particular, who worked in one—the factory became the symbol of the worst evils of culture: partiality, blind instrumentality, production without purpose that proceeds by perfectly sensible, but somehow hollow laws. But the worst thing about the factory was that it was not external to man; rather, it was a projection of himself, the measure of his goals and capabilities. The Victorian age was the first time, perhaps, that man could so clearly see himself dominated by his own mechanical nature, could see himself inscribed within his own suffocatingly artificial world.

It is difficult to estimate how far machine fear dominated Victorian thought as a metaphor, but the encroachment of the machine on human life seems to be behind a great deal of it. For instance, much of Victorian social thought is occupied with rejecting the partial view, dismantling systems of thought, and attacking inflexibility; at the same time, it is peculiarly reluctant to advocate alternative systems, as if new proposals only trapped one in new mechanisms. Machine fear could be said to account for the essential negativity of a work like *Culture and Anarchy*; opposing the ideal of an "organic" culture to different kinds of "machinery," Arnold says sweepingly, "What is freedom but machinery? What is population but machinery? What is coal but machinery? What are railroads but machinery? What is wealth but machinery? What are, even, religious organizations but machinery?"[5] Similarly, machine fear looms behind Carlyle's hypothesis, in *Sartor Resartus*, that man's understanding is only a machine for approximating Truth and is therefore always in need of adjustment (Carlyle uses clothes as a metaphor, but the principle is the same). Machine fear plays a role in Mill's liberal ideal of a perpetual give-and-take between factions—the dream that fragmented systems of thought can be stalemated by a non-system, thus yielding a higher order of unsystematized unity. And machine fear is behind the Victorians' faith in that chimera, the National Conscience, which, being organic, should have eliminated the need for prescribed systems of social order. Certainly, one of the most far-reaching of philosophical fears in Victorian England seems to have been the fear that subjectivity makes up a mechanical world around itself and that any thought or identity, if it could be seen from a larger perspective, would appear self-serving and self-sustaining, a mere function, a closed, pointless process—a machine.

With all this in mind, it appears almost perverse to elevate
the mechanical in Dickens as a metaphor for the experience of
excess. However, the Victorian attitude toward the machine—
inanimate or human—was not consistently one of distress. The
doctrine of progress held wide credence, and the sheer ingenuity
of new inventions compelled a certain universal fascination—for
some, a kind of fanaticism about machinery that they readily applied to human life. Bentham never saw anything wrong with a
mechanical approach to human nature. And Walter Houghton
claims that the strength, precision, and formidability of machines
became a model for Victorian moral standards.[6] Curiously, Dickens himself seems to have had two conflicting attitudes toward
the machine. The sketches in *Household Words* provide a convenient example of his ambivalence, since many of these sketches
can be sorted into two distinct categories. The first vehemently
denounces the wrongs inflicted by a rigid adherence to system;
there are attacks on the variously inhumane, mechanical operations of the Smithfield Cattle Market, the diplomatic corps, the
handling of English wills, and the Austrian government, to
name a few. The second category, however, celebrates the exercise of energy within closed systems, within mechanical operations, even as these operations seem to incorporate human lives.
These latter include the so-called process sketches, descriptions
of well-regulated trade procedures like glass-making, the refin-
ing of gold, or even the progress of a letter through the post
office. But the range of this kind of sketch also includes encomi-
ums on different forms of human mechanization; for example,
Dickens praises the smooth, secret efficiency of the London detectives and the rigorous, exhaustive cataloguing of the natural-
ist. In addition, there are cases in which Dickens advocates
greater degrees of mechanical regularity than had yet been
achieved—in the London cabmen, for instance, and in the pro-
cessing of unemployed laborers for emigration. It may be ob-
jected that when it comes to the post office or cabmen everyone
wants efficiency. But Dickens did not merely approve of systematic operations; he seemed instead to be fascinated with and

delighted by the spectacle of prodigious human energy expended through these mechanisms. In "A Preliminary Word" to *Household Words*, Dickens expressly defends his interest in the machine in general, claiming that the factory, "spitting fire and smoke upon the prospect . . . swart giants, Slaves of the Lamp of Knowledge, have their thousand and one tales, no less than the Genii of the East."[7] And as he looks over mechanisms of one kind or another, Dickens shows such a great love of them that it appears difficult to reconcile his enchantment here with the horror he expresses in the novels over the reduction of human beings to the status of machines. The most striking thing about these glorifications of mechanism are the ways in which Dickens celebrates mechanical processes that involve human relationships by recasting them in magical, romantic, and fairy-tale imagery. In a sketch called "Plate Glass," for example, the formula for glass, says the director, "is a secret, even to us. We give the man who possesses it a handsome salary for the exercise of his mystery"; the storage yard is like "the yard in which the cunning Captain of the Forty Thieves . . . stored his pretended merchandise"; female workers are "a bevy" out of "an Oriental storybook"; and young boys are glimpsed enviously by the wistful narrator as they descend into labyrinthine passages under the furnaces, where they "love to hide and sleep, on cold nights. So slept Defoe's hero, Colonel Jack."[8]

Dickens' fascination with machinery in *Household Words* might be taken as only a superficial attempt to arouse his readers' interest in the world around them, except that his contradictory attitude—love and hatred of mechanism—is not limited to his magazine. Dickens' own personality often seems divided between the man of extravagance and the man of discipline, the reckless madcap and the meticulous orderer of details.[9] Although analogies of this kind are often dangerously subjective, many of Dickens' personal habits do seem highly suggestive of the synthesis developed here. On the one hand, it goes without saying that Dickens was one of the most restless of men—he made his twenty-mile walk a daily adventure, claiming, "If I couldn't

walk fast and far, I should just explode and perish"[10]—and one
of the most playful. His propensity for emotional excess extended to his unabashed love of catastrophe; describing a nearly
fatal storm at sea to Forster, Dickens wrote gaily, "News! A
dozen murders in town wouldn't interest half so much!"[11] This
propensity can be seen, too, in his living beyond his means; Forster reports that Dickens was driven to pawning his gold watch
while on a brief vacation on the very day that *Master Humphrey's Clock* sold its first 60,000 copies.[12] On the other hand,
though, Forster reports in Dickens a great love of order, both in
household affairs, which he insisted he was more competent to
manage than his wife, and in regard to all conditions of his writing—the time, the place, the state of his desk and writing materials, the details of the finished work. Dickens worked quickly
but never sloppily.[13] We also know that he was a scrupulous, extraordinarily exacting businessman. His love of ritual, too, was
such that he met Forster in the same inn to celebrate Forster's
birthday and his own anniversary for twenty years running, and
he kept strictly to his superstitious practice of leaving London
on the first day of any publication.[14] But perhaps the ideal image
of Dickens' blend of prodigal energy and systematic discipline is
his method of publication itself; what must have been the dangerous, luxurious thrill of seeing one of his novels in print before
he knew exactly where he was going with it was matched by
Dickens' ability to keep the pacing of the novels strictly within
the twenty monthly numbers he had set for himself. Even more
remarkable, Forster tells us that Dickens never complained of
difficulties doing exactly what he wanted to do dramatically
within the space allowable for each number.[15] Forster sums up
nicely the absolute necessity of Dickens' wild energies' being put
in this kind of harness. "If he hadn't been famous, he would have
been a vagabond."[16] Conversely, Dickens merely exchanges conventional notions of mechanical regularity for unconventional
ones; as Kenner puts it, "The Dickens who hated the blacking
factory pridefully enslaved himself in a novel-factory."[17]

On a thematic level, Dickens' attitude toward mechanism re-

mains ambiguous. The fierce attacks on industry in *The Old Curiosity Shop* and *Hard Times* are never softened in any direct
way; yet it is significant that Dickens celebrated nature less and
less through the course of his career as an alternative to the
bleakness of industrial England. The pastoralism of *The Old Curiosity Shop*, which is threatened by industry, and the idyllic
country retreat from London available to Oliver Twist give way
to satires on romantic feeling about nature in Mrs. Skewton and
Harold Skimpole. Cloisterham in *Edwin Drood* is hardly depicted as a locus of natural freedom,[18] and although Little Dorrit has
passing longings for a more rustic life, her sphere of influence is
stronger within the confines of the city than outside of it, where,
traveling with her father's party, she feels lost and useless.[19] In
Little Dorrit, too, Doyce the inventor rescues Clennam finally
by restoring him to his position in some undefined—but "mechanical"—business; the pleasantest vengeance exercised in the
ending of the novel is the attack of the mechanical, robotlike
Pancks on Casby.

Dickens' double attitude toward machinery provides us with
a clue about the way he conceived human freedom, or at least
about the way he pursued it instinctively. Surprisingly, it suggests a kind of excess in Dickens that is not directly opposed to
human mechanicalness, as we might suppose it to be in view of
our previous notions about expenditure and restraint, but one
that in some way affirms mechanism as a metaphor for the liberating expenditure of human energies. Dickens never fully articulates this paradox on a thematic level in his work, and, in fact,
he explores the possibility of discovering human freedom within
mechanism only in a tacit way, through narrative style, which
communicates nonprogrammatically. Although, of course, it
would be reductive to see every aspect of Dickens' style as a
function of this one concern, nevertheless, much of what is dis-
tinctively Dickensian about his narrative voice is generated
from this mechanically excessive source.

The central impetus behind Dickens' narrative machine can
best be understood in terms of a certain dialectical tension be-

tween the voice of satire and the voice of parody. To a large extent, it is precisely his particular parodic voice—the tongue-in-cheek, mock grandiosity of his narrative prose—that is most recognizable as Dickensian. Significantly, this tension between satire and parody is clearest in the beginnings of Dickens' novels, at the point when we are first introduced to the narrative voice. To take up an early example, notice how, in the opening paragraph of *Oliver Twist*, Dickens' narrator satirizes relentlessly, but in a way that diffuses the object of his satire.

Among other public buildings in a certain town which for many reasons it will be prudent to refrain from mentioning, and to which I will assign no fictitious name, it boasts of one which is common to most towns, great or small, to wit, a workhouse; and in this workhouse was born, on a day and date which I need not take upon myself to repeat, inasmuch as it can be of no possible consequence to the reader, in this stage of the business at all events, the item of mortality whose name is prefixed to the head of this chapter.

For a long time after he was ushered into this world of sorrow and trouble, by the parish surgeon, it remained a matter of considerable doubt whether the child would survive to bear any name at all; in which case it is somewhat more than probable that these memoirs would never have appeared; or, if they had, that being comprised within a couple of pages, that they would have possessed the inestimable merit of being the most concise and faithful specimen of biography extant in the literature of any age or country. Although I am not disposed to maintain that the being born in a workhouse is in itself the most fortunate and enviable circumstance that can possibly befall a human being, I do mean to say that in this particular instance, it was the best thing for Oliver Twist that could possibly have occurred. The fact is, that there was considerable difficulty in inducing Oliver to take upon himself the office of respiration,—a troublesome practice, but one which custom has rendered necessary to our easy existence,—and for some time he lay gasping on a little flock mattress, rather unequally poised between this world and the next, the balance being decidedly in favour of the latter. Now, if during this brief period, Oliver had been surrounded by careful grandmothers, anxious aunts, experienced nurses, and doctors of profound wisdom, he would most inevitably and undubitably have been killed in no time. There being nobody by, how-

ever, but a pauper old woman, who was rendered rather misty by an
unwonted allowance of beer, and a parish surgeon who did such matters by contract, Oliver and Nature fought out the point between
them. The result was, that, after a few struggles, Oliver breathed,
sneezed, and proceeded to advertise to the inmates of the workhouse
the fact of a new burden having been imposed upon the parish, by setting up as loud a cry as could reasonably have been expected from a
male infant who had not been possessed of that very useful appendage,
a voice, for a much longer space of time than three minutes and a
quarter. (1)

A critical commonplace has it that *Oliver Twist* begins with a
satire on the workhouse. The point cannot reasonably be dis-
puted; the grim picture the narrator gives us of Oliver's birth,
attended only by the drunken pauper, Sally, and by the indifferent parish surgeon, establishes full well the irony in his argument that Oliver fared better in the workhouse than he would
have elsewhere. The overly delicate "in itself" with which the
narrator qualifies that argument points sarcastically to his real
feelings on the subject. With this introduction to the workhouse, too, we can only assume that the reason why the narrator coyly calls it "prudent" to conceal the name of his town,
though he gives it no fictitious name—which points up the relevance of the satire by ostentatiously refusing fictional disguise
—is because its workhouse would shame it. The early chapters
bear this assumption out. Any reader sensitive to satire also understands that calling Oliver an "item of mortality" and "a new
burden on the parish" are references to the callousness of the
institution and not a reflection of the narrator's own feelings
about Oliver.

And yet, what are the narrator's feelings about Oliver? The
narrator's antagonism toward the workhouse and toward genteel society, both expressed satirically, should not blind us to the
fact that Oliver does not fare much better with him. Oliver's
frailty is turned lightly into a joke about "faithful biography."
The reference to his breathing being "a troublesome practice"
stops just short of condescension, as do the descriptions of Oli-

ver's voice as a "useful appendage" and his crying as an "advertisement." Oliver is not attacked, but he is not treated with sympathy, either. He is a vehicle for verbal wit, nothing more. We should be careful, too, to see a difference between these seemingly gratuitous jokes and the narrator's pretences of roughness (the "item of mortality" reference, for example) that we can identify with the workhouse mentality. The oddity of the narrator's offhand, even opportunistic use of Oliver strikes one more forcibly when Oliver's mother dies several paragraphs later. One is tempted to say that we would be offended by the fun the narrator has at Oliver's expense if we were not assured of Dickens' liberal humanism through his satiric attack on the workhouse. But the effect of Dickens' narrative voice is even subtler here, in a way that his remark about Oliver's birth being of "no possible consequence" to the reader would seem to indicate; the reader understands very well that the jokes about literary biography, about breathing, and about crying—all of which are grounded in the possibility of Oliver's own imminent death—are skewed away from Oliver as a character. They are produced desultorily by the exaggerated, euphemistic formalism of the narrator's parodic tone. These are jokes which clearly have nothing to do with Oliver, nothing even to do with the story, and everything to do with the delight we and the narrator take together in the possibilities of verbal liberality inherent in parody. In and of itself the parodic voice, running away with the prose, and not the constraints of the satiric mode produces these jokes. Their digressive quality confirms the presence of a source of sniping, mocking energy independent of satiric intentions. What we are left with, then, is a curious doubleness in these paragraphs: a satiric voice making a pointed attack on the workhouse, and another, less restricted voice oriented in the same satiric way but unconcerned, even undiscriminating, as to the object of its fun.

Before proceeding, we should note that the most important aspect of the satiric/parodic mode is that it enables Dickens to construct a voice distanced in attitude from his own. We do not even hear the narrator's own voice, supposing for a moment that distinction has a real basis; the prose of Dickens' novels calls attention to itself as an impersonation, an affectation, a performance, and as such it can freely display its artificial, constructed qualities without impugning the narrator. The essential point about Dickens' satiric/parodic prose is just this: it displays itself as false, inauthentic. The long first two sentences here carry the reader along in a breezily efficient way, at a pace that is altogether too smooth and regular for sincere speech. The elaborate circumlocutions and long, well-balanced clauses serve to roll the narrative along like a roller coaster, which is partly why this prose is funny; it whirs along inhumanly fast. Together with the unfeeling tone of the narrator, which we strongly suspect to be feigned, the regular cadences of this prose approaches the inhuman energy of a machine. That very clockwork character is exactly its satiric quality. Satire always reduces its object to a thing, or a mechanical process, either by exaggerating the mechanical qualities it impersonates, or, as in this case, by indirectly imputing a mechanical atmosphere to what it attacks.

But there is an important distinction to be made about this affectation of mechanicalness. The voice of satire has a use; the falseness, the mechanicalness it impersonates is condemned. Satire remains righteously antagonistic to mechanical energy; it impersonates such energy only to mock it. In that sense, the satiric voice is conscripted in service of a single human intention—in this case, the attack on the workhouse. In Dickens, as everywhere else, satire employs the language of usefulness, and, in fact, Dickens' claims to social usefulness rest largely on his exposés of subjects like the workhouse, the Yorkshire schools, Chancery—the subjects of the introductory satires in his novels. The intention to satirize such objects may be laudable, it may be humane, but it remains single, narrow—in effect, a kind of work. It restricts language to an economy of purpose. Thus humanized, language loses the independent (though sometimes monstrous) life represented by the nonintentional energy of machines.

Parody, however, as Nabokov points out, is a more gratuitous exercise. The voice of parody escapes the restrictions of any useful economy. Even though it can only embody itself through the language of usefulness—the language of critical and intelligent satire—its intentions have been diffused. Parody is satire diverted away from usefulness, which is why the machine is such an appropriate metaphor for it; parody gives itself over to the very mechanicalness—free of human purpose—that satire condemns. Unlike satire, parody enjoys the mechanical qualities it exploits for their own sake, as a kind of verbal game. It manages to turn mechanicalness into a vehicle for the nonuseful, purposeless—and in this sense both mechanical and nonhuman —energy of play.

We can see in the *Oliver Twist* opening that by splitting him away from a singular satiric intention, Dickens has in effect made the parodic narrator into a machine—a parody machine— that operates with an unlimited, undisciplined kind of energy on whatever parodic object will fuel it. Like the satiric voice, parody seeks out the inorganic in human behavior and expression, but it does so with an eye to enjoyment rather than censure. In that sense, parody achieves the freedom of excess by imitating what is, in itself, restrictive. The paradox has been pointed out more gracefully by Sigurd Burckhardt in an essay on the gravity machine of *Tristram Shandy*. "Gravity is slavery, but since we will not grow wings by pretending that it does not exist, what little chance of freedom we have rests on our understanding; we would not be flying except that someone had the wit to discover that air is heavy."[20] While always held in check by the constraints of more limited satire (for example, Oliver cannot be directly attacked, and the workhouse must always be attacked), the voice of parody aspires to a certain freedom by stretching or exceeding the limits of the satirical usefulness of mechanism— which must nevertheless be present to produce the contrast, the gap. As we shall see, the generally relentless, machine-like freedom of Dickens' prose is constituted by the kind of human uselessness reflected chiefly, but not exclusively, in the tension between satire and parody.

Oliver Twist is not the only novel to begin with a parodic machine that tugs against the limits of a satirical point of view. A similar rhetorical strategy opens most Dickens novels. In *Dombey and Son*, the narrator sets out in the opening chapter to ridicule the house of Dombey and to introduce one nucleus of sympathetic characters, but his parodic tone seems to run away with the chapter and exercise its vengeance on everyone. Even Paul is "crushed and spotty in his general effect, as yet," and he is caricatured as a comic reflection of Dombey, with his fists "curled up and clenched" as if ready to do battle with the world. The narrator's enthusiasm for the exchanges between Dr. Parker Peps and Mr. Pilkins swamps the pathos of Fanny and Flo's attachment. And Fanny's death itself is lost in the comic treatment of Louisa. In the openings of both *Oliver Twist* and *Dombey and Son*, in fact, the deaths of mothers—which would normally be prime material for pathos in Dickens—are treated minimally and with the sole intention, it seems, of heightening the fun the narrator has with the general situation. This kind of runaway parody reaches its peak in the opening of *Martin Chuzzlewit*, which even a good number of Dickens' original readers found to be excessive, that is, too freely disengaged from the economy of any particular satire. And one of the most striking instances of the conflict is *Hard Times*; the furious energy of Dickens' satire of hard fact carries the narrator along into a highly comic but highly inaccurate rendition of Thomas Gradgrind. "He seemed a kind of cannon loaded to the muzzle with facts, and prepared to blow [the children] clean out of the regions of childhood at one discharge" (2), we are told. Or, "Thomas Gradgrind, sir— peremptorily Thomas—Thomas Gradgrind. With a rule and a pair of scales, and the multiplication table always in his pocket, sir, ready to weigh and measure any parcel of human nature, and tell you exactly what it comes to." As it turns out, Thomas Gradgrind is indeed an overly stern man, but he is not nearly the mechanical monster Dickens makes him out to be here. Gradgrind is not simply exaggerated in this opening, he becomes a victim of the exuberance of Dickens' passion for verbal excess. In fact, throughout the first two chapters of *Hard Times*, Dickens' frantic schoolroom scene seems borne along largely by Dickens' own relish for mechanical frenzy, which attains a level of manic energy sustained later on by no single character in the novel, not even by Bounderby. The intensity of the conflict between satire and parody at the beginnings of these novels is a good indication of its centrality as a force affecting various aspects of Dickens' style. In these openings, Dickens seems to be hurrying to establish both kinds of voice as a platform from which to launch other aspects of his narrative form.

Perhaps the most fruitful area in which to consider how Dickens' prose continues in a sustained way to exploit this tension between useful satire and useless parody is that most general category of his prose, writing which mocks the inauthenticity of prolix language. In fact, the most prominent source of comedy in Dickens is the very language, in all its bloated glory, of characters like Pecksniff, Chadband, Micawber. For all their idiosyncracies, these characters share a propensity for language that is in love with itself, that has become detached from human meaning and purpose and instead revels in its own sound and possibilities. And, relentlessly, Dickens ridicules the inflated diction, the ornate euphemisms, the self-serving egotism of their grandiose style, a mechanical, inhuman style. Dickens' hatred of these corrupters of language cannot be overstated; by locating the Circumlocution Office as the source of Britain's political evils, Dickens makes it plain he considers insincerity and abuses of language a serious moral problem.

No wonder, then, that Dickens allows his satire of prolixity to spill over into a general narrative posture, into what one critic has called the "preposterous" style.[21] Indeed, the centrality of Dickens' linguistic satire is evident in the pretentious posture his narrator takes up from the very first paragraph of his first novel.

The first ray of light which illuminates the gloom, and converts into a dazzling brilliancy that obscurity in which the earlier history of the public career of the immortal Pickwick would appear to be involved, is derived from the perusal of the following entry in the Transactions of the Pickwick Club, which the editor of these papers feels the highest pleasure in laying before his readers as a proof of the careful attention, indefatigable assiduity, and nice discrimination, with which his search among the multifarious documents confided to him has been conducted. (1)

The Latinate diction that blurs details and smothers the rhythm of these sentences, the convoluted syntax, the endless rolling clauses, the elaborate euphemisms, the redundancies, the addiction to adjectives—all help to render this prose inhumanly mechanical, since it takes its impetus not from a desire to communicate, but from the sheer ability of language to elaborate itself endlessly, meaninglessly. It would be tedious at this time in the history of Dickens criticism to catalogue all the discrete objects of Dickens' verbal satire. The point is simply that no one can miss the satiric intent of this prose. And Dickens critics from time immemorial have cited passages such as this in proof of Dickens' advocacy of a morality of style, his desire to see words clearly related to meaning and to achieve a sincerity uncontaminated by pomposity.

Nevertheless, the obvious question arises: at what point does Dickens' honest satirical intention give way to a parodic enjoyment of prolixity? While Dickens does satirize pomposity, he also seems to relish the potential for play in the euphonious non-meaning of pomposity. It cannot easily be denied that Dickens uses the self-serving, self-contained language of pomposity as a vehicle for his own flourishes and maniacal energy. When Mrs. Todgers asks Pecksniff, "How have they used you downstairs?" and Pecksniff responds, "Their conduct has been such, my dear madam . . . as I can never think of without emotion, or remember without a tear" (9), Dickens' gleeful interest in Pecksniff's meaningless linguistic energy penetrates the caricature. G. K. Chesterton, in fact, has written that Dickens "exaggerated Pecksniff because he really loved him."[22] The same could be said of innumerable Dickensian warblers. The endlessness of Flora Finching's speeches testifies not only to Dickens' bitter feelings

about Maria Beadnell, but also to the amount of linguistic variation he could squeeze out of Flora's hysterical desire to call attention to herself by bringing the words "Mr. Clennam" and
"Arthur" into conjunction. Joey Bagstock's obsession with his
name provides Dickens with an excellent opportunity to exploit
the capacity of a linguistic fixation—free of desires to communicate, free to spin its wheels uselessly—to give way to infinite
variation. Such characters present Dickens with a brilliant excuse for the transparently playful exercise of florid prose, and
the categories of possible linguistic play here overlap with the
categories of satirized prose: circumlocution, convolution, eu-
phemism—in short, nonsense. In all these characters, what ultimately attracts Dickens is exactly their disengagement from
sense and the resultant freedom of their language to expand and
fill up linguistic space—mechanically, according to its own laws
and not the laws of meaning. As J. Hillis Miller has remarked in
another context, Dickens has a double relationship to reality; his
firm grasp of it, often used to satiric effect, is also employed
against reality, to negate it in favor of freer kinds of artistic energies not constrained by realistic or satiric intent.[23]

Dickens' delight in the artificial excesses of his characters
spills over freely into the excesses of his own narrative prose.
Certainly, as readers we know that Dickens is at his best, his
liveliest, his most Dickensian in those passages in which he lib-
erally but indirectly spoofs the language of unnamed others.
Thus, in the narration of the *Pickwick Papers*, wine exerts a
"somniferous influence," Dr. Slammer is "indefatigable in paying
the most unremitting and devoted attention" to the widow, and
Mr. Tupman, "after experiencing some slight difficulty finding
the orifice in his nightcap, originally intended for the reception
of his head, and finally overturning his candlestick in his struggles to put it on . . . managed to get into bed by a series of complicated evolutions, and shortly afterwards sank into repose"
(2). Garrett Stewart has documented in great detail how Dickens' narrator's frequently outrageous language is a means to elegant variation, a means to employ stiff and tedious forms of

speech as vehicles for the exercise of parodic vitality. According to Stewart, in this way Dickens converts a sense of the limits of language, its artificialness, into a passion for expression.[24] In effect, by absorbing machine-like language into his own narration, Dickens out-machines the machine, performing with the very impersonal linguistic energy he can at the same time condemn in his characters. Of course, it is important to see that the presence of a satire on egotistical language alone allows Dickens to pursue the impersonation beyond the point of its usefulness as satire. But the only real difference between Dickens' prosy narrator and a character like Pecksniff is the clear indication in the novels that the narrator's language is self-consciously, deliberately artificial, which guarantees its purity precisely because it cuts that language off from any self-serving human intention. In one important sense, the narrator's prose is innocently vital because it is *more* meaningless than Pecksniff's.

The best guarantee we have that Dickens' satire on inorganic language is exceeded in his work chiefly through parody is simply Dickens' failure—despite his supposed belief in moral speech—ever to provide us with an example of a nonartificial, sincere language. As far as language is concerned, Dickens never creates a nonmechanical style; the normal speech of his characters is never free of rigid restrictions and formulas. One signal that we should suspect all language that lays claim to sincerity of being, in fact, inauthentically circumscribed, is the multitude of characters in Dickens who protest their sincerity and yet are clearly devious: Harold Skimpole, Uriah Heep, Joey Bagstock, Pecksniff, Carker. These satires on "sincere" speech should encourage us to examine very closely the sincerity of more well-intentioned characters. And, as our discussion of Esther Summerson suggested earlier, there is no such thing as a "selfless" language available even to Dickens' good characters.

It would be tempting to see Esther, David Copperfield, and Pip, the three prominent examples of first-person narrative in Dickens, as practitioners of a transparent style, and many Dickens critics have certainly made the attempt. Yet it seems hard to

deny that there is a masklike quality to the speech of these characters caused by their very desire to avoid linguistic transgression. This obfuscation is produced by the characters' verbal
repressiveness: their refusal to articulate certain kinds of
knowledge about themselves and others, and their use of rigid
formulas for self-effacement. When Esther tells us, "I was
brought up, from my earliest remembrance—like some of the
princesses in the fairy stories, only I was not charming—by my
godmother" (3), we feel her language self-consciously straining
in two directions—toward linguistic embellishment and vitality,
and toward a repression of any verbal impulse that might become self-serving. Tellingly, we measure Esther's goodness in
large part according to how well she restrains her native impulses to give her speech free reign. Thus, Esther seems virtuous when she breaks off her speech before announcing convic-
tions that she feels might be ungenerous.

> I ventured to take this opportunity of hinting that Mr. Skimpole,
> being in all such matters, quite a child—
> "Eh, my dear?" said Mr. Jarndyce, catching at the word.
> "—Being quite a child sir," said I, "and so different from other
> people—"
> "You are right!" said Mr. Jarndyce, brightening. (6)

More strikingly, Esther is virtuous when she shows herself picking her words carefully in order not to settle on dangerous
shades of meaning (which the reader assumes, anyway). "I had
always rather a noticing way—not a quick way, O no!—a silent
way of noticing what passed before me, and thinking I should
like to understand it better. I have not by any means a quick
understanding. When I love a person very tenderly indeed, it
seems to brighten. But even that may be my vanity" (3). Or
again: "I was wakeful and rather low-spirited. I don't know why.
At least I don't think I know why. At least, perhaps I do, but I
don't think it matters" (17). These repressions may guarantee
Esther's virtue, but they do not make for sincerity. If anything,
we are constantly aware of how much Esther conceals from us,

for fear of compromising herself. And Esther's reflexive turning
of her language away from herself toward other people as a defense against self-interest is often comically mechanical, as in
the last paragraph of *Bleak House*.

> "And don't you know that you are prettier than you ever were?"
> I did not know that; I am not certain that I know it now. But I
> know that my dearest little pets are very pretty, and that my darling
> is very beautiful, and that my husband is very handsome, and that my
> guardian has the brightest and most benevolent face that ever was
> seen; and that they can very well do without much beauty in me—even
> supposing— (67)

We are not meant to laugh at Esther, but we are meant to see
the effort in her innocence, and its unnaturalness. Esther's personality is a good machine, a machine built on undermining itself—a selflessness machine. Hugh Kenner, our current literary
expert on machines, remarks, "Wisdom is in part the ability to
tell one mode of counterfeit from the other, that which constitutes the aggressive environment from that which is benefi-
cent and homeopathic."[25]

Similarly, David Copperfield's reticence, his habitual dis-
claimers ("if I may say," "if I may so call it") too blatantly express a claim to honest speech by advertising the repressive
qualities of his narration. Like Esther, David never condemns or
accuses. Repeatedly, he refuses to give expression to his feelings about Steerforth. "Deeply as I felt my own unconscious
part in his pollution of an honest home, I believed that if I had
been brought face to face with him, I could not have uttered one
reproach. I should have loved him so well still—though he fascinated me no longer—I should have held in so much tenderness
the memory of my affection for him, that I think I should have
been as weak as a spirit-wounded child, in all but the entertainment of a thought that we could ever be re-united" (32). Often,
too, David describes himself attempting to speak to Steerforth
directly, but then shying away. "I had it in my thoughts to re-
monstrate with him upon his desperate way of pursuing any

fancy that he took—such as this buffeting of rough seas, and braving of hard weather, for example—when my mind glanced off to the immediate subject of our conversation again, and pursued that instead" (28). In addition, David's careful wording of accounts of his squabbles with Dora drains them of all passion. He miniaturizes their fights through verbal lightness, calling them "our first little quarrel," or "the Ordeal of Servants" (44), and he counterbalances even his deepest dissatisfactions with extenuations that deflect pure feeling into self-deprecation. "I did feel, sometimes, for a little while, that I could have wished my wife had been my counsellor; had had more character and purpose, to sustain me and improve me by; had been endowed with power to fill up the void which somewhere seemed to be about me; but I felt as if this were an unearthly consummation of my happiness, that never had been meant to be, and never could have been" (44).

But the goodness of David as a speaker demands certain exclusions that Dickens makes us well aware of; David's self-contained "honesty" results in an unnatural suppression of his hostile feelings, particularly for Heep—at one point, David wakes up in the night so uncertain as to whether or not he has killed Heep that he has to get up and check to make sure Uriah is still alive. Finally, too, it is Micawber who condemns Uriah, not David. And Dickens' reservations about the "sincere" voice are clearly revealed in the conflict we feel between David's speech and his ability to act. David can only remain an observer; his inability to intervene in the confrontation between Emily and Rosa Dartle confirms in him an unnatural, passive constraint that is signaled by his prose. Similarly, though her language may be pure, Esther's actions remain an enigma for critics, who cannot decide whether in her behavior she is purely selfless or deviously egotistical. So much for the efficacy of the "sincere" voice.

All of these repressive qualities of speech may help make these two characters good in a conventional sense, but they also turn Esther and David into machines—tightly regulated ma-

chines, but machines nevertheless. We need only place the passive, constricted voices of these two characters alongside the
vitality of Dickens' own speech to see how much they speak an
artificial language. In his letters or public statements, Dickens
would never say, "I must confess that I could not help feeling
rather angry with Mrs. Jellyby" (14), or, as David expresses
himself, "From the accumulated sadness into which I fell, I had
at length no hope of ever issuing again" (58). Compare Dickens'
remark to Collins: "I am dead sick of the Scottish tongue, in all
its moods and tenses."[26] And Dickens' accounts of his depressions were always blunt, as in "I want to escape from myself.
For when I *do* start up and stare myself seedily in the face, as
happens to be my case at present, my blankness is inconceiv-
able—indescribable—my misery, amazing."[27] It is difficult to
imagine Dickens ever expressing emotions like Esther's or David's in the buffered way they do. As much as we are aware of
David's or Esther's feelings, then, we are equally aware of their
restraint in giving voice to them.

Pip's speech is perhaps the most straightforward, the most
unrestricted of the three characters. Pip does not hesitate to accuse concisely. Of Mrs. Pocket, he tells us, "she had grown up
highly ornamental, but perfectly helpless and useless" (23).
Drummle strikes him immediately as "a sulky kind of fellow."
He is similarly direct about his own feelings; "it was highly
gratifying to me," he tells us when a clever answer of his to
Pumblechook "spoilt his joke, and brought him up short" (9).
Moreover, Pip's speech betrays none of the self-conscious awkwardness that marks David's and Esther's. And yet, part of the
reason Pip's speech comes across as relatively unconstrained is
that Dickens has suffused it with an overwhelming tone of melancholy self-rejection. Pip tells us very little about himself that
he does not bracket with gentle mockery. Of his feelings for Estella, he tells us, "I thought those were high and great emotions" (29). When describing his persistent courting, he says,
"Whatever her tone with me happened to be, I could put no
trust in it, and build no hope on it; and yet I went on against
trust and against hope. Why repeat it a thousand times? So it

always was" (33). His feelings for Biddy and Joe are always qualified with a "sense of my worthless conduct" (40). Pip himself reveals this pervasive attitude of self-deprecation and self-doubt best when he claims, "All other swindlers upon earth are nothing to the self-swindlers, and with such pretences did I cheat myself" (28).

Much more subtle and more graceful than the automatic repressions of Esther and David, Pip's habitual, inflexible need to renounce his previous attitudes and feelings, his need to turn his narrative into a confession, casts his speech in a similar kind of mechanical mold. From the first page, he is careful to tell us that his impression of his deceased parents and brothers is "unreasonably derived," a "childish conclusion," an "odd idea" (1). Certainly, Dickens did not mean to call attention to the automatic reflexes of Pip's speech to the same degree that he does with Esther's or David's (although 'this is partly because the latter two have much less that they specifically renounce as a way of purging guilt), but the reflexes are there nonetheless, if only as the signs of Pip's personality. And, most important, as a result, Pip's speech is never enthusiastic or playful (David Copperfield's, in the "Retrospects," is more so). It is always pained or wistful, instead.

It would be too harsh to claim that Dickens does not encourage us to practice the virtue of Esther, David, or Pip, or that Dickens does not take seriously and admire their linguistic economy, but the deliberate restrictions built into their voices make it plain that no organic freedom is available to Dickens' characters in terms of language. The only linguistic virtue Dickens can imagine is one in which he opposes one kind of machine to another—the virtuous, restrained machinery of his good character's speech to the rapacious machinery of others'. And even Dickens' impersonations of Esther's, David's, and Pip's voices have to be seen partly as a reflection of his interest in performing a mechanical role—however good, however restricted. The force of this argument leads us directly to a rationale for Dickens' indulgence in the more flamboyant exercise of his parodic machine. If speech, good or bad, is always mechanized, the only discreet avenue toward stylistic excess lies in freeing the self-generating, self-serving energy of the machine of language—with the aid of the purity guaranteed by parodic distance and by occasional assertions of satiric, moralistic outrage.

Still, it is crucial not to blur irrevocably the distinction between relatively good—that is, relatively more restrained—and bad uses of language in Dickens. Simply because the satire on pompous or mechanical language in Dickens is bracketed by his failure to imagine an unrestricted, moral language does not mean that the satire on language is perfunctory. On the contrary, Dickens' attack on linguistic abuses is quite real. If it were not, the parodic voice, unanchored, would drift off into pure nonsense. It is difficult to imagine how nonsensical Dickens' prose could become were it not for the counterweight of satire, which is always present in the background of his verbal play, always keeping it in check and tying it—sometimes tightly, sometimes loosely—to an economic purpose. Both these voices—the useful, moral, economical satire, and the excessive, playful, useless parody—are necessary to each other. It is only the tension between them that presents us with mutual but opposed satisfactions: the security of an attack that presumes to root out nonmeaning once and for all, and the dizzying energy of wit that seems to want to exceed and destroy the narrow limits and the meaning of that very attack.

The most important point about Dickens' style is that we never think of questioning the contradictory impulses behind his satiric and parodic voices. Is Dickens' satire on language finally moral? And if so, doesn't that morality implicitly condemn his enjoyment of his own linguistic excess? Or is the parody of linguistic baggage pure fun? And does that negate the serious attack on Pecksniffian abuses of language? Such questions never occur to us, and, posed in such a bald way, they appear sophomoric. Dickens' style remains both satiric and parodic at the same time. The distinction between the two is barely perceptible, yet it is certainly there. In this remarkable way, Dickens' style manages to reconcile drives for expenditure and for economy so subtly that the moral quandaries presented by his char-

acters' attempts to do the same are completly avoided. Dickens'
style *is* a delicate balancing of verbal excess within a moral
economy. As an indefinable presence, an attitude, a form of
mental activity, it sustains a kind of expenditure uncompro-
mised by the restrictions of form, having found a way to put
form to use in service of the boundlessness of pure energy—
which, paradoxically, can only be brought into existence by ani-
mating recognizable, mechanical forms like the voice of satire.

iii

The tension between satire and parody in his style allows Dickens to indulge the free exercise of energy in a language machine.
We need not locate this tension in every aspect of Dickens' style,
but we should examine Dickens' tendency to exploit this stylistic tension by leaning noticeably toward a disengagement of language from any strict economy of intentions. In this section, I
want to look at these diverse aspects of his style and the way
they, too, violate the limits of language by turning language into
a machine.

The most striking indication that Dickens delights in a non-
polemical, useless indulgence in mechanical impersonation for
its own sake lies in the fact that his prose often becomes comically mechanical when there is no object of satire, not even the
bloated figure of a prolix verbalizer, either as a character or as a
clear object of narrative attack. William F. Axton has shown
that, rather than taking up a number of satirical positions, Dickens' narrative runs on a spirit of "rootless burlesque,"[28] and
while that formulation is too simple as a general rule, in many
cases it seems to hold true. That is, Dickens' descriptive passages are often full of satiric devices that frequently do not express any obviously satiric intention at all. A good example is
this description of a Derby Day crowd at Epsom Downs.

All around me there are table-clothes, pies, chickens, hams, tongues,
rolls, lettuces, radishes, shellfish, broad-bottomed bottles, clinking

glasses, and carriages turned inside out. Amidst the hum of voices a
bell rings. What's that? What's the matter? They are clearing the
course. Never mind. Try the pigeon pie. A roar. What's the matter?
It's only the dog upon the course. Is that all? Glass of wine. Another
roar. What's that? It's only the man who wants to cross the course, and
is intercepted, and brought back. Is that all? I wonder whether it is
always the same dog and the same man, year after year! A great roar.
What's the matter? By Jupiter, they are going to start.

. . . Good gracious, look at the Grand Stand, piled high with
human beings to the top, and at the wonderful effect of changing light
as their faces and uncovered heads turn suddenly this way. Here they
are! Who is? The horses! Where? Here they come! Green first. No:
Red first. No: Blue first. No: the Favorite first. Who says so? Look!
Hurrah! hurrah! All over. Glorious race. Favorite wins! Two hundred
thousand pounds won and lost. You don't say so? Pass the pie![29]

There are a number of narrative devices here that can be satiric
because they play on the crowd's mechanicalness but are not
necessarily so: the competing interest of food and the race, the
emphasis on the crowd's unself-conscious repetition of emotion,
the idiotic confusion, the ironic predictability of the Favorite's
victory, the flippant, trivialized exchange of money, the haphaz-
ard estimation of the race's worth at the end, and, most important, the choppy, push-button pacing of the prose itself. Still,
the tone of the passage seems to enjoy the excitement of this
crowd behavior, distilling its pure energy as it elevates the mechanical in racing to the status of a robust traditional ritual.

Most of the holiday scenes in the novels are treated with the
same genial parodic tone, which clearly implies a cherishing of
robustly mechanical qualities in human behavior. In *Dombey
and Son*, Dickens' initial attack on the rigidity of Dr. Blimber's
establishment is moderated into affection for that rigidity by the
time of Mr. Toots' marriage.

The ceremony was performed in an admirable manner. Cornelia,
with her crisp little curls, "went in," as the Chicken might have said,
with great composure; and Doctor Blimber gave her away, like a man
who had quite made up his mind to it. The gauzy little bridesmaids

appeared to suffer most. Mrs. Blimber was affected, but gently so; and told The Reverend Mr. Alfred Feeder, M.A., on the way home, that if she could only have seen Cicero in his retirement at Tusculum, she would not have had a wish, now, ungratified. (60)

Unlike the satire on the workhouse in *Oliver Twist* or Dickens' general satire on pomposity, the satiric devices here are devoid of all satiric content. It would be difficult even to discover a covert satire on pretension exercised by the narrative pose. On the contrary, Dickens' mechanical pursuit of a satiric narrative posture without any object of attack actually seems to be a more or less patronizing guarantee of the innocence of the scene. A similar conjunction of innocence and mechanicalness runs throughout the more festive scenes in the *Pickwick Papers*. This encounter in the open countryside between the Pickwickians and a group of young ladies, all on their way to a wedding celebration, is representative.

The ceremony of introduction under such circumstances was very soon performed, or we should rather say that the introduction was soon over without any ceremony at all. In two minutes thereafter, Mr. Pickwick was joking with the young ladies who wouldn't come over the stile while he looked—or who, having pretty feet and unexceptional ankles, preferred standing on the top rail for five minutes or so, declaring that they were too frightened to move—with as much ease and absence of reserve or constraint, as if he had known them for life. It is worthy of remark, too, that Mr. Snodgrass offered Emily far more assistance than the absolute terrors of the stile (although it was full three feet high, and had only a couple of stepping stones) would seem to require; while one black-eyed young lady in a very nice little pair of boots with fur round the top, was observed to scream very loudly, when Mr. Winkle offered to help her over.

All this was very snug and pleasant. . . . (28)

What is both "snug and pleasant" for the reader in scenes like this is precisely the persistence of routine socialized behavior— the reluctance of the girls, the gallantry of Mr. Snodgrass—in contexts that, as Mr. Pickwick's lack of restraint here indicates, display such behavior as feigned; that is, the conventions of female timidity and male gallantry are exercised here with a good deal of detachment from real significance. These obviously mechanical forms of relationship are understood by all as simply the elaborate but empty, nonmeaningful channels through which erotic energy freely flows. And Dickens' prose aspires to the same innocent expense when it describes this kind of vital mechanicalness in a tone of automatic, energetic ridicule—"it is worthy of remark," "was observed to scream"—that nevertheless conveys no ridicule. Dickens' treatment of his holiday scenes—those moments in human life when excesses of emotion are most legitimate—in such a genially mechanical manner is a telling comment on his attitude toward the most satisfying means of expressing excessive, erotic energy.

In the same way, the actions of good characters are often described in blatantly mechanical terms, not to qualify those characters in any conceivable way, but as a gesture of endearment. With such characters, Dickens seems to be identifying the purity—the expansive, nonhuman freedom—of those characters' energy with their mechanical, purposeless discharge of it. In this way Noddy Boffin is first described in terms that would be appropriate to a wind-up toy. His robot-like "morning, morning, morning!" (5), his automatic interrogation of Wegg—who seems much more flexible in comparison when he hurriedly anticipates a Boffin question with "I don't know why"—and his fixation on Wegg's wooden leg all mechanize Boffin. Then, too, Dickens' description emphasizes Boffin's comical rigidity. "He wore thick shoes, and thick leather gaiters, and thick gloves like a hedger's. Both as to dress and to himself, he was of an overlapping rhinoceros build, with folds in his cheeks, and his forehead, and his eyelids, and his lips, and his ears" (5). And yet, these marks of mechanism in Boffin, which all contribute to his tremendous, cheerful energy, seem to be expressions of friendly sympathy on the narrator's part. Like the description of the race course, they are meant to signal pure, innocent vitality. And in passages like these, that is exactly the quality we associate with Dickens' own prose. The innocent exuberance of his predictably burlesque, tongue-in-cheek tone becomes a signal as to the innocence of his characters. A similar argument could be made about Dickens' treatment of the single gentleman's frequent but harmless "violent demonstrations" in *The Old Curiosity Shop*, Mr. Pancks' resemblance to a feisty tugboat in *Little Dorrit*, or the behavior of a number of other agreeably mechanical characters.

The same kind of disengagement of linguistic energy in Dickens' burlesque tone, to borrow the term from Axton, is featured in still other aspects of his style. When Dickens sets a grotesque scene, for example, it is often difficult to tell whether the grotesquerie belongs to the scene or to the disconnected energies of style, and whether the grotesquerie is meant to condemn or simply to luxuriate in its own absurdity, as in this portrait of Bunsby in *Dombey and Son*.

Immediately there appeared, coming slowly up above the bulk-head of the cabin, another bulk-head—human, and very large—with one stationary eye in the mahogany face, and one revolving one, on the principle of some lighthouses. This head was decorated with shaggy hair, like oakum, which had no governing inclination towards the north, east, west, or south, but inclined to all four quarters of the compass, and to every point upon it. The head was followed by a perfect desert of chin, and by a shirt-collar and neckerchief, and by a dreadnought pilot-coat, and by a pair of dreadnought pilot-trousers, whereof the waist band was so very broad and high, that it became a succedaneum for a waistcoat: being ornamented near the wearer's breast-bone with some massive wooden buttons, like backgammon men. (23)

Bunsby proves to be a genial character—not heroic, but certainly a part of the good characters' world. It would be a mistake to construe our introduction to him here as a warning. Rather, Dickens' style is simply running away with the narrative, relishing and elaborating the mechanical appropriateness of Bunsby's appearance to his surroundings without turning us against him in any way. It is clear that the energy here belongs solely to language and that the grotesque figure is only a vehicle for this energy, a vehicle which is elided to some extent in favor of the narrator's verbal exuberance.

There are, of course, cases in Dickens where the grotesque is truly grotesque—especially in the later novels—but in those cases, too, there is often a tension between the horrific scene and the possibilities such scenes open up to linguistic play. When the narrator of *Our Mutual Friend* describes Jenny Wren as "of the world, worldly; of the earth, earthy" (2.2), he is using her physical and psychological deformities as the pretext for elegant artifice. And though Eugene Wrayburn is at one point "shocked . . . at the thought of trifling with her infirmity," Dickens' narrator has no compunctions about ornamenting his treatment of Jenny's oddities with irrelevant verbal wit. At one point, in her argument with Fascination Fledgeby, Jenny cries, "'Oh my head!' . . . holding it with both her hands, as if it were cracking" (2.5). There are many characters in Dickens who might perform the same gesture without its being described in such physically acute terms. Similarly, Miss Mowcher in *David Copperfield* becomes an occasion for Dickens' verbal playfulness, so much so that the original for Miss Mowcher took offense.[30] The purely verbal symmetries and comic constructions are remarkable in David Copperfield's normally polite prose. "Throat she had none; waist she had none; legs she had none, worth mentioning; for though she was more than full-sized down to where her waist would have been, if she had had any, and though she terminated, as human beings generally do, in a pair of feet, she was so short that she stood at a common-sized chair as at a table, resting a bag she carried on the seat" (22).

Dickens has innumerable other devices for expanding the base of his mechanical verbal play. The coincidences of the novels, whether they are completely under control or not, have the effect of creating a world that, for all its variety, is closed in upon itself, systematized—a notion about the real world that Dickens was fond of remarking on.[31] Frequently, too, Dickens plays on the mechanical restrictions of language by juxtaposing contexts normally kept separate—Guppy's legalese during his proposal to Esther is a good example—or by refusing to supply the commonplace name for a behavior that the narrator describes literally, in all its automatized glory. Mr. Winkle's cowardice during his duel, for example, is executed in this way. "It is conjectured that his unwillingness to hurt a fellow-creature intentionally was the cause of his shutting his eyes when he arrived at the fatal spot; and that the circumstance of his eyes being closed, prevented his observing the very extraordinary and unaccountable demeanour of Doctor Slammer" (2). Most indicative of the range of this play, perhaps, is Dickens' habit of exploiting the artificial qualities of language itself—its inventedness, its arbitrariness—by pushing literalism to excess in the form of ingenious extended metaphors. Thus, in *Our Mutual Friend* we are told, "Being known on her own authority as Miss Abbey Potterson, some water-side heads, which (like the water) were none of the clearest, harboured muddled notions that, because of her dignity and firmness she was named after, or in some sort related to, the Abbey at Westminster" (1.6). And, in *Martin Chuzzlewit*, one of Pecksniff's ancestors was "a matron of such destructive principles, and so familiarized to the use and composition of inflammatory and combustible engines, that she was called 'The Match Maker'" (1). These comic metaphors and puns exploit the arbitrary resonances of words and phrases—the wheels and gears of language—to emphasize both the unnaturalness of linguistic interconnections and the way in which those channels, which render characters rigid through their own literalism, can be pursued as a kind of freedom for the narrator through the excessive energy of verbal play.

Dickens exploits mechanism in a larger way as a metaphor for excess through a process of narrative duplications that involves characters in a chain of functional resemblances, thereby undermining their singularity. For example, there are the deliberate parodies of one plot by another plot in the novels, as when the process of substitution by which Walter Gay replaces Paul as Flo's "brother" in *Dombey and Son* is mimicked by Susan Nipper's replacing Flo temporarily as Toots' partner, and by Bunsby's replacing Captain Cuttle as Mrs. MacStinger's. In a more pointed way, there is the common psychological trait—pride—

that unites Dombey, Edith, Carker, Skewton, and Bagstock in *Dombey and Son*, making them all imperfect behavioral echoes of each other and thereby mechanizing their actions. The same can be said of the variations and repetitions of the formula of selfishness in *Martin Chuzzlewit*, or the automatic craving after social respectability that unites such disparate characters as the Veneerings, the Podsnaps, Headstone, Hexam, Wegg, and Bella Wilfer in *Our Mutual Friend*. Perhaps the best example of a novel that proceeds by duplication of function is *Bleak House*, with its shifting analogies between the world of Chancery and the world of Fashion, its multiplication of detectives, and its innumerable minor refractions of character. For example, Richard's inability to settle on a profession is echoed by the needs of his tutor, Mr. Badger, for diverse authority in the matter of his wife; Esther's assumption of innocence and her book are echoed by Skimpole's assumption of innocence and his book; and the comic dominance of wife over husband is repeated *ad absurdam* in the Jellybys, the Pardiggles, the Bagnets, the Snagsbys, and the Dedlocks. All novelists may be said to pattern their work, but Dickens carries this patterning—the very machinery of novels—to an extreme, inscribing such characters completely within the pattern that generates the plot. His metered duplications create a chain of substitutions on the level of clearly defined mechanisms that undermines the subjective independence of single characters. Most important, by generating the plot through duplication, and also by working with stock narrative conventions borrowed from melodrama and the fairy tale—the formula of villain, gallant young man, and heroine; the certainty of the happy ending—Dickens turns his novels into machines with transparent working parts. The reader is less surprised by the turns in Dickens' plots—or, at least, in retrospect it is always difficult to imagine how Dickens would have ended a novel differently from the way he did end it—than by the details of style and the energy with which these turns are performed.

The most telling stylistic proof of Dickens' affirmation of the mechanical as a metaphor for energy without human content is that his spirit of parody extended to himself as well; Dickens was willing to dramatize his own deepest feelings as mechanical, to dissolve his own "serious" self into parody. For instance, though he spent much time and effort in philanthropic activities, Dickens did not hesitate to satirize philanthropy brutally in *Bleak House*. Similarly, his status as the voice of English domestic life did not stop him from satirizing eulogistic attitudes toward home and family through Pecksniff. More interesting, though, are the self-parodies that touch on dangerous personal ground. Dickens' manic pretense of having fallen in love with the queen must be seen as a self-dramatization of his constant and ultimately scandalous susceptibility to infatuation.[32] More daring still, Dickens sometimes signed his letters to Forster "Moddle"—the star-struck lover in *Martin Chuzzlewit* who, rejected by one girl, pursues her sister, much in the same way that Dickens romantically replaced one of the Hogarth girls with her sister, with Mercy being Mary and Charity, Kate. Then, too, Dickens ridicules Pecksniff's attempt to seduce Mrs. Todgers by invoking the memory of a dead loved one, which is similar to the way Dickens himself used to compare his wife's sister Georgina, for whom his feelings were at least ambiguous, to Mary Hogarth after her death.[33] Still another self-parody is the relationship of Quilp to Mrs. Quilp and to her mother, Mrs. Jiniwin, which bears a strong resemblance to Dickens' own relationship to Kate and to her mother.[34]

None of these biographical links are certain, of course, but the frequency of the pattern in Dickens of seeming self-parody is significant and richly suggestive. In all of these cases, the complex function of parody reveals its full potential as a vehicle for excess. A number of speculations can and have been made about the psychological satisfactions for Dickens; aside from the thrill of risk that might be involved in a perverse wish to give himself away—a wish he also displayed through his readings, which came close to revealing his murderous impulses, and by transposing the name Ellen Lawless Ternan into the Helena Landless of *Edwin Drood*[35]—these self-parodies can also be seen to provide Dickens with an ability to indulge a tabooed impulse with impunity. That is, they can be seen as an exhilarating sublimation, a disguised indulgence of his own excessive—because transgressive—desires. Though attacked through satire, these self-dramatizations would then give Dickens an opportunity to body forth his repressed wishes. But whatever else we can say about these self-parodies as gratifications, their presence also indicates that Dickens realized full well how these transgressive impulses of his are themselves diverted from true limit experience, how they are surrogates for the ultimate excess, for death. There is nothing more mechanical than the arbitrary substitution of an available lover for a lost one, nothing more clichéd than the romantically infatuated young man, nothing more common than a husband's hostility toward his wife and mother-in-law. The most interesting thing about these self-parodies, then, is that they gratify Dickens' search for limit experience, not merely through fantasy and wish-fulfillment, but through parody. In other words, by stressing and participating in the mechanical nature of his transgressive projects, Dickens does not perform his desires merely to satisfy them as they are in a sublimated way; instead, he achieves a kind of excess by taking up the most comically mechanical desires of his unconscious and by performing those desires with excessive spirit in a medium that renders them pointless, absurd, and unreal. By dramatizing impulses toward excess as mechanical, Dickens frees those impulses from their banal subjective form and uses them as vehicles for a kind of maniacal energy that claims to have no stake of its own in such impulses.

In light of this radical tendency of Dickens' mechanical prose to disengage itself from positive forms of human gratification and to delight in extreme parodic negativity instead, we can begin to evaluate the pervasive love of mechanism in Dickens' prose in more recognizable philosophical terms. In his style, localized satire and the laughter of superiority give way to what Baudelaire called the *comic absolu*[36]—art which directs its ridicule not against individuals or groups, but against the rigidity of all of nature. By refusing to define itself against those rigidities in some naturalized, organic way, however, and by immersing itself instead in rigid forms of expression, Dickens' style bypasses what is usually meant by "irony," the creation of a superior freedom through rejection. That is to say, the ironist is usually seen to achieve a kind of negative freedom through his rejection of the world. Paul de Man calls this process in romantic irony *dédoublement*; the ironist achieves freedom by opposing the self-as-consciousness negatively to the self-caught-up-in-the-world. The two can exist only in relation, one conscious of the other, but the very separation is a kind of freedom.[37] One theorist has defined this notion concisely. "Irony is the consciousness of the infinite negations of which free consciousness is capable in the exercise of its liberty."[38] But just as it is often difficult to find an object for Dickens' parody, so, too, it would be difficult to see in many instances (the Derby Day passage, for example) what an ironic consciousness in Dickens would be conscious of, or what it would negate. There is no dialectical opposition to this parody, no celebration of a subjectivity that is superior to particular attitudes or states of mind. Dickens' parody celebrates the energy of universal impersonation, not an aloof, subjective distance. It conforms more clearly to Jacques Derrida's notion of expenditure's goals. "[The] without-reserve of absolute expenditure . . . convulsively tears apart the negative side, that which makes it the reassuring other surface of the position; and it exhibits within the negative, in an instant, that which can no longer be called negative."[39]

Rather than producing an ironic consciousness that is detached from the world in a self-integrated way, Dickens dissolves rational consciousness in the exuberance of his excesses within mechanism. The freedom of Dickens as mechanical narrator is not his detachment from the role he assumes, but his freedom to expend himself excessively into the role, to lose himself in it once it is located in art as a mechanism without function or purpose. What we admire as readers is not the man implied behind the mask, but the extravagance of his involvement in the mask, the lavish details of the performance, the prodigal flourishes of the assumed role. We differentiate Dickens' energy from the human stereotypes that it animates, but only as energy, a something that consumes itself before our eyes, and not as a cold potency, a something held in reserve, a withheld judgmental consciousness. We should remember that Dickens so identified himself with his characters that he used to describe them on paper by transcribing his own appearance as he mimed them before a mirror. And as readers, our response to Dickens ideally is not reverence for the hypostatized aloofness of the ironist; it is, or should be, the kind of loss of conscious control before the narrator's exuberance that Dickens has described in one of the spectators at his readings. "There was a remarkably good fellow too, of thirty or so, who found something so very ludicrous in Toots that he *could not* compose himself at all, but laughed until he sat wiping his eyes with his handkerchief; and whenever he felt Toots coming again, he began to laugh and wipe his eyes afresh; and when Toots came once more, he gave a kind of cry, as if it were too much for him."[40] Dickens' unconcealed interest in producing tears and laughter in his readers, as we have already seen, is an index of this interest in staging an abandonment of consciousness. There are no values necessarily implied by this abandonment—Dickens' "remarkably good fellow" could have felt only the joy of Dickens' verbal energy freely giving itself up to the mechanism of Toots' personality.

The crucial point about Dickens' style is that he achieves a liberating abandonment only, paradoxically, through mechanism, through a willed and exuberant yielding to various kinds of restriction—elegant pomposity, the grotesque voice, the burlesque voice, the patterning of novels—all of which can be made not merely inflexible, but maniacally inflexible, as if they had a life of their own. Claude Lévesque summarizes this principle, the way in which excess can be achieved through deliberate restriction, in his interpretation of Bataille's search for madness as limit experience.

It is not a question of paradoxically opting for madness instead of reason, of putting nonsense in the place of sense, because nonsense is at the very limit of sense and therefore implies it. On this matter Bataille is as explicit as he can be: he writes: "Le plus étrange dans ce voyage aux limites de l'être, je n'abandonne pas la raison"; "Le raison seule accède à ce vertigineux, qui échapperait si cela n'était intangible en nous." . . . Bataille does not believe in the possibility of experience outside of language and its possibilities. You leave language through language just as you leave the domain of the project through a project.[41]

In Dickens' world, the freedom of excess is, not a freedom of opposition, but a kind of distraction, a slippage of consciousness as it acts a part in the world, aware that its energy uses those parts only as vehicles for its own expense.

iv

It is tempting to assume that Dickens' use of mechanical narrative devices, which tacitly allow his verbal energies to surpass the normal economics of meaning, somehow marks a final liberation of energy from restrictions in his novels. The vitality of his prose in the burlesque mode or in the freer moments of the parodic mode seems completely expended in a profitless enthusiasm. But as this study has made clear, all excess short of death is implicated again in some form of economy. Pure excess is always a tendency or at best a moment, never an achievement —which is why conflicts like the tension between satire and parody are necessary to heighten it. And in terms of Dickens' narrative style, while one impulse behind that style does push it to surpass certain limits of usefulness and to approach the more open reaches of impersonal energy, that impulse establishes another kind of limiting presence in the process. Dickens' narrator may not define himself as superior, in the manner of the ironist, yet there is a stabilizing presence created by this narrator's mechanical dissipation of energy. And, as we shall see, this stabilizing presence facilitates—for Dickens' Victorian readers, at least—yet another kind of loss.

Ultimately, the machine-like voice in Dickens has a subtle component of reserve; it implies a certain stable ground for its freedom. Dickens' narrator, when he is so completely negative, is projected as a thoroughly neutral, impersonal presence. This impersonal presence, as we have already seen, is not one that employs its reserve, its ironic freedom, in service of a superior subjectivity—as, say, the narrator of a Hemingway novel does. Dickens' narrator never uses parody to promote a particular point of view, because the parody is exuberant rather than rational, sympathetically involved rather than satirically detached. The narrator willingly and, one might almost say, lovingly becomes and acts out what he parodies. And yet, because of the transcending freedom implied by that very excessiveness, the narrator does become, in a certain sense, a stable point, an omniscience that the reader is always able to identify as a generous but unequivocal sovereign, implying security, stability, and community. The paradox is difficult to grasp, since outright, unrestricted parody is something we have considered to be subversive and not constitutive of communal values. But a comparison of several pathetic/parodic passages will show how Dickens' parodic voice, even in its excessive "uselessness," represents a subtle containment of loss.

In 1841, Dickens' pet raven, the one used as a model for Grip in *Barnaby Rudge*, suddenly died. Dickens sent a letter to Maclise describing the death.

Yesterday afternoon he was taken so much worse that I sent an express for the medical gentleman (Mr. Herring), who promptly attended, and administered a powerful dose of castor oil. Under the influence of this medicine, he recovered so far as to be able at eight o'clock p.m. to bite Topping. His night was peaceful. This morning at daybreak he appeared better; received (agreeably to the doctor's directions) another dose of castor oil; and partook plentifully of some warm gruel, the flavor of which he appeared to relish. Towards eleven o'clock he was so much the worse that it was found necessary to muffle the stable-knocker. At half-past, or there-abouts, he was heard talking to himself about the horse and Topping's family, and to add some incoherent expressions which are supposed to have been either a foreboding of his approaching dissolution, or some wishes relative to the disposal of his little property: consisting chiefly of half-pence which he had buried in different parts of the garden. On the clock striking twelve he appeared slightly agitated, but he soon recovered, walked twice or thrice along the coach-house, stopped to bark, staggered, exclaimed *Halloa old girl!* (his favorite expression), and died.

He behaved throughout with a decent fortitude, equanimity, and self-possession, which cannot be too much admired. . . . Were they ravens who took manna to somebody in the wilderness? At times I hope they were, and at others I fear they were not, or they would certainly have stolen it by the way. In profound sorrow I am your bereaved friend C. D. Kate is as well as can be expected, but terribly low as you may suppose. The children seem rather glad of it. He bit their ankles. But that was play.[42]

Forster, caught up with Dickens' comic tone well enough to play along, records: "unable from the state of his feelings to write two letters, he sent the narrative to Maclise under an enormous black seal, for transmission to me." Of course, it is difficult to specify Dickens' real feelings here, but the important point is that the parody is not felt to be cruel or hardhearted, even though it undermines the typical human reaction to death; as in the above-mentioned treatment of Boffin, there is even something affectionate in Dickens' treatment of the bird's thinglike mannerisms, a kind of love for the bird's very way of dying. But this affection is affection firmly rooted in distance, in the breezy serenity of the parody. It is an affection that emphasizes its own inability to be ruffled by death. It tells us: this is, after all, the death of a bird. The mechanized, parodic enthusiasm of the narrative voice here is disengaged from the pathetic subject matter in a way that is ultimately comforting. Dickens' tone comprehends death in a generous joviality that survives death—as machines do—that is simply not related to the world in which birds die. The narrative tone is almost patriarchal, indulgent of suffering the way a father would indulge a spoilt child—which is exactly how Dickens once described his relationship to his work.[43]

The death of a raven is one thing, of course, and human pathos is another. But Dickens' parodic tone—which cannot be

identified as comic, as harsh, or as satiric, but which is somehow
transcendent, clearly sovereign—remains an integral part of his
sentimental death scenes. Some of the same devices used to describe the raven's death can be found in the death of the orphan
John in *Our Mutual Friend*.

> "Him!" said the little fellow. "Those!"
>
> The doctor was quick to understand children, and, taking the
> horse, the ark, the yellow bird, and the man in the Guards, from
> Johnny's bed, softly placed them on that of his neighbor, the mite with
> the broken leg.
>
> With a weary and yet a pleased smile, and with an action as if he
> stretched his little figure out to rest, the child heaved his body on the
> sustaining arm, and seeking Rokesmith's face with his lips, said:
>
> "A kiss for the boofer lady."
>
> Having now bequeathed all he had to dispose of, and arranged his
> affairs in the world, Johnny, thus speaking, left it. (2.9)

The comic disposition of worldly goods, the abrupt, mechanical
exit, the "favorite expression" of the dying child—all are absorbed directly into the scene, not as comic diversions, but as
the very substance of the narration. It would be inappropriate
to call this narrative voice comic; the orphan's death is a dominantly pathetic scene. Still, the parodic voice is fused into this
scene in an odd kind of mixture, one that implies neither ridicule
nor pity. What this voice does instead is insist on the mechanical
narrator's difference from the scene he has created. It "miniaturizes" the death scene and effectively distances it from the
narrator's sphere of being. The impression the reader has is that
the narrator comprehends the death scene in a way that recognizes the element of loss and even increases it through a sympathetic contrast of Johnny's pathetic mechanical movements and
the abyss into which they dissolve, but in a way that transcends
loss; the narrator, through his mechanical distance, occupies an
impersonal but creatorly role.

It would not be inappropriate to invoke again the Master-

Slave dialectic to explain the authority achieved by the narrator here. In a sense, the parodic narrator displays his affinity with death through parody; he violates the normally sacrosanct limits of sense and in a very real way launches himself into an open-ended, sometimes violent and cruel, dizzying world of speech that most of us would never dare free ourselves enough to enter. We feel in Dickens' parodic narrator a potential for verbal violence that surpasses our own capacities for explosive expression. There seems to be no limit to the lengths Dickens' narrator will go to in the exercise of his inexhaustible energy. And in this way, the parodic narrator reclaims the status of a superior being, a master, an author. No wonder that Dickens' narrative voice is able to justify itself as one of the most authoritative, controlling voices in English literature; its excessive freedom is the condition for this authority.

Moreover, the parodic elements in scenes like the death of the orphan John help tie potentially tragic scenes back to the rest of Dickens' prose. Rather than representing a radical rupture in the Dickensian world, Johnny's death is presented against the background of an unruffled voice that quietly but firmly calls to mind the well-oiled, well-ordered Dickens world in its entirety. It need hardly be said, too, that one of the elements in that world is the network of values of liberal humanism associated with the satiric half of Dickens' disengaged narrator. The inextricable blend of parodic and satiric voices in Dickens makes it possible for the reader to associate the austere, limitless authority of the parodic narrator's voice with specific, conservative values—a kindly attitude toward children, for example, or the underlying reverence for social communities discussed in the previous chapter. In a very complex way, Dickens' mechanical voice hints at mastering authority at the same time that it endows that limitless authority paradoxically with a particular set of conservative values, making it an infinitely benign but infinitely powerful master.

The resulting tension between tragic loss and a stabilizing, masterful, parodic overtone helps create the kind of conflict that facilitates emotional release. We saw in Chapter 2 how one powerful inducement to yield to our feelings of grief is the presence of a secure yet sympathetic other, which is exactly what Dickens' narrator becomes. It is perhaps one of the most skillful aspects of Dickens' style that he was able to create this sense of infinite detachment in his narrator through parody and at the same time personalize the narrator enough so that he did not undermine the pathos of the scene for his Victorian readers through an affected ironic or aggressive superiority. The blend of parodic and satiric overtones attempts to balance in a very delicate way the tension between extreme states of loss and an infinite comprehension of loss.

This same strategy is at work in more subtle ways in all of Dickens' pathetic death scenes, though it does not necessarily focus on the victim but can use other characters as vehicles of parody instead. Even in the death of Little Nell, for example, the parodic voice is given great play through Nell's grandfather, who obsessively, mechanically refuses to accept the death. The narrator's lengthy treatment of the grandfather, which, on the one hand, heightens suspense and, on the other, reinforces our sense of the narrator as a masterful impersonator of the rigid, prepares us for the violation of his blunt announcement that Nell is dead. In the death of Jo in *Bleak House*, too, the parody focuses on Snagsby's attempt to make everything right with money, on Jo's mechanical repetition of the "Our Father" and his pathetically conventional desire to make his own will (this particular keynote does Dickens' parodic narrator great service), and on the broken-cart metaphor, which becomes so rampant and regular that it calls attention to the narrator's verbal abilities. Even Jo's pauper dialect, which Dickens has used elsewhere to comic effect, helps keep up the parodic overtones. "Different times, there was other genlmen come down Tom-all-Alone's a-prayin, but they all mostly sed as the t'other wuns prayed wrong, and all mostly sounded to be a-talking to theirselves, or a-passing blame on the t'others, and not a-talkin to us.

We never knowd nothink. *I* never knowd what it wos all about"
(47). In all these scenes, the parodic tone does not invoke comedy. What it does most of all, is invoke the impersonal authority
of the narrator's voice as the proper tension to balance against
the reader's desire to yield to grief.

This relationship between the authoritative parodic voice
and the reader's sense that he may safely abandon himself to
emotion in the presence of that voice—a relationship that is sug-
gestively like the contrast between brutality and vulnerability
that underlies all of *The Old Curiosity Shop*—provides us with
a further clue to our earlier question about why Dickens should
open his novels with more than usually extravagant parodies.
Only when the narrator's authority has been established through
his razor-sharp, seemingly omniscient critical faculties can he be
used as an effective counterpoint for more naive emotional aban-
donments. In effect, the narrator's all-inclusive intelligence and
critical powers, his mechanical ruthlessness, open a verbal space
in which Dickens' Victorian readers could suspend critical faculties and give way to naive emotion. From suspecting all motives and all behavior along with the narrator, the reader is
enabled to entrust the all-powerful narrator alone with that responsibility and to suspect none himself; the narrator's limitless
intelligence thus permits a sacrifice of rational control on the
part of readers.

Perhaps the best illustration of this principle is the way
Dickens often ridicules minor good characters when they are
first introduced, only to soften toward them later. For example,
Susan Nipper in *Dombey and Son* is originally called "Spitfire,"
and we are told she was "so desperately sharp and biting that
she seemed to make one's eyes water" (3). Tom Pinch is "far
from handsome certainly," has "a ludicrous habit . . . of thrusting his head forward," and is "one of those strange creatures
who never decline into an ancient appearance, but look their
oldest when they are very young, and get it over at once" (2).
Barkis is "of a phlegmatic temperament, and not at all con-
versational—I offered him a cake as mark of attention, which he

ate at one gulp, exactly like an elephant, and which made no more impression on his big face than it would have done on an elephant's" (5). Similar slanders are directed at the first appearances of Sleary, Caddy Jellyby, and Wemmick. Dickens' first impulse with these characters—which reflects a larger impulse affecting the overall form of his novels—is to establish a critical perspective immediately, one which is often needlessly grating and which calls attention to its own freedom from restraint. Once this authoritative, impersonal attitude is established, Dickens can allow it to recede somewhat into the background, both as the facilitator of sentiment and its limit.

So it is, too, that the parodic voice in Dickens, once established as an overriding context, can recede into the background as the restraining context for Dickens' more naive narrative voices—the rapturous voice, or the sentimental voice. Garrett Stewart has pointed out how what he calls the "lyric voice" in Dickens—the voice of David Copperfield's "Retrospects"—is an ageless kind of writing in which assertion and self-will dissolve into an identityless emotional flux.[44] David Copperfield, for example, introducing one of his "Retrospects," says "let me stand aside" and then lets the "phantoms" of memory proceed past him (43); the atmosphere of these passages is suffused with references to the dreamy dispersion of self he feels through remembrance. David sees everything through a mist, or "in a dream"; he registers surprise at frequent dissociated images of himself; he asks his visions questions like, "Why does Traddles look so important?" (43), as if he had no control over these projections himself. Similarly, the "lyric" voice that ends *Martin Chuzzlewit* with a portrait of Tom Pinch aspires to a kind of dissolution of self; the narrator tries to merge his prose with the contentless, nondiscursive chords of Tom's music and ends the novel with a fantasied dissolution of Tom and his sister into that music, which interrupts the progress of time and makes present merge with past and future. "As it resounds within thee and without, the noble music, rolling round ye both, shuts out the grosser prospect of an earthly parting, and uplifts ye both to Heaven!" (54).

These passages in Dickens are the closest he ever comes to directly expressing "excessive" emotion; that is, in these passages Dickens invites the reader directly to feel the dissolution of personal boundaries that he can evoke only indirectly in numerous other aspects of his work. But it is interesting to note that these effusions are made possible partly through their relationship to the restraining authority established by the parodic voice. The extremely brief rhapsody over Tom Pinch, for example, is preceded by a lengthy and very harsh—for the last chapter of a Dickens novel—comic treatment of Mercy Pecksniff's being jilted at the altar by her intended, Augustus. The four "Retrospects" of *David Copperfield* each follow chapters that end with the freest kind of comedy possible in David's polite book, all involving the Micawbers. The systematic appearance of the Micawbers—which in two cases out of the four are gratuitous tidbits dropped at the end of otherwise very serious chapters—at these key moments seems an attempt on Dickens' part to use his strongest exercise of the parodic voice as a springboard to "lyric" emotion. Only by giving over a certain amount of stabilizing authority to Dickens' mechanically acute narrator can the reader yield to the abandonment of control called for in these passages.

In one way or another, emotional writing in Dickens is always balanced by the presence of an intelligent, mastering parodist. Even the more exclusively sentimental Christmas sketches begin with the firm intonations of the parodic voice. "A Christmas Carol" is perhaps the most striking; the comic repetition of the fact of Marley's death, the fun with the expression "dead as a doornail," the tongue-in-cheek mention of Scrooge's "solemnizing" the day of the funeral with a bargain—all strike a parodic posture that solidly establishes the authoritative personality of Dickens' narrative machine. And the balancing of these kinds of narrative forces—the direct emotional excesses backed by the overriding stability of an authorial voice—are brought into their most direct conjunction in Dickens' endings. Here, the sentiment springing from our vague sense of nostalgia at "losing" the good characters is enhanced and contained by the genial parody that defines the atmosphere around the heroic couple by miniaturizing secondary characters, like Charley's brother Tom in *Bleak House*, who is "always falling in love with somebody, and being ashamed of it" (67), or like Bates in *Oliver Twist*, who becomes "the merriest grazier in all Northamptonshire" (53). In *David Copperfield*, it is Traddles who is miniaturized, being described whimsically by the narrator in his new role as "Patriarch" at the same time that he remains "exactly the same, unaffected fellow as he ever was" (64). These friendly satiric references all represent attempts on Dickens' part to balance Esther's blissful marriage, Oliver's "perfect happiness," and David's "beautiful serenity."

This doubleness, in all its interwoven forms—the economy of authoritative intelligence, the excess of sentiment; the economy of satire, the excess of parody—is at the heart of Dickens' narrative style and accounts for the fact that, rather than consisting of a single texture, Dickens' style is a rhythm of constrictions and expansions,[45] sometimes spaced across many pages, sometimes fused as a dynamic within the same voice. Finally, it is probably futile to try to isolate the dialectical components of Dickens' narrative voice in this way; certainly, any systematic analysis must fail. Yet, however limited the description of the workings of Dickens' dialectical language machine that is developed here, I hope it creates an awareness of his stylistic complexity that will contribute to his readers' greater admiration of Dickens' genius.

Chapter 7

The Fairy Tale

Everything possible to be believed is an image of truth.

—William Blake, "The Marriage of Heaven and Hell"

If they have not died, they are still alive.

—Traditional fairy-tale ending

Dickens' stylistic freedom through excess is always a negative one, in the sense that all excess is negative; it is founded upon a loss. The energy released through Dickens' writing is negative energy because it is exhausted without being able to recuperate, in some valuable way, the artistic play that it generates. What distinguishes Dickens' parodic voice from his satiric voice is precisely its uselessness, its tendency to escape rational purpose and values. At its purest moments, the energy of that voice is expended without leaving the positive trace of a meaning behind. But Dickens did want to present some kind of final, positive image of this experience, which is why his novels always move from parody to romance. Though Dickens' novels may begin in absolute skeptical negativity, they end in unqualified images of satisfaction. In the presentation of these positive images, of course, Dickens is faced with the problem that haunts most novelists: the problem of imaging infinite (or "negative") novelistic experience in a finite form.[1]

Dickens is usually assumed to have resolved the dissonances of his world in an image of the bourgeois marriage that is too conventional to be taken seriously. He thus fails to address either metaphysical or pragmatic issues satisfactorily, and he certainly never brings them into agreement. But as long as the question of conclusiveness is posed in this traditional way—as the problem of a disjunction between transcendent experience and meaning recuperated as a limited form of experience in the world—the question is self-circumscribing. What is at stake in Dickens is not a prescription for a final, transcendental positivity; what is at stake is the affirmation of a purity of loss. Since by definition loss does not want to be recuperated, the question for the ending of Dickens' novels becomes: how does the narrative affirm loss as a form of human action in a way that mitigates its terror? Dickens *did* want to end his novels with a positive image, but not necessarily with a positive image of recuperated meaning, or even of recuperated loss. Rather, as we saw in Chapter 5, Dickens wanted to present a positive image of loss itself, drained of its violent and aggressive qualities. Instead of simply retreating from impulses toward ultimate excess, in his endings Dickens wanted to image the very goal of excess—that which is beyond the limits of human life, the impersonal flux of union and continuity—in a desirable way. In Dickens' novels, this project extends beyond the symbolic level discussed previously in regard to endings and becomes also a question of stylistic enthusiasm, of voice: first, through certain stressed qualities of the positive images in Dickens' "happy endings," and second—but more importantly—through appeals to a narrative genre that renders even these images obviously mechanical, thus freeing the energy that animates them.

In the first place, Dickens' eternally conclusive image of the bourgeois marriage certainly does not express the violence of excess, but it does express the wish underlying all expenditure, the wish that loss may produce "union." In Dickens' endings, as in those of all Victorian novels, we are presented with marriage as an act, not as a state. As indicated previously, we should be careful to observe a difference between the social or ideological meaning of the state of marriage and the experience of timelessness that marriage as an act can produce for characters. Esther Summerson repeatedly insists on this timeless quality in her marriage, and her version of timelessness exceeds even the vehicle of marriage that creates it, since timelessness extends to everyone associated with Esther in *Bleak House*, married or unmarried. Of Charley, Esther says, "I might suppose Time to have stood still for seven years"; of Jarndyce, "I have never known the wind to be in the East for a single moment, since the day when he took me to the porch to read the name" (67). And even a disillusioned Pip at the end of *Great Expectations* sees "no shadow of another parting" (59) from Estella. In one way or another, all of Dickens' novels feature an ending moment that dissolves both the flow of time—which engenders separations— and the estrangements between characters, resolving them all into an uninterrupted state of bliss that Bataille would call "continuity," the eroticized formlessness that is ontologically prior to the discontinuity of human life. In his endings, Dickens takes positive—in the sense of nonviolent—images of expenditure, images of rest rather than of energy, and he pushes these images to the point at which they become images of a purer loss, irreconcilable with the world. This is the reason why Dickens' happy endings have a nostalgic quality to them; the happy ending is an image of loss contained now within a soothing metaphorics of union. We saw in Chapter 5 how Dickens' endings are based in hidden movements of excess, but it is also important to recognize that the ending represents marriage itself as an act that ends experience, rather than as a beginning or a continuation of experience. Dickens' typical sorrow at taking leave of his characters is partly sorrow over their being rarefied beyond the range of his pen—that is, beyond the possibility of meaningful, alterable existence in the world.

In the second place, these positive images, in which loss is embodied in a conservative form, are treated stylistically in vaguely parodic terms similar to those Dickens uses to free the energy of narrative parody from the rigid, mechanical stereotypes that it animates. So it is that we feel Dickens' tone to be slightly condescending at the end of his novels even toward his good characters. The more affirmative way to put this is that Dickens miniaturizes his good society in a way that seems to remove it from the realm of plausibility. But to raise the issue of style in this way is to raise the great question always asked of Dickens' work: did Dickens really believe in his domestic conclaves as plausible images of blissful life on earth? What exactly is the status of the good society in Dickens' novels as an image of human action?

Surely, Dickens did believe in the values represented by hearth and home, but it is possible to see in his attitude two different levels of belief. We know, for example, that for all his defense of the home, Dickens was a less-than-perfect husband himself. Johnson points out that he never regarded his wife as an equal,[2] and it is difficult to understand why he tortured Kate with his love for Mary,[3] or why he made her visit Ellen Ternan after declaring to Kate his love for the actress.[4] In addition, Dickens often neglected his children. His daughter Katie said of Dickens during the time of his separation from his wife, "He did not give a damn about any of us. We were the most miserable and unhappy household imagineable."[5] We also know that Dickens had nothing but contempt for the ordinary domestic novel.[6] These inconsistencies do not necessarily make Dickens a hypocrite, or a bad husband—whatever we understand that to mean—but they do tend to imply that there was some kind of doubleness in Dickens' attitude toward conventional marriage. Significantly, Forster tells us that Dickens could be convinced only with considerable difficulty that *Household Harmony* might be a bad title for a magazine about to appear immediately after his separation from Kate.[7] Strangely, too, Dickens' audience at the first readings supported him wholeheartedly throughout the separation, continuing to cherish his stories of connubial bliss despite what they knew of the author's blasted home life. On both sides, belief in marriage as a value seems willing to dispense with the reality, or at least to have slightly different expectations from life and from literature, and to take slightly different satisfactions from the two. Dickens himself casts this doubleness in harsh terms through the artistic doubleness of Jenny Wren; the doll's dressmaker takes great pains in the construction and care of her dolls, yet she hates real children. This kind of doubleness indicates that the question of Dickens' actual beliefs is irrelevant to the novels; the real question is, what did Dickens do with the convention of bourgeois marriage as a writer? And what happens to the convention when it is projected in his novels? Very simply, such conventions operate only as fairy-tale values.

Dickens' fairy-tale marriages emerge from the same source as many of his stylistic idiosyncracies—in a parodic movement that expends energy profitlessly and experiences a pleasure in loss. How the fairy tale parallels Dickens' parodic voice will become apparent if we consider for a moment what a fairy tale is. From a certain perspective, the fairy tale can be seen as a substitute for, rather than a reflection of, reality. According to Jean Starobinski, for example, the fairy tale expresses what is literary about literature—its desire to stage experience that is not possible in the limited state of nature, but which is possible as an act of free consciousness. The goal of the fairy tale, Starobinski says, is to make the literal meaning of a story insubstantial and to emphasize instead its figural meaning.[8] In this view, the fairy tale does not represent a state of affairs in nature, since it is obviously not true, and it does not take our credence on a mimetic level; rather, the fairy tale is an image of the kind of felicity man can imagine but can project only in language. For this reason, the fairy tale calls attention to its artificiality, its unreality, its claim to a separate, purely linguistic status. That is, by emphasizing its formal unreality, the fairy tale seems to embody desires without tying them to real and, therefore, inevitably limited solutions. In other words, through the fairy-tale device Dickens' stories are deliberately presented as mechanical, as artificial, to elide the conservative ideological content of the conclusions without actually negating that ideology. Paradoxically, by stressing their conventionality, their mechanicalness, these endings aspire to the more organic world of pure story.

Though we tend to think of fairy tales as naive, self-consciousness is actually indispensible to the form. As Starobinski points out, many great fairy tales—the *1001 Nights*, for instance, or the fables of Gozzi and Hoffmann—are framed by explicit hopes that the world of story can cure the melancholy of characters within the fairy tale. The fairy-tale story itself is often presented as the magical cure for the particular melancholy at hand.[9] Something of this belief in the magically primal power of stories lies behind Captain Cuttle's announcement to Florence—"I know a story, Heart's Delight" (49)—as an introduction to his producing Walter; Cuttle's fairy-tale story echoes Polly's fairy tale at the beginning of *Dombey and Son*, in which she tries to present Florence with an image of the restoration of her mother, but Cuttle—a better storyteller—actually makes his story work. Cuttle's self-conscious fabrication of an innocent but potent world of story at the critical juncture of the novel is telling: the very naiveté of fairy tales is often deliberate, as an expression of their claim to primal truth. No wonder that even the most serious analysts of narrative often tend to think of fairy tales as being closer to the organic well-springs of narrative than to the literature generated by mere individuals. What this deliberate fabrication of naiveté implies, ultimately, is that the pretended naturalness of the fairy tale conceals very real, socially determined values; the purity of the fairy tale is illusory. But the illusion is powerful, and, in Dickens' case, it is an indispensible element in the effect of his endings.

The most important feature of the fairy-tale voice, then, for our purposes, is that it always tries to circumvent any subjective assertion of temporal values by aspiring to the pure world of story. In the fairy tale, we are asked to believe in the absence of merely personal authorship and of any personal avowal of values. By being traditional, and even mechanically formulaic, the fairy tale aspires to an objective or impersonal status, denying its partiality. And through this deliberate gesture toward the world of story, the fairy tale tries to break itself free of determined meaning. The consequence of this aspiration toward narrative purity is that even the figural meaning of the fairy tale is not meant to be reduced to temporal terms. Starobinski claims that when fairy tales do provide morals, these morals are either obviously tacked on or they are enigmatic, belonging to a different order of knowledge;[10] even a psychoanalyst like Bruno Bettelheim, who is interested in the use fairy tales are put to by children, insists that fairy tales are never meant to be explained.[11] Dickens himself hated the reduction of fairy tales to moral lessons—he protested vehemently, for example, against Cruikshank's use of fairy tales as lessons in temperance.[12]

As an intention, at least, the fairy-tale voice does not remain tied to the conventions it employs—for the very reason that those conventions are so obvious—any more than the parodic voice is tied to the objects of satire it uses as a springboard. Instead, the fairy tale is a kind of benign parody of the real, deliberately stressing itself as intention and not as prescription. Like the parodic voice, the fairy-tale voice is a narrative machine; it uses the conventions of the happy ending, along with its other obvious clichés and repeated motifs, in exactly the same way that Dickens' parodic voice uses the conventions of mechanical behavior—that is, to elide the mimetic substantiality of those conventions in favor of mimetically ungrounded and therefore free images of continuity. Thus, John Harmon and Bella Wilfer's home is frequently described as a doll's house to express an impossible kind of harmony, one that negates any conceivable conflicts they might have—specifically, one wants to say, over Harmon's deception. Similarly, Jarndyce's fairy-tale role as Esther's guardian helps to eliminate questions about the plausibility of his nonsexual interest in her. Character psychology is partially suspended here in favor of a larger, purely formal, narrative resolution. Aside from these specific images of marriage, Dickens' endings generally insist on their pure existence as stories by calling attention to their fictional status. When Mr. Dombey and his grandson disappear into the ending of *Dombey and Son*, we are told, "as they go about together, the story of the bond between them goes about, and follows them" (62); the ending in *A Tale of Two Cities* is projected as a story told by Darnay to his future grandson; and besides telling us that the story of Nell is repeated by Kit to his children, and by Master Humphrey to his circle of friends, *The Old Curiosity Shop* ends, "Such are the changes which a few years bring about, and so do things pass away, like a tale that is told" (72).

A closer look will reveal all of Dickens' concluding marriages to be presented as fairy-tale marriages, as resolutions which lack psychological or social content because they are dictated by the naive power of story. Of John Westlock and Ruth Pinch we are told, "They went away, but not through London's streets! Through some enchanted city, where the pavements were of air; where all the rough sounds of a stirring town were softened into

gentle music; where everything was happy; where there was no
distance, and no time" (53). This enchanted city is not merely an
ornamental way of describing Ruth's bliss; it posits a state of
being that exists only on the level of story, as the negation of
worldly space and time. The more prosaic descriptions of Tom
and Ruth Pinch's bourgeois domestic economy earlier stress the
difference between the substantiality of that arrangement and
the insubstantial, purely fictional quality of Ruth's marriage.
So, too, David Copperfield loves Agnes "with a love unknown on
earth" (60). Even *Little Dorrit*, which ends more grimly, perhaps, than any other Dickens novel, concludes with a modest appeal to the fixed destiny of the fairy-tale world; before they
leave the Marshalsea to be married, Arthur and Little Dorrit
ritually burn his mother's letter, while Arthur asks, "Does the
charm want any words to be said?" (2.34). And at the church,
Little Dorrit's "old friend" holds open the worn marriage regis-
ter for her to sign and comments, "This young lady is one of our
curiosities, and has come now to the third volume of our Registers. Her birth is in what I call the first volume; she lay, asleep
on this very floor, with her pretty head on what I call the second
volume; and she's now a-writing her little name as a bride, in
what I call the third volume." Earlier, the volumes of the regis-
try had been called a "sealed book of Fate" (1.14). Then, too,
Little Dorrit's marriage cannot but remind us of the fairy tale
she had earlier told Maggy, about a "tiny woman" who possesses
a "shadow of Some one," which she will take to her grave with
her (1.24). Little Dorrit's fairy tale comes true in a way that
even she had not foreseen; this fairy tale posits a union of the
"tiny woman" and the "Some one" only in death. And, as we saw
in Chapter 5, Little Dorrit and Arthur must go through a kind of
deathlike loss—the separation from the world both experience
through the loss of their fortunes—before they can be united.

The marriage of John Harmon and Bella Wilfer is the union
most explicitly merged with the conventions of the fairy tale.
We are told that "the two walked away together with an ethe-
real air of happiness, which, as it were, wafted up from the

earth and drew after them a gruff and glum old pensioner to see it out" (4.4). This character is then given a fairy-tale sobriquet, "Gruff and Glum"; Mr. Wilfer is so frightened by this apparition that "his conscience might have introduced, in the person of that pensioner, his own stately lady disguised, arrived at Greenwich in a car and griffins, like the spiteful Fairy at the christenings of the Princesses, to do something dreadful to the marriage service." Bella's movements are described as a fairylike gliding; "the church-porch having swallowed up Bella Wilfer for ever and ever, had it not in its power to relinquish that young woman, but slid into the happy sunlight, Mrs John Rokesmith instead." And at the marriage dinner we are told that there are even "samples of the fishes of divers color that made a speech in the Arabian Nights"; that the dishes are "seasoned with Bliss"; and that "the golden drink had been bottled in the golden age." The fairy-tale references suffusing the wedding—barely glanced at here—are inexhaustible, making this marriage seem the focal point for all the fairy-tale motifs scattered throughout *Our Mutual Friend*; together they make this marriage, the last to be described in Dickens' novels, seem to address itself to the primitive world of story and to dissolve any reality in the love of John and Bella into a fairy-tale connection that exceeds the world.

In this way, Dickens uses the fairy-tale voice to move beyond the conventions of his happy endings—specifically, the resolution of marriage—into the world they intend, a world of rest that is on the other side of loss, a world which, as our study of expenditure makes clear, is something that consciousness can imagine, can even intend as the goal of action, but cannot fully realize in the world. The reader of Dickens' novels is not left with marriage as a meaning, a prescription for happiness—if he were, the bachelorhood of characters like Tom Pinch, Jarndyce, or Mortimer Lightwood would be disturbing. Instead, conservative, fairy-tale marriages become metaphors for an affirmed experience of timelessness and of satisfied, excessive desire; the fairy-tale marriage presents a positive image of that which surpasses or destroys meaning, exceeding significance by dissolving itself into the pure mechanism of narrative convention. Thus, for Dickens, the fairy tale is a terrorless image of loss itself, and fairy-tale marriages aspire to an absence of ideological or social content—they constitute a kind of infinite loss—by merging with traditional narrative structures. In other words, positive expressions of loss or rest in Dickens depend paradoxically on the operation of a linguistic and narrative machine that never ceases its operation.

Through the fairy-tale voice in Dickens, the happy ending is lifted above the status of a worldly economy, an image only of what can be retained. As if to insure this excess, there is no observable progress developed to produce the happy ending; it is not earned by any of the characters[13] and therefore does not form a strategy of exchange or reward—it cannot realistically be reimplemented; it is "useless." In sum, Dickens employs an image of what recuperated loss might be like—marriage—only in a kind of recognition that thought cannot escape the necessity of temporal form, what Bataille calls "the self-evidence of meaning."[14] That is, the restoration of a significance to loss is inevitable in thought and in language—inevitable even in terms of this study of Dickens, which tries (despite an understanding of the paradoxical quality of the labor) to affirm a temporal, useful meaning in expenditure. But through the very predictability of fairy-tale marriage Dickens can use his conventional image in such a way as to push it, too, toward a euphoria of absence, toward a recognized fairy-tale impossibility that is the very condition of its value for Dickens and for his reader.

Notes

Introduction

1. Paul de Man, *Blindness and Insight* (New York: Oxford Univ. Press, 1971), p. 9.

2. I find myself partially sympathetic, for example, to the central argument of Gerald Graff, in *Literature Against Itself* (Chicago: Univ. of Chicago Press, 1979), that much of literary postmodernism merely rationalizes the powerlessness and consumer orientation of capitalist society. Graff, however, too dogmatically insists that literature must be divided into mimetic and autonomous categories, and thus falls victim to the extravagantly rigorous logic of the nonmimetic critics he chastises. By playing both ends off against the middle and risking no compromise or alternative, Graff's complaint is itself too complacently consumed. A more important influence is the work of Kenneth Burke, especially his ideas about "substance" as motive or intention. In *A Grammar of Motives* (Berkeley: Univ. of California Press, 1969), p. 57, Burke claims, "An epithet assigns substance doubly, for in stating the character of the object it at the same time contains an implicit program of action with regard to the object, thus serving as motive." Burke reasons further, "even when statements about the *nature of the world* are abstractly metaphysical, statements about the *nature of these statements* can be . . . empirical" (p. 58).

3. Robbe-Grillet's description might be "the sublimation of a difference"; *For a New Novel: Essays on Fiction*, trans. Richard Howard (New York: Grove, 1965), p. 60. For Lévi-Strauss, such artificial resolution of conflict points to a final relativity of meaning and value; see especially *The Savage Mind* (Chicago: Univ. of Chicago Press, 1966). However, as Nietzsche wrote long ago in *The Will to Power*, such skeptical attitudes toward truth covertly express a nostalgia for absolute certainties and an obsession with illusory kinds of moral purity. Furthermore, it would not be unfair to see the deconstructive critic as a version of Nietzsche's "ascetic priest"; a de facto rejection of all assertion, Nietzsche argues, is itself an assertion and a covert claim to power.

4. Stanley Diamond, *In Search of the Primitive* (New Brunswick, N.J.: Transaction Books, 1974), p. 153.

5. See Diamond's remarks in "The Inauthenticity of Anthropology: The Myth of Structuralism," in ibid., pp. 292–331.

6. I do not consider myself original in my theoretical goals. Critics like René Girard, Kenneth Burke, or Georges Bataille make similar kinds of compromise assumptions.

7. These ideas, absurdly abbreviated here, are all expressed in "Differance," *Speech and Phenomena, and Other Essays on Husserl's Theory of Signs*, trans. David B. Allison (Evanston, Ill.: Northwestern Univ. Press, 1973), pp. 129–60; and in *Of Grammatology*, trans. Gayatri Chakravorty Spivak (Baltimore: Johns Hopkins Univ. Press, 1976).

8. de Man, p. 106.

9. Derrida and de Man, of course, occupy an extreme position in a theoretical debate about the epistemological possibilities of literature. But the basic assumption that makes their work possible—the assumption that literature reflects an "inorganic" human consciousness of the world, and not the real world itself—permeates most contemporary discussion. One has only to look at a critic with opposing views about human flexibility like Frank Kermode to see the pervasiveness of this common groundwork. See especially *The Sense of an Ending* (New York: Oxford Univ. Press, 1966), in which Kermode discusses the "artificial" aspects of epistemology reflected by our very interest in positing fictional endings.

10. See Jacques Derrida, "Structure, Sign, and Play in the Discourse of the Human Sciences," in *The Structuralist Controversy: The Languages of Criticism and the Sciences of Man*, ed. Richard Macksey and Eugenio Donato (Baltimore: Johns Hopkins Univ. Press, 1970), pp. 147–64.

11. See "The Rhetoric of Blindness: Jacques Derrida's Reading of Rousseau," in *Blindness and Insight*, pp. 102–41. De Man's criticism of Derrida, interestingly enough, claims that Derrida, in his deconstructive project, creates desires for presence where they do not exist so that he may deconstruct them—in this case, in Rousseau. But de Man then sets aside Rousseau as a rare instance of the "unblinded author" without investigating the wonderful consequences of such a category; instead, he proceeds to claim that "blindness is part of the specificity of all literature" (p. 141).

12. Ultimately, as William E. Cain points out in "Deconstruction in America: The Recent Literary Criticism of J. Hillis Miller," *College English* 41 (1979): 367–82, this thematization results in a return to the

notion that the author "controls" his text—an undermining assertion
of extralinguistic authorial control that is implicit in most deconstructive projects. Cain also argues that deconstructive criticism privileges
a certain kind of knowledge about literary texts; deconstruction itself—or at least the intention to deconstruct—becomes "truth."

13. See James Kincaid, *Dickens and the Rhetoric of Laughter* (Oxford: Clarendon, 1971), especially pp. 12–14. Kincaid also claims that
comedy in Dickens is "subversive," but this notion is not developed in
Kincaid's book, which continues to see laughter as an educative, rhetorical tool.

14. Several recent critics have observed this tendency, though not
to similar conclusions: William F. Axton, in *Circle of Fire* (Lexington: Univ. of Kentucky Press, 1966), discusses a "rootless burlesque"
in Dickens' prose; Garrett Stewart, in *Dickens and the Trials of
Imagination* (Cambridge: Harvard Univ. Press, 1974), concentrates
on Dickens' love of negating the real through fantasy; and Robert
Garis, in *The Dickens Theater: A Reassessment of the Novels* (Oxford: Clarendon, 1965), analyzes Dickens' work for its "performative"
rather than its "psychological" content. J. Hillis Miller is perhaps
the most thorough of these critics, though he pursues his argument
to unfortunate nonmimetic lengths. See "The Fiction of Realism:
Sketches by Boz, Oliver Twist, and Cruikshank's Illustrations," in
Dickens Centennial Essays, ed. Ada Nisbet and Blake Nevius
(Berkeley: Univ. of California Press, 1971), pp. 1–69; or "The Sources
of Dickens's Comic Art," *Nineteenth-Century Fiction* 24 (1970): 467–76.
On the other hand, critics who attempt to recuperate Dickens at his
more nonsensical moments to a system of direct social analysis seem to
be stretching a point. See, for example, Raymond Williams, "Social
Criticism in Dickens: Some Problems of Method and Approach," *Critical Quarterly* 6 (1964): 214–27. Williams admits that Dickens' political
and social views are often either contradictory or ignorant, but he tries
to rescue Dickens as a social thinker by praising his vision of man, a
vision implicit in his nonsensical style, which tends to reduce characters to functions of their social or material environments. What Williams does not see, though, is that his approach opens the floodgates to
a vision of behavioral functionalism in Dickens that is social only in
part, one which contains an interest in human mechanization that is
purely parodic in origin.

15. The best Barthesian descriptions of play are to be found in
Barthes by Barthes, trans. Richard Howard (New York: Hill & Wang,

1977). The classic Derridean formulation is in "Structure, Sign, and Play . . . ."

16. I must state here that I reject most of these writers' alternative ideals, particularly the mystical irrationalism of Brown and the luxurious "pleasures" of Barthes.

17. See Sigmund Freud, *The Complete Introductory Lectures on Psychoanalysis*, trans. and ed. James Strachey (New York: Norton, 1963), p. 571: "And now the instincts that we believe in divide themselves into two groups—the erotic instincts, which seek to combine more and more living substance into ever greater unities, and the death instincts, which oppose these efforts and lead what is living back into an inorganic state." Freud later relaxed the distinction between erotic and death drives, but he still wanted to compartmentalize them in such a way as to make them separate but interdependent. The closest Freud ever comes to identifying the two drives is in *Beyond the Pleasure Principle*, trans. and ed. James Strachey (New York: Norton, 1961), p. 57, where he observes, "The pleasure principle seems actually to serve the death instincts."

18. Georges Bataille, *Death and Sensuality*, trans. Mary Dalwood (New York: Walker, 1962), esp. pp. 12–38. In many contemporary psychoanalytic discussions, life and death drives are still kept separate. But much of the confusion dissolves if we broaden our notion of death to include experiences of significant limitlessness, and not just biological death. Ernest Becker, for instance, in *The Denial of Death* (New York: Free Press, 1973), defines this notion by opposing the life/death drive to repression. According to Becker, the urge to confront life in some authentic way is equivalent to a desire for maximum meaninglessness, on the assumption that all human meaning is arbitrary, invented as it is to shield us from the knowledge of our mortality; maximum meaninglessness, of course, is only completely realized by dying. Thus, the life and death drives merge as an impulse to strip away illusion. Becker, it should be noted, ultimately argues for "necessary repression" of this life/death drive, and he projects "hero worship" as the form of repression that denies death reassuringly while it also channels human energy productively. Becker bleakly claims that "the question of human life is: on what level of illusion does one live?" (p. 202). Of course, it is finally impossible to prove the existence of a life/death drive; I hope only that my study of Dickens will shed as much light on this subject as Bataille's concept has shed for me on Dickens.

19. See Georges Bataille, *La part maudite* (Paris: Les Éditions de

Minuit, 1967), pp. 21–46 for a discussion of *dépense*. Bataille's theory of expenditure is ultimately derived from a concept of biological determinism, i.e., that the primary activity of all forms of life is growth, and that when a group of organisms reaches a limit to growth, it either forcibly overcomes the limit or it expends the energy of growth in internal depredations. Bataille applies this notion broadly to history, economics, anthropology, and analyses of class antagonisms. See also *Death and Sensuality* for a discussion of expenditure in its psychological aspect, as an escape from discontinuity into continuity. Though Bataille focuses mainly on areas of radical expenditure—on violence and sexuality—his principles are easily extended to more modest kinds of activity.

20. But see "Les consequences du non-savoir," in *Oeuvres complètes* (Paris: Gallimard, 1976), VIII, 190–98.

21. One such charge is made by René Girard in *Violence and the Sacred*, trans. Patrick Gregory (Baltimore: Johns Hopkins Univ. Press, 1977), p. 222. Girard, of course, claims that the function of violence is to create order in society, which accounts for his hostility to Bataille. But the two thinkers are more similar than it would appear; both see the survival of society as dependent on its ability to legitimate and control acts of violence. Their differences largely amount to a question of emphasis. While one cannot help wondering what the common criminal would say about Girard's notion that violence has a social function, nevertheless, the potential for a hyperaesthetic flaunting of eroticism is inherently dangerous in Bataille. One has only to consider his novels, in particular *The Story of the Eye*, trans. Joachim Neugroschel (New York: Urizen, 1977) and *My Mother*, trans. Austryn Wainhouse (London: Jonathan Cape, 1972).

22. The form of my argument here bears a resemblance to Richard Barickman's in "The Comedy of Survival in Dickens's Novels," *Novel* 11 (1978): 123–43. Barickman sees Dickens' characters as "walling up covert gratifications of the forbidden desires" (p. 134). But Barickman sees these "covert gratifications" only as the realization of aggressive identities, not the achievement of forbidden loss.

Chapter 1: Storytelling

1. This perception is clearly articulated by J. Hillis Miller, "Introduction," *Bleak House*, by Charles Dickens, ed. Norman Page (Baltimore: Penguin, 1971), pp. 11–36.

2. On this instance of solipsism in Dickens, see Dorothy van

Ghent, *The English Novel: Form and Function* (New York: Holt, Rinehart, and Winston, 1953), p. 126.

3. J. Hillis Miller demonstrates how, in Dickens, imagination and reality are both made up; *The Form of Victorian Fiction* (Notre Dame: Univ. of Notre Dame Press, 1968), pp. 36–44.

4. Though Dickens celebrated work as a moral value, he seldom valued it as an experience. See the discussion of this point in Chapter 5. See also Alexander Welsh, "Work," in *The City of Dickens* (Oxford: Clarendon, 1971), pp. 73–85, for a good discussion of the differences in the attitudes of Dickens, Carlyle, and other Victorians toward work as the expression of moral virtue and as an experience. Welsh argues that these differences constitute a "contradiction between doctrine and theme," and he notes that the value of work in Victorian novels is almost always defined negatively, rather than embodied in a positive ideal.

5. Sören Kierkegaard, *The Sickness Unto Death*, trans. Walter Lowrie (Garden City, N.Y.: Anchor, 1954), p. 163: "For the self is a synthesis in which the finite is the limiting factor, and the infinite is the expanding factor. Infinitude's despair is therefore the fantastical, the limitless"; and pp. 166–67: "But while one sort of despair plunges wildly into the infinite and loses itself, a second sort permits itself as it were to be defrauded."

6. John Carey, *The Violent Effigy* (London: Faber and Faber, 1973), commits precisely this mistake. Carey's documentation of Dickens' interest in violence is invaluable. It is significant, too, that Carey balances his catalogue of violent interests with a treatment of Dickens' reciprocal desires for order. But Carey never analyzes the relationship and leaves the reader to assume only that Dickens' interest in both violence and order was eccentric.

7. For a good selection of these early warnings, see Ioan Williams, *The Novel and Romance* (New York: Barnes and Noble, 1970).

8. See Nancy Aycock Metz, "The Artist's Reclamation of Waste in *Our Mutual Friend*," *NCF* 34 (1979): 59–72, for a catalogue of these sketches. Metz, however, rather than seeing an attraction to waste here, an attempt to found life on death, claims that Dickens is making an argument about the economy of art; her perspective is that of an ecologist.

9. "Continuity" is Bataille's term for the state of selfless union we imagine to exist beyond death. See *Death and Sensuality*, trans. Mary Dalwood (New York: Walker, 1962).

10. This observation, together with the bland conclusion that

Dickens was "able to see almost everything from two opposed points of view," is made by Carey, pp. 12–16.

11. See, for example, Jack Lindsay, *Charles Dickens* (London: Dakers, 1950), esp. p. 164; and James R. Kincaid, *Dickens and the Rhetoric of Laughter* (Oxford: Clarendon, 1971), pp. 17–19.

12. *The Letters of Charles Dickens*, ed. Walter Dexter et al. (Bloomsbury: Nonesuch Press, 1937–38), I, 647–48.

13. John Forster, *The Life of Charles Dickens* (New York: Doubleday, 1886), p. 163.

14. Quoted in Lindsay, p. 164.

15. Forster, p. 654.

16. Georges Bataille, from *Hegel, la mort et le sacrifice*, quoted in Derrida, "A Hegelianism Without Reserves," trans. Allan Bass, *Semiotext(e)* 2, no. 2 (1976): 30.

17. See Kincaid, p. 17.

18. See George Ford, *Dickens and His Readers* (New York: Norton, 1955), p. 50.

19. *The Letters of Charles Dickens*, II, 679.

20. See Kincaid, p. 18.

21. Quoted in ibid., p. 19.

22. Lindsay makes this point, pp. 377–78.

23. Forster, p. 386.

24. See "Personal" in Harry Stone, ed., *Charles Dickens' Uncollected Writings from Household Words* (Bloomington: Indiana Univ. Press, 1968), p. 586.

25. Forster, p. 646.

26. Quoted in Lindsay, p. 452.

Chapter 2: Melodrama and Sentimentality

1. I am thinking, in particular, of Philip Collins, *Dickens and Crime* (London: Macmillan, 1962).

2. See Edmund Wilson, "Dickens: The Two Scrooges," *The Wound and the Bow* (New York: Oxford Univ. Press, 1941), pp. 1–104.

3. *The Letters of Charles Dickens*, ed. Walter Dexter et al. (Bloomsbury: Nonesuch, 1937–1938), I, 633.

4. See Peter Brooks, *The Melodramatic Imagination* (New Haven: Yale Univ. Press, 1976), pp. 36–44. Many of my thoughts in this paragraph were inspired by Brooks' study.

5. See ibid., pp. 15–17.

6. *The City of Dickens* (Oxford: Clarendon, 1971), p. 106.

7. So claimed Friedrich Brie, an influential Swiss professor. Quoted in Mario Praz, *The Hero in Eclipse in Victorian Fiction*, trans. Angus Davidson (London: Oxford Univ. Press, 1956), p. 127.

8. Quoted in George Ford, *Dickens and His Readers* (New York: Norton, 1955), p. 61.

9. See Ford, p. 108.

10. See Jack Lindsay, *Charles Dickens* (London: Dakers, 1950), p. 473.

11. John Forster, *Charles Dickens* (New York: Doubleday, 1886), p. 479.

12. Both phenomena have been noted often enough, but their local historical causes remain unaccounted for. The traditional explanation, that the Victorians were "repressed" and that their sublimations were consequently more intense, seems parochial and inadequate. S. C. Chakraborty, in *'Sentiment' and 'Sentimentality': Their Use and Significance in English Literature* (1951; rpt. Norwood: Norwood Editions, 1976), argues that sentimentality was the historical manifestation of a shift in Western thought from conceptions of impersonal transcendence to conceptions of a personal, individualistic one. But the argument seems to lack historical precision, if only because, like most critics who have written on sentimentality, Chakraborty considers it to be strictly an eighteenth-century phenomenon. Peter Brooks' argument about melodrama shares this same notion of a shift in metaphysical values toward the personal, but such a shift has been located by literary critics and by art historians in every historical period following the Renaissance. The question one wants to ask of such analyses, regardless of their functional plausibility, is: why then, should our strategies in the twentieth century have changed?

Perhaps the most convincing analysis is proposed by Richard Sennett in *The Fall of Public Man: On the Social Psychology of Capitalism* (New York: Random, 1978). Sennett proposes that melodrama and a histrionic theater flourish in a time when public life is perceived to be separate from private life. Rather than searching for the complexities of motivation *behind* public expression, Sennett argues, the audience to melodrama accepts conventional motivations as the occasion for kinds of emotional display that are not permitted in private life. Sennett claims that the balance between a convention-controlled public life and a more spontaneous private life signaled by the excesses of eighteenth- and early nineteenth-century theater is a healthy one, a balance that our contemporary obsession with intimacy as the guarantor of authentic experience has disrupted. I would argue, however, that even the twentieth century's emphasis on intimate excess requires conventions for the focusing of emotional display—for example, the nondemanding, "non-neurotic" norms for sexual experience that control the so-called liberations of what is coming to be called "the therapeutic society."

13. This notion informs most of Bataille's social analyses in *La Part maudite* (Paris: Les Éditions de Minuit, 1967).

Chapter 3: Villains

1. See George Brimley, from *The Spectator*, reprinted in Philip Collins, ed., *Dickens: The Critical Heritage* (New York: Barnes & Noble, 1971), p. 283—or virtually any of the other reviews in this section of Collins' book.

2. The best collection of views on the subject is probably Ernest Becker, *The Denial of Death* (New York: Free Press, 1973, esp. pp. 11–66.

3. *The City of Dickens* (Oxford: Clarendon, 1971), p. 120.

4. Girard employs the term "masochistic mediation" to describe fascination with obstacles for their own sake. See *Deceit, Desire, and the Novel: Self and Other in Literary Structure*, trans. Yvonne Freccero (Baltimore: Johns Hopkins Univ. Press, 1965), pp. 176–92. But Girard is interested in the masochist's pursuit of a metaphysical presence beyond the obstacle, whereas Dickens' villains are more interested in the unrecuperated expense of violent energy such obstacles make possible.

5. This scene and the quarrel about Quilp's nose are noted by A. E. Dyson, *The Inimitable Dickens* (London: Macmillan, 1970), p. 30, and by Steven Marcus, *Dickens: From Pickwick to Dombey* (New York: Basic Books, 1965), p. 159, respectively. All three of us, however, pursue different ends.

6. See A. E. Dyson, *"The Old Curiosity Shop:* Innocence and the Grotesque," *Critical Quarterly* 8 (1966): 118–19.

7. *Love's Body* (New York: Vintage, 1966), p. 162.

8. See *Death and Sensuality*, trans. Mary Dalwood (New York: Walker, 1962), pp. 12–36.

9. Marcus, p. 148, refers to remarks made by José Ortega y Gasset in *The Dehumanization of Art*, trans. Helene Weyl (1948: rpt. Princeton: Princeton Univ. Press, 1968).

10. *The Letters of Charles Dickens*, ed. Walter Dexter et al. (Bloomsbury: Nonesuch, 1937–38), I, 261–62.

11. For a more elaborate reading of this scene, see Michael Steig and F. A. Wilson's excellent article, "Hortense vs. Bucket: The Ambiguity of Order in *Bleak House*," *Modern Language Quarterly* 33 (1972): 289–99.

12. Girard, p. 153.

13. This brief summary is taken from Alexandre Kojève, *Introduction to the Reading of Hegel*, trans. James H. Nichols, Jr., ed. Allan Bloom (New York: Basic Books, 1969), pp. 3–30.

14. This claim is made by J. Hillis Miller, *Charles Dickens: The World of His Novels* (Bloomington: Indiana Univ. Press, 1958), p. 173.

15. See Georges Bataille, *La part maudite* (Paris: Les Éditions de Minuit, 1967), pp. 35–41, for a discussion of the way in which the bourgeoise-capitalist elite exercises its wealth, not by spending its own capital, but by wasting the lives of the lower orders.

16. For a discussion of Orlick as an allegorical echo of Pip's own guilt, see Julian Moynihan, "The Hero's Guilt: The Case of *Great Expectations*," *Essays in Criticism* 10 (1960): 60–79.

17. Girard, pp. 185–90.

18. J. Hillis Miller, "Introduction," *Bleak House*, by Charles Dickens, ed. Norman Page (Baltimore: Penguin, 1971), pp. 11–34.

19. My summaries here are taken from Kojève, pp. 3–30, and from Girard, who says, "The impulse toward the object is ultimately an impulse toward the mediator" (p. 10). Girard also claims that "for Hegel, the reign of individual violence is over" (p. 110), and he argues that the novel's subject can no longer be violence itself, but that it must be the structure of internal mediation.

Chapter 4: Heroes

1. See, for example, Edmund Wilson, *The Wound and the Bow* (New York: Oxford Univ. Press, 1941), p. 103: "Dickens in his moral confusion was never able to dramatize himself completely, was never in the last phase of his art to succeed in coming quite clear."

2. This tendency is exemplified by Michael Steig, "The Central Action of *The Old Curiosity Shop*, or Little Nell Revisited Again," *Literature and Psychology* 15 (1965): 163–76; and by Leonard F. Manheim, "Thanatos: The Death-Instinct in Dickens' Later Novels," in L. Manheim and E. Manheim, ed., *Hidden Patterns: Studies in Psychoanalytic Literary Criticism* (New York: Macmillan, 1966), pp. 113–31.

3. For a discussion of the *pharmakon*, see René Girard, *Violence and the Sacred*, trans. Patrick Gregory (Baltimore: Johns Hopkins Univ. Press, 1977), p. 95.

4. See Alexandre Kojève, *Introduction to the Reading of Hegel*, trans. James H. Nichols, Jr., ed. Allan Bloom (New York: Basic Books, 1969).

5. This passage is a variant quoted in Charles Dickens, *Great Expectations*, ed. Louis Crompton (New York: Bobbs-Merrill, 1964), p. 436.

6. See, for example, Julian Moynihan, "The Hero's Guilt: The Case of *Great Expectations*," *Essays in Criticism* 10 (1960): 60–79.

7. See Edgar Johnson, *Charles Dickens: His Tragedy and Triumph* (New York: Simon and Schuster, 1952), pp. 482–83.

8. From the manuscript. See Charles Dickens, *The Old Curiosity Shop*, ed. Angus Easson (Baltimore: Penguin, 1972), p. 702.

9. See Garrett Stewart, "The New Mortality of *Bleak House*," *ELH* 45 (1978): 443–87, for an excellent discussion of Esther's voidlike qualities. Unfortunately, Stewart sees this "deadness" of Esther's only as a negative quality, something she must overcome, rather than as an integral goal of her innocence.

10. See Joseph I. Fradin, "Will and Society in *Bleak House*," *PMLA* 81 (1966): 95–109.

11. Even Forster complained, in an unsigned review from the *Examiner* quoted in Philip Collins, ed., *Dickens: The Critical Heritage* (New York: Barnes & Noble, 1971), "We suspect that Mr. Dickens undertook more than a man could accomplish when he resolved to make her the *naive* revealer of her own good qualities. We cannot help detecting in some passages an artificial tone, which, if not self-consciousness, is at any rate not such a tone as would be used in her narrative by a person of the character depicted" (p. 291).

12. See, for example, William F. Axton, "The Trouble with Esther," *Modern Language Quarterly* 26 (1965): 545–57; or Alex Zwerdling, "Esther Summerson Rehabilitated," *PMLA* 88 (1973): 429–39.

Chapter 5: Endings

1. *Dickens and the Trials of Imagination* (Cambridge: Harvard Univ. Press, 1974), p. xvii.

2. Frank Kermode makes this point about a number of novelists in *The Sense of an Ending* (New York: Oxford Univ. Press, 1966), p. 129.

3. See, for example, Roland Barthes, *The Pleasure of the Text*,

trans. Richard Miller (New York: Hill & Wang, 1975), p. 11, for his concept of "tmesis." Barthes argues that the classical novel is not read linearly, even if it is written as a closed form, but that the reader—by skimming, rereading, looking up from the book—imposes his own gaps on the plot. For Barthes, it is the interface between linearity and formlessness that is crucial in reading.

4. This summary, obviously, does not do justice to Kermode, though it is faithful to the main lines of his thought. It should be noted that, for Kermode, order is finally consoling because it allows for communication and human community.

5. *Beginnings: Intention and Method* (New York: Basic Books, 1975). I am drawing mainly on remarks made in Chapter 3, "The Novel as Beginning Intention," pp. 79–188.

6. I am aware that Said speaks of "beginnings" as a radical departure for novelists, but Said's sense of beginnings is explicitly finite. In fact, he claims, "My thesis is that invention and restraint—or, as I shall call them, 'authority' and 'molestation,' respectively—ultimately have *conserved* the novel because novelists have construed them together as *beginning* conditions, not as conditions for limitlessly expansive fictional invention. Thus the novel represents a beginning of a precisely finite sort insofar as what may ensue from that beginning" (p. 83).

7. The assumption that endings can only be approached as epistemological statements of one kind or another divides critics neatly into two camps. The first, favoring "open" form, looks to literature as a description of phenomenal reality—see Alan Friedman, *The Turn of the Novel* (New York: Oxford Univ. Press, 1966), or Beverley Gross, "Narrative Time and the Open-Ended Novel," *Criticism* 8 (1966): 362–70. The second, favoring "closed" form, looks to literature as a description of thought—see David H. Richter, *Fable's End: Completeness and Closure in Rhetorical Fiction* (Chicago: Univ. of Chicago Press, 1974).

8. I should note that my description of endings sets me against Alan Friedman's thesis, in *The Turn of the Novel*, that contemporary novels aspire to ethical openness, while nineteenth-century novels remained morally "end-stopped." Friedman cites *Bleak House*, which I discuss later in this chapter, as a preeminently "end-stopped" novel (p. 25). My description of endings attempts to break down the condescension implied by such theories, which privilege twentieth-century epistemology.

9. It is by now an aesthetic commonplace to say that there is no such thing as a negative in literature, even when concepts or metaphors are presented in negative forms. The best discussion I know of is Kenneth Burke's in "The Definition of Man," in *Language as Symbolic Action* (Berkeley: Univ. of California Press, 1966), pp. 11–12. In Burke's argument, once they are repeated sequentially, images such as freedom and determination cannot negate each other but can only enter into a dialectical relationship of mutual limitation.

10. *A Grammar of Motives* (Berkeley: Univ. of California Press, 1969), p. 230.

11. Interview, *Wisconsin Studies in Contemporary Literature* 6 (1965): 8.

12. Said makes this point on p. 79.

13. This principle is basic to all Derridean thought. Perhaps the best discussion is in "Differance," *Speech and Phenomena, and Other Essays on Husserl's Theory of Signs*, trans. David B. Allison (Evanston: Northwestern Univ. Press, 1973), esp. pp. 140–42.

14. See Jacques Derrida, "Structure, Sign, and Play in the Discourse of the Human Sciences," in Richard Macksey and Eugenio Donato, ed., *The Structuralist Controversy: The Languages of Criticism and the Sciences of Man* (Baltimore: Johns Hopkins Univ. Press, 1970), pp. 247–64.

15. "An Introduction to the Structuralist Study of Narrative," *New Literary History* 6 (1975): 271.

16. See especially *Writing Degree Zero*, trans. Annette Lavers and Colin Smith (New York: Hill & Wang, 1967), pp. 9–13.

17. This is almost a universal assumption among Dickens critics. For the consummate summary of the position, see G. W. Kennedy, "Dickens's Endings," *Studies in the Novel* 6 (1974): 280–87. I do not wish to argue that Dickens' endings do not attempt to escape conflicts that are pragmatically insoluble, but only that such escapes are themselves actions and not just impossible wishes.

18. *A Grammar of Motives*, p. 475.

19. See, for example, Northrop Frye, "Dickens and the Comedy of Humors," in Roy Harvey Pearce, ed., *Experience in the Novel* (New York: Columbia Univ. Press, 1968), pp. 49–81. Frye argues convincingly that the major paradigm of the Dickens plot is the overcoming of obstacles in the form of an "obstructing society" by a "good society," but Frye also asserts that the "humors" of each society are merely identical, in ways that he connects to obsessive "organization."

20. I am echoing Burke's comments in "Terministic Screens," in *Language as Symbolic Action*, pp. 44–62. Much of my discussion of symbolic shifts was inspired by thoughts in this essay. Burke argues impressively that very few linguistic terms are positive and that the rest are dialectical. He then builds a case for symbolic drama in literature, which, for Burke, is a development of symbolic terms that works toward modifying the dialectical position of significant ideas, actions, and images.

21. Françoise Basch, *Relative Creations* (New York: Schocken Books, 1974), esp. p. 65.

22. See Michael Steig and F. A. Wilson, "Hortense vs. Bucket: The Ambiguity of Order in *Bleak House*," *Modern Language Quarterly* 33 (1972): 289–99. Steig and Wilson argue compellingly that Bucket and Tulkinghorn represent good and bad versions of social order; however, they never acknowledge any personal motives on Bucket's part, except in terms of what they call his "repressed" sexuality.

23. See John T. Smith's excellent article, "The Two Endings of *Great Expectations*: A Reevaluation," *Thoth* 12 (1971): 11–17. Smith points up Pip's deliberate refusal to recognize Esther's rejection of him.

24. "Metaphysical desire" is the key concept in *Deceit, Desire, and the Novel: Self and Other in Literary Structure*, trans. Yvonne Freccero (Baltimore: Johns Hopkins Univ. Press, 1965).

25. See, for example, Mordecai Marcus, "The Pattern of Self-Alienation in *Great Expectations*," *The Victorian Newsletter* 26 (1964): 9–12; or Ruth Vande Kieft, "Patterns of Communication in *Great Expectations*," *Nineteenth-Century Fiction* 15 (1962): 325–34. I do not argue that Pip's final love for Estella does not coincide with an image of "self-knowledge" that allows him to feel tenderness for Estella, but only that it is impossible to see his love as either fulfilled or complacent at the end of the novel; that is, Pip never escapes desire.

26. Georges Bataille, *La Part maudite* (Paris: Les Éditions de Minuit, 1967), pp. 107–24.

27. The echoes of Derridean terminology here are intentional, though the effect of my reading is hardly structuralist. Dickens, I have argued, finds a way to fracture restrictive human structures—specifically, in *A Tale of Two Cities*, the behavioral structure of rivalry—in the interest of human freedom and originality, even if this disruption of structure requires death. Nevertheless, the presence of rigid linguistic and behavioral structures in the novel gives point to Dickens' attempt to exceed them. For perhaps his most complete statement on linguistic structure, see Jacques Derrida, *Of Grammatology*, trans.

Gayatri Chakravorty Spivak (Baltimore: Johns Hopkins Univ. Press, 1976). For an interesting statement by Derrida on Georges Bataille's defiance of the concept of restrictive structure, see Jacques Derrida, "A Hegelianism Without Reserves," trans. Allan Bass, *Semiotext(e)* 2, no. 2 (1976): 25–55.

28. For a detailed account of this and other Victorian excesses, see John Morley, *Death, Heaven, and the Victorians* (Pittsburgh: Univ. of Pittsburgh Press, 1971).

29. Both attitudes are expressed by Morley and by James Stevens Curl, *The Victorian Celebration of Death* (London: David and Charles, 1972).

30. See Curl, p. 20.

31. See John Gross, *"A Tale of Two Cities,"* in *Dickens and the Twentieth Century*, ed. John Gross and Gabriel Pearson (Toronto: Toronto Univ. Press, 1962), p. 191.

32. See Welsh, "Work," in *The City of Dickens*, pp. 73–85, for a good discussion of differences in the attitudes of Dickens, Carlyle, and other Victorians toward work as the expression of moral virtue and as an experience. Welsh calls these differences a "contradiction between doctrine and theme," and he notes that the value of work in Victorian novels is almost always defined negatively rather than embodied in a positive ideal.

33. "The Dynamic of Time in *The Old Curiosity Shop,*" *NCF* 28 (1973): 133.

34. This aspect of Swiveller's character has been well documented by James R. Kincaid, *Dickens and the Rhetoric of Laughter* (Oxford: Clarendon, 1971), pp. 99–104.

35. In "A Christmas Tree," Dickens recollects Little Red Riding Hood as "my first love. I felt that if I could have married Little Red Riding Hood, I should have known perfect bliss"—*Selected Short Fiction* (Baltimore: Penguin, 1976), p. 130. Other aspects of "Little Red Riding Hood" are applicable to *The Old Curiosity Shop*, notably, the identity of sex and death, and the eventual recovery of the "dead" girl.

36. *Death and Sensuality*, trans. Mary Dalwood (New York: Walker, 1962), pp. 155–62.

37. *The Pleasure of the Text*, p. 7.

38. However, this position has been taken by Leslie Fiedler in "Good Good Girl and Good Bad Boy," *No! in Thunder: Essays on Myth and Literature* (Boston: Beacon Press, 1960), pp. 257–65.

39. See Jerome Meckier, *"The Old Curiosity Shop:* Dickens' Contrapuntal Artistry," *Journal of Narrative Technique* 2 (1972): 199–207,

for a detailed account of Dickens' skill in preparing his readers for the conclusion of the novel.

40. I am thinking mostly of the charge of Steven Marcus, *Dickens: From Pickwick to Dombey* (New York: Basic Books, 1965), p. 142, that the novel tries "to disengage itself from energy."

41. Harry Stone, ed., *Charles Dickens' Uncollected Writings from Household Words* (Bloomington: Indiana Univ. Press, 1968), p. 13.

42. José Ortega y Gasset, *Meditations on Quixote*, trans. Helene Weyl (New York: Norton, 1963), p. 137.

Chapter 6: Mechanical Style

1. Quoted in Herbert Sussman, *Victorians and the Machine: The Literary Response to Technology* (Cambridge: Harvard Univ. Press, 1968), pp. 1–2.

2. Lewis Mumford, *Technics and Civilization* (New York: Harcourt, Brace & World, 1934), p. 237. Mumford divides technological history into three periods, the eotechnic (water and wind), the paleotechnic (coal and iron), and the neotechnic (electricity and metallurgy). The second and third division are implicitly confirmed in Siegfried Giedion. *Mechanization Takes Command* (New York: Oxford Univ. Press, 1948), esp. pp. 49–77. Giedion locates the important developments in standardization and the interchangeability of parts at the beginning of the nineteenth century. Significantly, the same sort of philosophical extrapolations are made in two important recent works of cultural history. Fernand Braudel, in *Capitalism and Material Life, 1500–1800*, trans. Miriam Kochan (New York: Harper & Row, 1973), chooses 1800 as a rough dividing line between humanity's use of technology as a pragmatic solver of immediate problems and the flowering of technology as an infinitely expanding field disconnected from necessity. Michel Foucault, in *The Order of Things: An Archaeology of the Human Sciences* (New York: Random House, 1970), chooses the same point in time to divide the history of knowledge into a classical period of discursiveness and a modern period of structural systematization.

3. Mumford, p. 246.

4. Sussman, pp. 1–2.

5. Quoted in Sussman, p. 11.

6. *The Victorian Frame of Mind* (New Haven: Yale Univ. Press, 1957), p. 198.

7. Harry Stone, ed., *Charles Dickens' Uncollected Writings from Household Words* (Bloomington: Indiana Univ. Press, 1968), p. 13.

8. Ibid., pp. 213–14.

9. The dual nature of Dickens' personality is noted by John Carey in *The Violent Effigy* (London: Faber & Faber, 1973), but without an overriding principle of synthesis.

10. John Forster, *The Life of Charles Dickens* (New York: Doubleday, 1886), p. 76.

11. Ibid., p. 203.

12. Ibid., p. 158.

13. Ibid., p. 159.

14. Ibid., p. 102 and p. 158.

15. Ibid., p. 124.

16. Ibid., p. 636.

17. Hugh Kenner, *The Counterfeiters* (Garden City, N.Y.: Anchor, 1968), p. 136.

18. For a good reading of the fallen state of nature in *Edwin Drood*, see Roy Roussel, "The Completed Story in *The Mystery of Edwin Drood*," *Criticism* 20 (1978): 383–402.

19. This observation, as well as a number of good observations about Dickens' aversion to romanticized nature, is made by R. D. McMaster, "Dickens, the Dandy, and the Savage," *Studies in the Novel* 1 (1969): 133–46.

20. "*Tristram Shandy*'s Law of Gravity," *ELH* 28 (1961): 88.

21. Garrett Stewart, *Dickens and the Trials of Imagination* (Cambridge: Harvard Univ. Press, 1974), p. 5.

22. G. K. Chesterton, *Charles Dickens: A Critical Study* (1906; rpt. New York: Schocken, 1965), p. 231.

23. J. Hillis Miller, "The Sources of Dickens's Comic Art," *NCF* 24 (1970): 467–76. Miller overstates the argument, however—here and also in "The Fiction of Realism: *Sketches by Boz, Oliver Twist*, and Cruikshank's Illustrations," in *Dickens Centennial Essays*, ed. Ada Nisbet and Blake Nevius (Berkeley: Univ. of California Press, 1971), pp. 1–69. In his argument against Dickensian mimesis, Miller discredits any notion of satiric intentions on Dickens' part. It seems a strange argument, since so many hundreds of thousands of readers have felt the force of Dickens' satirical attacks, and in view of Dickens' explicit statements about his intentions to remedy social conditions (not to mention the actual effect of his books on institutions like the workhouse). Dickens clearly has more in mind than narrow politi-

cal satires, but Miller goes astray in attributing an unequal priority to the nonmimetic aspects of Dickens' text. On this debate see also Gerald Graff, *Literature Against Itself* (Chicago: Univ. of Chicago Press, 1979), pp. 175–78.

24. Stewart, "The Pickwick Case: Diagnosis," in *Dickens and the Trials of Imagination*, pp. 3–29. Stewart says explicitly, "Dickens never loses sight of the possible excess, the ready comedy of circumlocution and variation" (p. 7).

25. Kenner, p. 167.

26. *The Letters of Charles Dickens*, ed. Walter Dexter et al. (Bloomsbury: Nonesuch, 1937–1938), II, 646.

27. Quoted in Edgar Johnson, *Charles Dickens: His Tragedy and Triumph* (New York: Simon & Schuster, 1952), p. 878.

28. William F. Axton, *Circle of Fire* (Lexington: Univ. of Kentucky Press, 1966), p. 194.

29. Stone, pp. 306–7.

30. See Johnson, pp. 674–75.

31. See Forster, p. 76.

32. According to Jack Lindsay, *Charles Dickens* (London: Dakers, 1950), one of Dickens' younger children is said to have remarked on one of Dickens' depressions by saying to a guest, "Poor papa is in love again" (p. 248). The parody of his feelings for the queen is legendary; Dickens carried on the pretense for days, involving many of his friends in it. Forster quotes this letter to a "befuddled" Landor: "I have fallen hopelessly in love with the Queen, and wander up and down with vague and dismal thoughts of running away to some uninhabited island with a maid of honor, to be entrapped by conspiracy for that purpose. . . . It is too much perhaps to ask you to join the band of noble youths (Forster is in it, and Maclise) who are to assist me in this great enterprise, but a man of your energy would be invaluable" (p. 155).

33. Lindsay quotes a letter from Dickens to Mrs. Hogarth. "I trace in many respects a strong resemblance between her mental features and Georgina's—so strange a one at times, that when she and Kate and I are sitting together, I seem to think that what has happened is a melancholy dream from which I am just awaking" (p. 230). And in *Martin Chuzzlewit*, written at roughly the same time, Pecksniff moons similarly over Mrs. Todgers:

"You are very like her, Mrs. Todgers."

"Don't squeeze me so tight, pray, Mr. Pecksniff. If any of the gentlemen should notice us."

"For her sake," said Mr. Pecksniff, "Permit me. In honour of her memory. For the sake of a voice from the tomb. You are *very* like her, Mrs. Todgers! What a world this is!" (9)

34. The last three examples have been pointed out by Lindsay, pp. 193, 238.

35. See also ibid., p. 393.

36. For a good discussion of Baudelaire's notion of ironic comedy, see Paul de Man, "The Rhetoric of Temporality," in Charles Singleton, ed., *Interpretation: Theory and Practice* (Baltimore: Johns Hopkins Univ. Press, 1968), pp. 194–98.

37. See ibid., esp. pp. 196–98.

38. Jean Starobinski, "Ironie et mélancholie: Gozzi, Hoffmann, Kierkegaard," in *Estratto da Sensiblitá e Razionalitá nel Settecento* (Florence, 1967), p. 458. The translation is my own.

39. Jacques Derrida, "A Hegelianism Without Reserves," trans. Allan Bass, *Semiotext(e)* 2, no. 2 (1976): 32. Derrida's comments seem aimed partly at Kierkegaardian irony, which conceives of the temporal self and ironic consciousness as two sides of the same coin.

40. Forster, p. 664.

41. Claude Lévesque, "Batail+ Beyond Bounds," trans. M. L. Taylor, a paper delivered at the State University of New York at Buffalo on Nov. 15, 1977.

42. Forster, p. 165.

43. Ibid., p. 721. Dickens said, "I have such inexpressible enjoyment of what I see in a droll light, that I dare say I pet it as if it were a spoilt child."

44. See "Appendix: A Note on the Narrative Imagination," in Stewart, *Dickens and the Trials of Imagination*, pp. 231–40.

45. Ibid., p. 238, writes, "One is enticed by widespread and various evidence to call it almost the essential genius of Dickens's prose to go forward through contrastive patterns of tone and registration."

Chapter 7: The Fairy Tale

1. Georg Lukács, *The Theory of the Novel*, trans. Anna Bostock (Cambridge: MIT Press, 1971), pp. 71–72, expresses the problem. "Either the fragility of the world may manifest itself so crudely that it will cancel out the immanence of meaning which the form demands, or else the longing for the dissonance to be resolved, affirmed and absorbed into the work may be so great that it will lead to a premature closing of the circle of the novel's world."

2. Edgar Johnson, *Charles Dickens: His Tragedy and Triumph* (New York: Simon & Schuster, 1952), p. 131.

3. Jack Lindsay, *Charles Dickens* (London: Dakers, 1950), p. 131, reports that Dickens frequently told his wife of his dreams about Mary, and that the *Miscellany*'s notice of Mary's death referred to her—tactlessly, to say the least—as Dickens' "chief solace."

4. See Gladys Storey, *Dickens and Daughter* (1939; rpt. New York: Haskill House, 1971), p. 96.

5. Quoted in Lindsay, p. 298. There is much evidence that Dickens did help his sons find careers, but one cannot be sure whether he was seriously interested in them, or whether he simply wanted to be free of them financially. Katie Dickens' account would seem to indicate the latter; see Gladys Storey, pp. 92–94.

6. See Harry Stone, ed., *Charles Dickens' Uncollected Writings from Household Words* (Bloomington: Indiana Univ. Press, 1968), p. 621n.

7. See John Carey, *The Violent Effigy* (London: Faber & Faber, 1973), pp. 16–17.

8. "Ironie et melancholie: Gozzi, Hoffmann, Kierkegaard," in *Estratto da Sensibilitá e Razionalitá nel Settecento* (Florence, 1967), p. 425. My translation. Starobinski, of course, is drawing heavily on the work of the Russian Formalists.

9. Ibid., pp. 437–41.

10. Ibid., p. 428.

11. Bruno Bettelheim, *The Uses of Enchantment* (New York: Vintage, 1975), p. 12.

12. See Angus Wilson, *The World of Charles Dickens* (New York: Viking, 1970), p. 23.

13. I am aware that I am disagreeing with an entire tradition of Dickens criticism, but I am not the first; see Alexander Welsh on "grace" in Dickens' endings, *The City of Dickens* (Oxford: Clarendon, 1971), pp. 68–72.

14. Discussed by Jacques Derrida in "A Hegelianism Without Reserves," trans. Allan Bass, *Semiotext(e)* 2, no. 2 (1976): 49.

Index

Index 281

Harlowe, Clarissa, 26
Hegel, G. W. F., 81, 99, 109;
  Hegelian, 90. *See also* Master-
  slave dialectic
Hemingway, Ernest, 234
Hoffman, E. T. A., 249
Hogarth, Catherine (Kate), 36, 40,
  229, 248
Hogarth, Mrs. George, 229
Hogarth, Georgina, 229
Hogarth, Mary, 54
Household Harmony, 248
Household Words, 32, 39, 40, 201; "A
  Preliminary Word," 193, 202;
  "Plate Glass," 202
Humanism, 6, 8, 9, 14

Jeffrey, Francis, Lord, 57
Joyce, James, *Finnegan's Wake*, 137

Kafka, Franz, *The Castle*, 139
Kenner, Hugh, 203, 216
Kermode, Frank, 3, 137–39, 258
  (n. 9)
Kierkegaard, Sören, 25; *The
  Sickness Unto Death*, 25

Landor, Walter Savage, 274 (n. 32)
Lévi-Strauss, Claude, 4, 6
Linguistics, structural, 5
Little Dorrit, 16, 19, 67, 82, 132, 153,
  191, 204, 225, 252; Henry Gowan,
  21, 38, 192; Arthur Clennam, 51,
  154, 192, 213; Mrs. Clennam, 51,
  73, 79, 101, 102, 154, 192; Rigaud
  (Blandois), 51, 64, 68, 73, 79, 83,
  85, 88, 90, 101–2; Mr. Merdle, 61;
  Mr. Pancks, 65; Affery Flintwich,
  73, 79, 102; John Baptist
  Cavalletto, 83; Daniel Doyce, 121;
  Amy Dorrit, 129, 154, 192; William
  Dorrit, 129, 192; Miss Wade, 192;
  Flora Finching, 198, 212, 213
"Little Red Riding Hood," 186
Love, romantic, 131, 132
Lytton, Edward Bulwer-, 76

Maclise, Daniel, 234, 235
Macready, William, 36
Marcel (in *A Remembrance of
  Things Past*), 139
Martin Chuzzlewit, 37, 39, 114, 210,
  227, 228, 229, 240, 272 (n. 32);
  Anthony Chuzzlewit, 14, 70, 71;
  Mrs. Harris, 20, 89; Mark Tapley,
  20; Sarah Gamp, 20; Martin
  Chuzzlewit, Sr., 33; Pecksniff, 33,
  37, 61, 62, 104, 198, 211, 212, 214,
  220; Jonas Chuzzlewit, 38, 62, 64,
  70–71, 74, 79, 82, 84, 90; Tom
  Pinch, 38, 48, 54, 71, 109, 127, 128,
  239, 241, 252, 253; Ruth Pinch, 48,
  54, 251, 252; Charity Pecksniff, 48,
  54, 251, 252; Mercy Pecksniff, 71,
  79, 241; Montague Tigg, 71; Mrs.
  Todgers, 212; Augustus Moddle,
  241; John Westlock, 251
Master Humphrey's Clock, 203
Master-slave dialectic, 81–82, 109,
  236. *See also* Hegel, G. W. F.
Mediation, masochistic, 69–71;
  mediator, 93
Melville, Herman, *The Confidence
  Man*, 139
Mill, John Stuart, 200
Miller, J. Hillis, 3, 6, 94, 213, 257
  (n. 14)
Milton, John, 132; *Paradise Lost*, 19,
  26
Moreau, Frédéric, 139
Mumford, Lewis, 199

Nabokov, Vladimir, 25, 208
The National Enquirer, 26
New criticism, 2
Nicholas Nickleby, Wackford
  Squeers, 47
Nietzsche, Friedrich, 257 (n. 3)
Novel, 25; nineteenth-century
  English, 131; and romance, 193;
  Victorian, 165, 246. *See also*
  Theory, literary